Criminal Practices

JULIAN SYMONS

Criminal Practices

Symons on Crime Writing 60s to 90s

MACMILLAN

First published 1994 by Macmillan London

an imprint of Macmillan General Books
Cavaye Place London SW10 9PG
and Basingstoke

Associated companies throughout the world

ISBN 0-333-61446-1

135798642

A CIP catalogue record for this book is available from
the British Library

Typeset by CentraCet Limited, Cambridge
Printed and bound in Great Britain
by Mackays of Chatham plc, Chatham, Kent

Acknowledgements

For permission to reprint articles and reviews, thanks are due to the following newspapers and periodicals:

The Times, the *Sunday Times*, the *Guardian*, the *Listener*, the *New York Times Book Review*, the *New York Review of Books*, the *Times Literary Supplement*, *Punch*, the *London Magazine*, the *Reporter*, the *Author*.

'The Case of Sherlock Holmes' originally appeared as introduction to *The Complete Adventures of Sherlock Holmes*, published by Martin Secker & Warburg, 1981.

The articles about Poe and John Mair were written as introductions to the World's Classics edition of Poe's *Selected Tales* and the Twentieth Century Classics edition of John Mair's *Never Come Back*, published by Oxford University Press.

'The Hound of the Baskervilles' was written as an introduction to the novel, published by the Folio Society, 1987.

'The Mistress of Complication' appeared in *Agatha Christie, First Lady of Crime*, edited by H. R. F. Keating and published by Weidenfeld & Nicolson, 1977, and 'An Aesthete Discovers The Pulps' in *The World of Raymond Chandler*, edited by Miriam Gross, published by Weidenfeld & Nicolson, 1977.

The articles about Erskine Childers and Edgar Wallace were originally introductions to paperback editions of *The Riddle of the Sands* and *The Mind of Mr J. G. Reeder*, both published by J. M. Dent.

The article about John Franklin Bardin was originally an introduction to the Penguin *John Franklin Bardin Omnibus*, published in 1978. The recollections of Ross Macdonald first appeared in *Inward Journey*, edited by Ralph B. Slipper (1984).

'Chekhov's Only Novel' was written as an introduction to his *The Shooting Party*, published by André Deutsch, 1986.

I am grateful to all the publishers concerned for permission to reprint these pieces, in some cases slightly abbreviated.

Contents

Contents

Introduction

(i) Crime Past

Early in 1958 I received a note from Leonard Russell, literary editor of the *Sunday Times*, asking if I would like to become the paper's crime reviewer, writing two pieces a month for £600 a year. A couple of years earlier I had ended a decade-long stint writing a weekly book column for the *Manchester Evening News* because I felt myself suffering from what might be called reviewer's fatigue. But the prospect of writing about crime stories and nothing else was attractive, the pay was fair or even handsome for the late fifties, and I said yes. The association thus casually begun has lasted for, at the moment of writing, thirty-five years. For the first twenty of them I had no agreement, so that the arrangement could have been terminated without notice.

I had written two or three pieces for the *Saturday Book*, a yearly volume Leonard edited with great success in the years after the War, and had been to parties he and his wife Dilys (the *Sunday Times* film critic) gave at their house in Albion Street. Leonard was exuberant, impatient, temperamentally generous, prone to enthusiasm that quickly faded: not the kind of person I found naturally sympathetic. We had had brushes in the past, when he was adviser to a short-lived publishing firm called the Falcon Press, for which I edited a selection from Johnson, and they were renewed when he invited me to choose my 'Hundred Best' crime stories and write a piece about each of them, promising that they would be handsomely publicized in the paper. So they were: but it was typical of Leonard that he should improve on his original idea, suggesting that I enlist the help of critics, historians and other writers in the genre when making the final choice. Accordingly, a number of selctions were made by Agatha Christie, Cyril Hare, C. P. Snow, Nicholas Blake, Rex Stout, Assistant Commissioner R. L. Jackson of the CID, Leonard's wife Dilys, and several critics.

The books they chose were often those I would have picked myself (I was especially pleased that Dilys chose John Mair's thriller *Never Come Back*), but this was hardly *my* Hundred Best, although I reluctantly agreed to what I felt was an adulteration of a Symons-pure selection. When Leonard looked at the final choice of ninety-nine books – another idea of his was that the paper's readers should select the hundredth – he was horrified to find that almost a third of them were out of print. What, he asked, was the point of publicizing books that readers would not be able to find in the shops? I replied that crime stories, more than other fiction, tended to move in and out of print. Eric Ambler's *The Mask of Dimitrios* was out of print when the list appeared, yet was acknowledged as a classic and reissued two or three months later. Leonard remained unhappy about this. I don't think he went so far as suggesting I should rejig the list to include only books immediately available, but he certainly thought I could have made some more popular choices. On my side I felt the list would have been more coherent if the choice had been made by a single person – me. The hundredth book was Ernest Raymond's *We, The Accused*, a work I would never have chosen.

Three years later Leonard and I fell out again, when after the success of a book I wrote about the literary thirties he commissioned two long articles about British reactions to the Spanish Civil War, to appear in consecutive weeks. I learned later that the editorial supremo Denis Hamilton had been away when the articles were delivered, and when he saw them disliked the attitude from which they were written so much that he put an interdict on the second piece, although it eventually appeared in a much truncated form. Looking back, I am sure Leonard Russell tried to do his best for me and I dare say considered me ungrateful. I suppose it could be said I was lucky to survive as a contributor. At the time, though, these incidents plus Leonard's habit of occasionally postponing or even dropping my crime column without telling me made for an uncomfortable relationship.

I found reviewing on the paper much easier when Jack Lambert succeeded Leonard as literary editor. From my point of view Jack was the model of what somebody in his position should be, allowing me all the freedom I wanted, punctilious in telling me if cuts were needed because room had unexpectedly to be made for late advertisements, careful never to impose his will because he preferred his opinion to mine. He never questioned the substance of what I wrote, although occasionally raising an eyebrow at details. An instance of his impeccable behaviour has stayed in my memory. A reviewer's particular pleasure is reading a good first book, finding a diamond among the zircons. In 1962, after reading Len Deighton's *The Ipcress File*, I rang Jack to tell him I had discovered a splendid new thriller writer. I asked if I could have an extra review to say so, in addition to my fortnightly column. 'You really think it's that good?' Jack said. 'All right.' My extra piece appeared. Several months later I learned that Jack, a great reader of crime stories, had started the book and put it aside before my telephone call as unreadably complex and unbearably smart. Others would have made their own opinion clear, or simply said no to my request. I think and hope Jack Lambert enjoyed his years of literary editorship. He was a witty, sharply intelligent writer who abandoned other possible careers, in particular that of dramatic critic, for the pleasures of shaping the literary columns, and eventually the arts pages, of a newspaper.

For a crime column to appear twice a month in a paper was unprecedented. I wrote the column for more than a decade, received the whole flood of crime stories that came into the paper (reviewers usually get only a small selection), and so read thousands of books in the genre during that period. But 'read' needs inverted commas, for many of the books that piled up on my desk were ill-written, poorly crafted rubbish. Twenty pages were often enough to tell me I should not be reviewing the book, and when two or three others by the same writer had proved equally inept I was likely to give later work no more than a cursory glance to see if some ingenuity of plot went a little way towards redeeming the execrable writing.

The experience was instructive. Until I was threatened by burial under this mass of rubbish I had not realized the full weight of it. The fact is that ninety per cent of crime stories, mystery stories, thrillers, are written by people with no feeling for language, place or character. Once I had understood that, there followed a desire to make distinctions in my column, to abandon the alkaline flatness of most writing about crime stories in favour of something sharper, sometimes even picric. The good should be praised, the eccentric tolerated, the bad excoriated, especially if a well-regarded name was on the title page.

What could be more reasonable? Yet after such knowledge, what forgiveness? The approach did not make me universally loved. Margery Allingham asked that her books should be kept out of my hands, and at the Crime Writers Association a motion was proposed (though decisively defeated) that I should be expelled until such time as I understood a critic's duty to be helpful towards all writers. Some friends took lukewarm reviews or buffetings calmly, others showed a sense of injury. After a decade I began to question my own reactions, felt myself growing stale. I no longer opened each new package with an expectation turning to delight when it proved to contain a first novel to be praised, but instead with the expectation that these volumes would be the mixture as before and that I should be faced with the problem of saying something fresh about them. I told Jack I wanted a change and, ever-amiable, he put me to reviewing novels. I suggested Edmund Crispin as my successor, in part because I knew his approach to be very different from mine, and he wrote the crime column until his death. In recent years the paper's literary editors have had less interest in the crime genre and have given it less space, although a book by an acknowledged master or mistress (John le Carré, P. D. James, Ruth Rendell) is likely to receive special treatment. As for me, within a lustrum I was finding 'straight' novels less interesting than good crime stories, and was allowed to give them up in favour of writing about poetry, biography, social history, with an occasional dash of fiction, a box of literary allsorts that has suited me very well.

Did my crime column have any effect on the general perception of crime stories? I hope and believe my activities in the sixties, followed by the publication of *Bloody Murder* in 1972, played a part in making the distinctions between the genuine and the gimcrack widely acknowledged today. Certainly I learned a good deal during the period. Looking again at that Hundred Best I blush for some of my choices. *The Pit-Prop Syndicate, The Bellamy Trial, The Nursemaid Who Disappeared, The Pleasantries of Old Quong, Venetian Bird, A Case to Answer, Above the Dark Circus* – how many readers would be able to put names to the authors of all these books, let alone claim to have read them? And these titles were not pressed on me, except in one or two cases like *The Nursemaid Who Disappeared*, which I chose rather than another Philip Macdonald title because it was in print. If I were playing the agreeable Hundred Best parlour game today, however, I doubt if anything by Philip Macdonald would make the grade. Nor would several other writers then included now find a place. Time deals more harshly with crime stories than with other fiction, in part because it so insistently embodies the manners and morality of its period, even though on a superficial level.

No doubt some of my now-regretted inclusions were due to my imperceptiveness, but more to the point is the fact that in the fifties the crime story was still comparatively in its infancy. In terms of characterization, attention to forensic detail and police procedure, and truth to the lives and language of the many millions of people below the upper and middle classes, the best British crime stories were immensely inferior to those written now. Things developed differently in the United States with the emergence of writers through the pulp magazines, although the results were little nearer to reality. Chandler, and even Hammett, took a romantic view of their principal characters, and if Ross Macdonald avoided such romanticism in his later books it was at the cost of making his detective Lew Archer a conduit rather than a character. Of course there are few gains without losses, and it is true that not many stories written nowadays compare, in the cunning and deceptiveness of their plotting, with the best of Christie and Sayers, Anthony Berkeley, John Dickson Carr or Ellery Queen. Such cunning is an integral part of many fine crime stories, just as the plot (neglected or despised in so much modern fiction) is a vital element in all of them. Yet often these plot devices were so artificial, so nearly incredible, that they made the books containing them no more than entertaining verbal or visual puzzles to which some kind of story was attached.

Perhaps also I was lucky to have been reviewing in a decade that saw not merely a changed approach in the crime story, but also developments in subtlety, sophistication and style. In it le Carré and Deighton emerged as the first thriller writers comparable with Eric Ambler, and the sixties saw also the flowering of Patricia Highsmith's extraordinary talent, and the beginnings although not the best of P. D. James and Ruth Rendell.

(ii) About This Collection

No more than a sizeable minority of the pieces that follow came from those *Sunday Times* reviews. The reason is simple. Splendid though it was to be given space for writing about crime stories twice a month, the space was still limited and I was expected to deal with a minimum of four and a maximum of six books within it. Reviews like the special one already mentioned were unusual, and even praise of *The Ipcress File* was confined to three or four hundred words, space enough to say hurrah or express disappointment, but not to give reasons in much detail. The pieces that follow, more leisurely and written at greater length, mostly give my reasons for saying yes, no or perhaps.

It was a pleasure to be able to consider the Sherlock Holmes stories, and the man himself, more closely than I had been able to do elsewhere. Perhaps there is nothing new of major importance to be said about the saga, but I don't recall seeing any other comment on Holmes's curious failure to make use of developments in fingerprinting and ballistics, or any serious question about what Belgian painters it can have been who 'entirely absorbed' Holmes's attention in a Bond Street gallery.

The introduction to an edition of *The Riddle of the Sands* was an act of homage to the most extraordinary one-off in the history of the adventure story, a wonderful book even or perhaps especially for those who don't like mucking about in boats. I was particularly pleased to be able to bring back into print two other singletons. Chekhov's only novel was brought to my attention by one of the many correspondents who over the years have pointed out omissions from *Bloody Murder*. In this case my interest was roused particularly by the statement that Chekhov had anticipated by forty years the device used by Agatha Christie in *The Murder of Roger Ackroyd*. The book is a curiosity rather than a masterpiece, but certainly deserved better than the neglect of Chekhov scholars. Neglect had also been the fate of John Mair's *Never Come Back*. Although it had been included in that Hundred Best at the instance of Dilys Powell, I lobbied publishers unsuccessfully for years in the attempt to get it reprinted. One expressed admiration but said it had only a period attraction, another turned it down because a character was called simply 'the Jew' and the book might therefore be thought anti-Semitic. Others were lukewarm. Its appearance caused only a small ripple of critical interst, but a TV version was made, lively enough although lacking the book's individual flavour.

Dates are appended to all the pieces. In some cases they show my fluctuating feelings about a writer, as in the views of le Carré and Chandler. I am among a minority who found the later Smiley books over-written and infuriatingly rather than fascinatingly tortuous, and a smaller minority who admired *The Night Manager*. And a belief that Chandler has been over-praised is expressed in the pieces about him. If I were writing a fourth article today my feeling that many of his one-liners smell of the lamp would be more strongly emphasized. I am astonished that some of my juniors think otherwise, and can only regard them as mistaken.

In some other instances the dates are important. The piece about Patricia Highsmith was written in 1969. For me her talent reached its peak in the early sixties, and was maintained through a series of tense, disturbing novels for more than a decade. Since then there has been a slow decline, associated with her obsessive liking for Tom Ripley, the most popular but not the most convincing character in her books. The profile of P. D. James was commissioned by the *New York Times*, who found what I wrote 'too literary'. A revised version appeared in the paper's magazine but I preferred the original, which is printed here for the first time. Again the date should be noted in relation to the fact that *A Taste For Death* is called her best book (I would still think that), and to the later blossoming of her career as a BBC governor, a speaker much in demand, and her accession to the House of Lords as Baroness James of Notting Hill.

Agatha Christie was one of the targets in a recent TV series called *J'Accuse*, the accusation being that she was a bad and snobbish writer. When approached by the programme-maker I said I should like to say something as counsel for the defence. I should have known better. My twenty minutes of chat was cut to a few phrases which, taken out of context, seemed to endorse the programme's theme. The articles here represent an attempt to come to terms with the disparate elements in her personality, and her writing skills. When one has admitted the justice of much that is said against her, why does she remain so readable, and years after her death so widely read? If I don't provide the answer I have at least asked the question. A similar question should be asked about another often denigrated writer, Edgar Wallace.

The reminiscences of John Creasey and Ross Macdonald need no comment, except perhaps that Creasey was a more complicated character than my brief sketch conveys, and could be an interesting biographical subject. I hope the respect and affection I felt for Ross Macdonald come through as they should, and the interview with Eric Ambler may also be considered as an act of homage to the man who turned the thriller into an adult entertainment with something to say about the kind of society we live in. Simenon has also, of course, provided adult entertainment in the crime story. I have always felt an ambivalence about the work, probably connected (as of course it should not be) with distaste for his personality.

The pieces about real-life characters and cases are perhaps interesting chiefly because they show a writer of fiction trying to cope with the improbabilities and absurdities of the actual. What crime novelist would dare to invent the saga of Hiss's typewriter (about which Allen Weinstock's book by no means says the last word), and what serious writer of spy stories would contemplate creating a figure so outrageous as Colonel Z? One learns with the years that the improbabilities acceptable in fiction are not identical with those of life. Those in fiction, or in crime fiction, should ideally be logical; those of life are mostly random, or the results of coincidences too preposterous for fictional use.

Looking at this selection from a much greater number of articles written over the last four decades (and it is still a dereliction on my part to have written nothing at length about Sciascia, Dürrenmatt, Sjöwall/Wahlöö), what comes through is the variety of the crime story, the ability of writers as different as le Carré, James and Highsmith to find scope for what they wanted to do in fiction under crime's umbrella. The scope it offers to writers is as great as that afforded by any other contemporary approach to fiction. Anything that can be done by, say, Martin Amis or Ian McEwan can be done in the crime story. Indeed, both Amis and McEwan have taken sidelong looks at the form in recent novels. With the exception of Highsmith, who has lived in Europe for many years, American names are absent from this paragraph, and the omission is deliberate. It seems to me that the recent American writers, often praised for ruthless realism, produce for the most part sensational or sentimental sex-grills designed to titillate, written in hard-shelled but soft-boiled sub-Hemingway prose. In that view, as in much else, I am content to be out of fashion.

Julian Symons
April 1994

BRITAIN

The Sherlock Holmes Case

(i) Holmes the First: the Genius

The man with whom Dr Watson casually agreed to share rooms at 221B Baker Street had a distinctive appearance. 'In height he was rather over six feet, and so excessively lean that he seemed to be considerably taller. His eyes were sharp and piercing . . . and his thin, hawk-like nose gave his whole expression an air of alertness and decision. His chin, too, had the prominence and squareness which mark the man of determination.' His handshake was powerful, as the doctor discovered at their first meeting, but the ink and chemical-stained hands had an extraordinary delicacy of touch.

When they began to live together the doctor found that Sherlock Holmes had some unusual, and as many would think disagreeable, habits. These ranged from smoking strong tobacco and performing chemical experiments to strumming on the violin, sometimes playing recognizable airs, but more often scraping carelessly at the fiddle thrown over his knee. He often lay on the sofa hardly speaking, and with a dreamy vacant look that made Dr Watson suspect him of using narcotics. Before long this suspicion was confirmed, when Holmes began to inject himself three times a day with a seven per cent solution of cocaine, varying this with morphia. This went on for months, so that his forearm and wrist became dotted with innumerable puncture-marks, and at last Watson was moved to protest. In reply Holmes said that he had found, as others have done since, that the drugs were 'so transcendently stimulating and clarifying to the mind' that their secondary action was comparatively unimportant. The doctor warned him indignantly that although the brain might be stimulated, it was by 'a pathological and morbid process which . . . may at least leave a permanent weakness'. He spoke as a medical man who felt some responsibility for his companion. Holmes says that he does not question the facts, but remarks simply that he craves for mental exaltation, and has recourse to drugs when life fails to provide it.

He is, he arrogantly claims, the only unofficial consulting detective in the world, 'the last and highest court of appeal in detection'. Scotland Yard detectives ask for his help when they find themselves out of their depth, 'which, by the way, is their normal state'. Dr Watson finds that his friend has a varied and curious range of knowledge, which includes 'profound' learning in chemistry, including in particular the action of poisons, and a remarkable geological skill which enables him to tell different sorts of soil from each other at a glance. He beats dead bodies with a stick to verify how far bruises may be produced after death. He has written a monograph on 140 kinds of tobacco ash, another on the tracing of footprints, and a third on 'the influence of a trade upon the form of the hand, with lithotypes of the hands of slaters, sailors, cork-cutters, compositors, weavers and diamond-polishers'.

The fields of his ignorance are far wider than those of his knowledge. He knows nothing, Watson observes as he jots down points about Holmes at an early stage of their friendship, about literature, philosophy or astronomy, and very little about politics. This is demonstrated in the most emphatic way when he asks who Thomas Carlyle might be, and shows total ignorance of the solar system. Would such knowledge be useful to him as a detective, he asks? Certainly not. 'A man's brain originally is like a little empty attic', and cannot find place for everything. A skilful workman will keep in the attic only tools which may be useful, and will reject everything else. 'It is of the highest importance, therefore, not to have useless facts elbowing out the useful ones.' Watson sums up the character of his friend, when explaining why Sherlock Holmes had no room in his make-up for any emotion, especially that of romantic love:

He was, I take it, the most perfect reasoning and observing machine that the world has seen, but as a lover he would have placed himself in a false position. He never spoke of the softer passions, save with a gibe and a sneer . . . Grit in a sensitive instrument, or a crack in one of his own high-power lenses, would not be more disturbing than a strong emotion in a nature such as his.

Such is Sherlock Holmes as we know him first, in two of the four novels, *A Study in Scarlet* and *The Sign of the Four* — the original title, although Conan Doyle soon dropped the second definite article, perhaps feeling that its repetition was clumsy — and in the opening story of the *Adventures*. He changed a great deal later on, and already in the second novel showed some knowledge of literature, but the original portrait is particularly interesting. It sprang from the contemporary need to conceive a man of genius.

Victorian society seems to us remarkable in its assurance. The dogmatic certainty felt by people in all classes about the inevitable expansion of the British Empire and the sacredness of property, and the acceptance of a natural division between gentlemen and players, masters and men, appear to us astonishing. In the late nineteenth century there might be argument about the forms of religion, but faith in the Established Church and belief in the existence of a supreme being was almost unquestioned, and this spiritual faith had practical importance in reconciling the poor to their lot. Optimistic utilitarians, although they recognized that the poor must always exist, were cheered by the ways in which the general human condition improved each decade with new discoveries in medicine, science and engineering. This society, in which material possessions among the upper and middle classes grew by geometrical rather than arithmetical progression, flourished under the rule of laws which particularly protected property and those who owned it, and punished transgression against the rights of property-owners with great severity. Such an order of things seemed to those who principally benefited from it to be a natural one. They felt no uneasiness about their right to occupy the premier position in society, and did not doubt that all was for the best in the best of all possible worlds.

That is how we feel the Victorians looked upon their society. The view is not wrong but it is incomplete, for these feelings existed beside their opposites. In saying this one does not refer to the tiny minority of socialists and violent radicals who wished to change the state of things altogether, for in Queen Victoria's Britain they had no power and were of little importance. It was among scientists and intellectuals in particular that doubt was felt about the quality and the lasting nature of this broad-bottomed society in which lip-service was paid to religion, but everything was really judged in terms of breeding and money.

A man like John Tyndall, whose researches into the nature of light, heat and electricity had led to important and practical results, was typical of many scientists and engineers in his attitude to such questions. As a scientist, Tyndall was bound to believe in rational explanations of natural phenomena, and so to be drawn towards agnosticism. Yet if he could not believe in a supreme God, Tyndall wished ardently to believe in a superior man, who was not ruled solely by practical and commercial considerations. He found such a man in Thomas Carlyle, as a generation of Oxford students found him a little later in John Ruskin. Both envisaged a new and better world, Ruskin in terms of manual labour and individual craftsmanship, Carlyle in the light of a hero who must come to redeem the desperate state of Britain, a kingdom sunk in spiritual sloth and materialist greed. Carlyle's lectures on heroes began with Odin and Mahomet but ended with Napoleon and Cromwell, and as he grew older this Victorian prophet saw the hero more and more in terms of a military dictator who would get rid of Parliament, destroy the idle aristocrats who did nothing for their country but shoot partridges, and force those unwilling to work to do so by means of whip and chain. Such a hero would not obey the law because he would be above it, and he would substitute for the pettifogging procrastination of Parliament the spiritual values of a hero. The way in which a modern Cromwell could best serve his country, Carlyle said meaningfully to 'Our Only General', Sir Garnet Wolseley, was by sending those people in the Houses of Parliament about their business.

Few went as far as Carlyle, but many in the last quarter of the century felt the need for a hero. Their own lives were ruled by material considerations, yet they needed a figure who would symbolically express in his actions their own imagined finer selves. They were practical people, aware above all things of the value of money; he would care nothing for financial matters. The hero would outrage their regular habits by his eccentricity, would feel nothing of their own respect for orders from above, and might upon occasion flout the law. He would have none of their worshipful feeling for those above themselves in station, yet he would not be a political radical but rather a man outside society, even though he would always be acknowledged as a gentleman. He would not feel their own ordinary sentiments of human love, and must inevitably be an egotist because of the intensity with which he pursued his desired ends. This desired Victorian hero was a kind of superman, although it was a few years before Nietzsche's work was translated, so the title of the *Übermensch* would have been unknown.

This tendency towards turning fallible human beings into stainless myths can be seen to some degree in the slang phrase 'All Sir Garnet' (all correct) derived from Wolseley's name, but most clearly in the career of General Gordon. Here was a man who paid no regard to money, transformed a force of Chinese irregulars into what was called 'The Ever Victorious Army', was unmarried, and in the months before he was sent out to Khartoum was chiefly concerned with discovering the burial place of Jesus Christ. In life many people found Gordon frantically irritating, others thought him a kind of holy fool, and others still that he was half-mad. After his death at Khartoum, however, clubs and boys' homes were named after him, and the real erratic man was forgotten as he took on the features of the perfect Victorian hero. It was entirely in keeping with the creation of a heroic myth that Gordon stained-glass windows should have decorated churches.

Sherlock Holmes was the fictional counterpart of General Gordon. The superman hero was brought to literature in his person. He was deeply egotistical, careless of worldly concerns, a misogynist to the verge of misanthropy. He took little interest in things that concerned the ordinary man, and this alienation was clearly expressed in his drug-taking. Why does Holmes take drugs? Because 'I abhor the dull routine of existence' – that is, the lives most people live. And there are twenty occasions on which he flouts or breaks the law. When he has come to a decision the matter is settled, regardless of what the law or Scotland Yard may think.

This is Sherlock Holmes the First, the pure genius with no concern for anything or anybody outside his work. 'I really cannot congratulate you,' he says when Watson breaks the news that he is to marry Mary Morstan, adding that he himself will never marry 'lest I bias my judgment'. Not a very agreeable fellow, Holmes the First, and some thought of this kind must have occurred to his creator. Perhaps Conan Doyle found so self-centred a man increasingly difficult to write about, perhaps the shift from novels to short stories made after *The Sign of the Four* necessarily involved a change of character.

In any case, the Sherlock Holmes we meet in the three great collections of short stories, the *Adventures*, the *Memoirs* and the *Return*, and in the books that follow them, no longer takes drugs, shows a good deal of knowledge in many matters of which Holmes the First knew nothing (he is able to make a comparison between the battles of Waterloo and Marengo, to mention one of a hundred instances), and feels sympathy for many of his clients, especially if they are young gentlewomen. At the same time Conan Doyle realized that there must be no sacrifice of Holmes's genius. One achievement of the short stories and the later novels is that they present a genius who has the aloofness and other-worldliness which the audience of the time demanded, yet is not just an observing and reasoning machine but also a human being.

(ii) Holmes the Second: the Human Being

There are signs of this new, human Holmes in the very first short story, 'A Scandal in Bohemia'. Irene Adler, we learn in the opening line, will always be *the* woman to Holmes, and certainly he never shows again the open admiration he feels for this contralto who played at La Scala and was then prima donna at the Imperial Opera of Warsaw. (Her real-life original was probably the actress Lola Montes.) Holmes shows here also, for the first but not the last time, an indifference to hereditary nobility which should earn acquittal on the charge of snobbery sometimes made against him. When the affair is settled he is cold, and indeed almost rude, to the King of Bohemia when he observes: 'She seems indeed to be on a very different level to your Majesty,' and ignores the kingly hand offered to him at parting. He rejects an emerald ring by way of payment, taking only Irene's photograph. Could there be a more romantic gesture?

This story sets the keynote for the new Sherlock Holmes. In the future he will often be irascible and impatient, but in spite of those words of Watson's enshrining him as a perfect reasoning and observing machine, he is much more than that. He resists an inclination to horsewhip the scoundrel who deceives short-sighted Mary Sutherland, feels pity and admiration for Helen Stoner who consults him in the matter of the speckled band, and is deeply sympathetic to Hatty Doran, the Californian heiress who acknowledges that she has treated Lord St Simon 'real bad'. These are three instances from the *Adventures*, the first book of short stories. They all concern women, but Holmes is capable of equal charity to his own sex when he thinks it deserved. It is in the *Adventures* also that he tells Mr Holder that his son 'has carried himself in this matter as I should be proud to see my own son do, should I ever chance to have one'.

Holmes's charity is often dispensed, it might be said, from on high, in the sense that it often ignores or runs counter to the law. 'You don't mind breaking the law?' he asks Watson in 'A Scandal in Bohemia', and the respectable doctor blithely answers: 'Not in the least.' So the pattern has been set. There are four cases in the *Adventures* in which Holmes moves outside the law, and by the time of the *Case Book* he is saying with a touch of world-weariness: 'I suppose I shall have to compound a felony as usual.' Yet Holmes the reasoning machine has not been forgotten. He remains a Victorian superman, he is still egotistical, but his law-breaking and law-making now take place in the service of hapless men and women. It is to fulfil a superior Holmesian ideal of justice that he stands by while the blackmailer Charles Augustus Milverton is plugged full of bullets, permits a cheating student to go free in the hope that a bright future awaits him in Rhodesia, and with Watson's agreement brings in a 'Not Guilty' verdict in favour of a man who has shattered another man's head with a poker 'as though he were a rotten pumpkin'. As he remarks in the last of these cases, he would rather play tricks with the law of England than with his own conscience.

This then is the mature Sherlock Holmes, a man sometimes brusque but always tender-hearted, irritable upon occasion with his obtuse friend the doctor, but deeply distressed when through him Watson runs into unexpected danger. The writing of the novels and stories spanned forty years of Conan Doyle's life, and by the time of the *Case Book* the Sherlock Holmes presented in the first two novels had, except in a physical sense, become a changed man.

(iii) Holmes + Watson = Conan Doyle

The original model for Sherlock Holmes was Dr Joseph Bell, one of Conan Doyle's professors at Edinburgh, who in the manner of the detective was able to make deductions which showed him at a glance that a patient was a left-handed cobbler. The model for Watson was Conan Doyle's secretary, Major Wood. But as soon as those statements have been made, some qualification is necessary. Dr Bell always said Conan Doyle had greatly exaggerated his deductive ability, and certainly many of Holmes's deductive flights go far beyond the instances given to us of Dr Bell's powers; and although Major Wood looks remarkably like the Watson generally shown to us on the screen, Conan Doyle looks like him too, particularly in photographs taken in middle age. (Neither of them much resembles the Watson given us by the stories' most famous illustrator, Sidney Paget.)

Conan Doyle not only resembled Watson in appearance. Part of him was similar to Watson in character. The figure he presented to the world was that of bluff, extrovert British citizen, with strongly held conventional views on many matters like the virtues of the British Empire and the outrageous absurdity of modern art. So far Conan Doyle was Dr Watson, or perhaps it should be said that Conan Doyle perfectly understood Watson, sympathized with his decency and even with his obtuseness, and felt Watson represented much that was stable and good in British life.

But if part of Conan Doyle was Dr Watson, another and to us more interesting part was Sherlock Holmes. From his Irish ancestors Conan Doyle inherited a Celtic streak that ran through his life and his writing. From early manhood he was interested in the supernatural, and in his last decade he became an ardent propagandist for spiritualism. In relation to spiritualism he was credulous, but in dealing with the criminal cases that concerned him because of his desire to put right official injustices, he showed deductive powers of which Holmes might have been proud:

He held the paper close to his eyes and rather sideways, proving not only a high degree of myopia but marked astigmatism. The idea of such a man scouring fields at night and assaulting cattle while avoiding the watching police was ludicrous to anyone who can imagine what the world looks like to eyes with myopia of eight dioptres.

That is not Sherlock Holmes talking, but Conan Doyle giving one reason why the Parsee solicitor George Edalji was innocent of the crimes for which he had received a seven-year sentence. The mental acuity and powers of observation shown by Conan Doyle in such investigations, and the ingenuity of his various suggestions for protective devices to be used by soldiers and sailors during World War I belong to the Celtic side of his nature. His mind was strongly practical, but the Celtic streak made him also a man fascinated by all kinds of unlikely speculations.

It is this blend of speculation and rationalism, of Holmes and Watson, in Sir Arthur Conan Doyle, that helps to give the stories their unique flavour. The solutions to the problems are always reached by reason, but there is something disturbing about many of them that leaves one with a shiver after the rational explanation. 'The Copper Beeches' terrified me as a child and adolescent, with that request by the permanently smiling Mr Rucastle that his new governess should cut off her luxuriant chestnut hair, and wear a dress in a particular shade of electric blue. So did the livid yellow face that watched Mr Grant Munro from the cottage near to his house, and the description of the resident patient, Mr Blessington, when he is found hanged:

The neck was drawn out like a plucked chicken's, making the rest of him seem the more obese and unnatural by the contrast. He was clad only in his long night-dress, and his swollen ankles and ungainly feet protruded starkly from beneath it.

The neck drawn out like a plucked chicken's, those swollen ankles – and the electric blue dress – are memories that have stayed with me. So has the 'peculiar yellow band, with brownish speckles, which seemed to be bound tightly round [the] head' of Dr Grimesby Roylott, the 'horrid red, spongy surface' of the wound where Victor Hatherley's thumb has been 'torn right out from the roots', and the terribly emaciated figure whose mouth is covered with sticking plaster, met by the innocent Greek interpreter Mr Melas. Many of the effects in these stories belong to the dark side of the moon. It does not seem that Conan Doyle intended or even recognized these effects, but it is such touches of the macabre that play a large part in making us read these tales again and again. They have the rarest quality of detective short stories in their own or any period, that of imagination.

(iv) The Unimportance of Sherlock's Limitations

If we compare a Sherlock Holmes novel with a good modern story from a technical point of view, the former may seem a broken-backed affair, in the sense that a long explanatory section from the past is embedded in three of the novels. Readers have been known also to complain that in the fourth, *The Hound of the Baskervilles*, they know the villain's identity too soon for their pleasure. The short stories have received their share of criticism, one historian going so far as to say that they are often loose, obvious, imitative, trite and repetitious. Perhaps, then, one should say something about Sherlock's limitations, and why they are of little importance.

One criticism often made is that the deductions which so much astonish Watson and others are capable of more than one explanation. True enough, but this is a criticism of such wretched meanness that those who make it seriously must be incapable of enjoying any imaginative intellectual flight. The fourteen deductions made by Holmes from a battered old felt hat in 'The Blue Carbuncle', the way in which Mycroft and Sherlock cap each other's observations in 'The Greek Interpreter', give delight both in their cleverness and by the rhythms of their phrasing. Yes, those deductions about Mr Baker's foresight, his moral retrogression and other things might properly be called conjectures, and Mycroft's conclusion drawn from a man wearing ammunition boots is daring rather than convincing, but properly viewed (that is, viewed by admirers) such things enhance rather than damage our belief in Holmes the superman. Those opening passages in which Holmes demonstrates his genius, instead of merely announcing it like most fictional detectives, are perfect overtures to the feats of deductive skill that lie ahead. One mark of the later stories' inferiority (with exceptions like 'Wisteria Lodge' and 'The Bruce-Partington Plans') is the rarity of those dazzling openings, and the general lack of surprising deductions.

It is similarly beside the point to complain that some of the puzzles are not very puzzling, particularly to a modern reader. Certainly this is true, and one could go further and say that in a number of stories there is no puzzle at all, of the kinds cunningly devised and carefully solved by writers X, Y and Z. But this truth is of no importance, because X, Y and Z can do nothing except construct puzzles. Take away the puzzle, and the story is sawdust. Take away the puzzle from a Holmes story, and almost everything is left: the genius of Holmes, his relationship with Watson, and the rich Victorian romanticism that suffuses the novels and most of the stories. Who ever read 'The Dancing Men', or the other code stories, for the puzzle? It is the fascination of the little dancing men on the page, or of the questions and answers in 'The Musgrave Ritual', that draws us back to them. Conan Doyle was a story-teller, especially a teller of short stories, and these tales are finely presented and beautifully told. That many of them also contain baffling puzzles adds to our pleasure, but is not the origin of it.

There is a more serious case to be made, and I don't think anybody has ever made it, against the nature of Holmes's methods. Those brilliant openings demonstrate his powers of observation, but are rarely directly concerned with deductive methods. The methods are said to be scientific, and certainly they compare well with the astonishing blunders of Lestrade and Athelney Jones (it is worth noting that the only detective positively praised by Holmes, Inspector Baynes of 'Wisteria Lodge', is not a London man, but belongs to the Surrey constabulary). When we compare Holmes's forensic practice with the best scientific knowledge of the time, however, he often seems strangely ignorant.

Startling advances in scientific deduction were made in the last quarter of the nineteenth century, particularly through the anthropometrical method of Alphonse Bertillon. If, Bertillon said, you measured a man's height, head, ears, arms, fingers and feet, it would be found that no two men were identical. Anthropometry, which was extended so that a card called the *portrait parlé* was issued for everybody in police custody (it showed a picture, plus eleven different measurements), had many triumphs, and was used by the police of almost every country in Europe until the end of the century.

The Bertillon system is mentioned twice in the stories – in 'The Naval Treaty' when Holmes, in conversation with Watson, expresses 'his enthusiastic admiration of the French savant', and in *The Hound of the Baskervilles* when Holmes is annoyed by Dr Mortimer's reference to Bertillon as the greatest expert in Europe 'to the man of precisely scientific mind'. It is true that the British police were lukewarm about anthropometry, but they did keep some measurement records and one would have expected Holmes to make use of the system, at least in cases involving known criminals.

More remarkable is the way in which Holmes ignores fingerprints. The possibility that fingerprints might be unique had been mooted in the 1870s, a murder in Buenos Aires was solved in 1892 through the identification of a bloody thumb-mark on a door, and in 1900 Sir Edward Henry devised a workable registration system for the recognition of prints. He was appointed head of the CID, and fingerprinting was made the official identification system in Britain.

All this seems to have passed Holmes by. In 'The Norwood Builder' he suggests how the bloody thumb-mark (an echo of the Buenos Aires case?) could have been forged, and in 'The Three Gables' the inspector mentions the possibility of 'finger-marks' on a sheet of paper, a remark the detective ignores. There is not a single case in which Holmes shown any interest in possible prints. Nor does he seem to be aware of the developments in ballistics by which bullets could be identified through the rifling on a gun barrel.

Conan Doyle must have known of these advances in forensic science, and it is surprising that even in the later stories, some of them written in the 1920s, he did not allow Sherlock Holmes to show such knowledge. Perhaps he simply did not bother to do so, but it is more likely that he felt Holmes's methods to have been so firmly fixed early on that they should not be changed. It is more romantically impressive, more appropriate to a superman, to be able to distinguish 140 different varieties of tobacco and be familiar with 42 different impressions left by tyres, than to be making fingerprint and ballistic tests. If these were Conan Doyle's reasons for ignoring such modern discoveries, he was perfectly right. Sherlock Holmes comes through to us as a man with a genius for his occupation, and this effect would have been lessened if we had been given details about the nuts and bolts of forensic investigation which no doubt he used. Such details are for the groundlings of detection, not for the eagles.

(v) The Lasting Myth

The myth endures. The characters casually invented by the young doctor practising without great success at Southsea are not only immortal in themselves, but have sprouted a monstrous progeny on film and TV, in worlds where Sherlock Holmes meets Jack the Ripper and Sigmund Freud, or preserves a bombsight from the plans of Moriarty. Almost every year a member of the Sherlock Holmes Society publishes a book about the contradictions in the canon, sometimes suggesting that Holmes is real and Conan Doyle a fiction. The sitting room at 221B Baker Street may be seen in the 'Sherlock Holmes' pub along with relics of the cases, and the Post Office acknowledges letters written to the detective at Baker Street, just as they do letters written to Father Christmas. Groups and societies, sometimes with names as eccentric as The King of Scandinavia's Own Sherlockians, flourish in almost every country.

For the Victorians and Edwardians the myth took its power from the quality of Holmes as superman, dispenser of justice outside the law. Today we are inclined to distrust such supermen, and the myth's endurance is based upon different qualities. The stories exist for us bathed forever in the warm sunlight of Victorian certainties (we glimpse it always through those London fogs), in a world where a hansom is always conveniently at hand, trains are waiting to take travellers from London to the sinister suburbs, and Holmes is able to deduce that a man stayed in 'one of the most select London hotels' from the fact that he paid eight shillings for a bed and eightpence for a glass of sherry. 'There are not many in London which charge at that rate.' Holmes, Watson, Lestrade and Stanley Hopkins and the rest are for us period pieces, belonging to a world which ended with the First World War. There can be no better example of Conan Doyle's artistic tact than the fact that the last Sherlock Holmes story takes place on 2 August 1914.

Yet although this period flavour has its differing charm for each succeeding generation, the power of the myth rests on other pedestals as well. Conan Doyle did not think very highly of the Holmes saga, believing that it kept him from more important work, yet it was in these tales and not in the historical novels he valued so much that his imagination ran free. Critics have said that both Holmes and Watson are two-dimensional figures, and they are right in the sense that they exist only in the context of the puzzles presented to Holmes, and that neither is ever involved in any personal emotional conflict. They are 'characters', it is said, rather than human beings. This is true, yet the relationship of these 'characters' to each other and to their world is extraordinarily convincing. The power of such mythical figures transcends the usual considerations, so that we do not question their actions or motives as we would those of ordinary human beings. Holmes and Watson live in the world of Don Quixote and Sancho Panza, not in that of Edwin Clayhanger and Soames Forsyte.

One hopes that in the end Conan Doyle understood this, and became reconciled to the fact that the man he sent to his death over the Reichenbach Falls was to be his lifelong companion. It must be said, however, that the probability is otherwise. Once, talking in Amsterdam about detective stories, I had in the audience people who had listened to Conan Doyle at a lecture he gave there shortly before his death in 1930. His subject was spiritualism, but many of the questions were about Sherlock Holmes. The lecturer abruptly refused to answer them, telling the questioners that he had nothing more to say about the detective or his cases.

In the preface to the last collection of stories, Sherlock Holmes's creator struck a gentler note. These lighter sketches, as he called them, had not after all affected his more serious writing. It might be, he thought, that there was some fantastic limbo in which such minor children of the imagination as Dickens's cockneys and Thackeray's worldlings still existed. If such a fancy was indulged, 'Perhaps in some humble corner of such a Valhalla, Sherlock and his Watson may for a time find a place.' In suggesting a time limit for these particular inhabitants of Valhalla, Sir Arthur Conan Doyle was, as in some other things, too modest.

(1981)

(vi) *The Hound of the Baskervilles*

It was in December 1893 that purchasers of the *Strand Magazine* read, with delight but dismay, 'The Adventure of the Final Problem', the dismay springing from the apparent death of Sherlock Holmes. The sound of public protest was loud and did not, as Doyle had expected, fade away, but instead became one of Wagnerian power. Newspaper editorials, pleas from Conan Doyle's mother and from friends, were joined to thousands of letters like one from three 'ardent admirers' in Baltimore urging the author to 'Favour us with another one of your works on the famous detective Sherlock Holmes'. After several years Conan Doyle gave way and wrote *The Hound of the Baskervilles*, although he made it clear that this was an early adventure. Later he accepted Holmes's immortality, brought him back from the Reichenbach Falls, and published another novel and three collections of short stories.

The *Hound* originally appeared, like the earlier short stories, in the *Strand*. 'The Coneydoil or Shurlacombs,' *Punch* said, 'likes to run through the *Strand* with his tail in parts – all of them strong and healthy – then he collects it all together.' The first instalment carried a footnote acknowledging the help of 'my friend, Mr Fletcher Robinson', and the published volume was dedicated to him. The two men had met in South Africa during the Boer War, which Robinson attended as correspondent of the *Daily Express*, Conan Doyle as member of a volunteer hospital unit, and then historian of the war. They liked each other, played golf together on returning to England, and later talked about writing a story in collaboration. Robinson told his companion of Dartmoor legends, including one involving a spectral hound, and made his own notes for 'The Ipplepen Hound, A Gruesome Tale of Dartmoor'. However, he never wrote the story, and when Conan Doyle said in dedicating a copy of his own book to Robinson that the journalist had inspired it, and that his name 'should properly appear above my own', he exaggerated his debt. Fletcher Robinson gave him an idea that was perhaps the original inspiration of the story, but we may be thankful that it was not called *The Ipplepen Hound*.

The book Conan Doyle wrote is by general agreement the most successful of the four Holmes novels. It is the only one that follows a continuous narrative, without a long excursion back into the past. For modern readers, as no doubt for those of 1901, it is evident, right from the opening scene in which Holmes makes deductions from a walking stick left in the Baker Street apartment, that Sherlock is in sparkling form. He is a little hard on Watson in this first chapter, but anybody who reads the tales in the order that they were written will soon realize that this is a Holmes much less anti-social and authoritarian than the character met in the earlier novels and short stories. Although he orders a pound of the strongest shag tobacco when puzzled by the Baskerville problem, there is no hint of anything like his resort to the cocaine bottle at the end of the *The Sign of Four*. The two opening chapters are classic Holmes, including as they do the surprising deductions, the appearance of the interestingly eccentric medical client who covets Homes's skull ('Would you have any objection to my running my finger along your parietal fissure?'), and one of the near approaches to the fictitious, legendary 'Elementary, my dear Watson', which industrious researchers still hope to find. And these opening chapters end with one of the most evocative phrases in the whole canon: 'Mr Holmes, they were the footprints of a gigantic hound.' The story ran through nine issues of the magazine, and Conan Doyle was well aware of the need to provide a cliff-hanger to close each instalment. That first one is particularly memorable.

Are there still readers, eighty years and more after the Hound first leapt over the Moor, to whom the secret of Sir Charles Baskerville's death will come as a surprise? I think it must be assumed such readers exist, and that secrets should not be given away. It will do no harm to say, however, that in this story it is lightly hidden, and likely to be discovered by readers before

Sherlock Holmes reveals it two-thirds of the way through. As in the other Holmes novels, Conan Doyle was less concerned with the mystery than with the tale. He was always interested in the supernatural and the occult, and what caught his imagination in those talks with Fletcher Robinson was the idea of the hound that had the appearance of being outside ordinary animal creation, a survivor perhaps from the Lost World Conan Doyle was to invent a few years later. Since this was a Sherlock Holmes story there must be a rational explanation, but the author let his imagination play around the irrational one. The legend of the 'great black beast . . . larger than any hound that ever mortal eye has rested upon' that tore out the throat of Sir Hugo Baskerville, was made more disturbing by an evocation of Dartmoor which owed much to imagination. Dartmoor bogs there were, but nothing like the great Grimpen Mire in which ponies perished, and the Moor with its barrenness, its vastness, and its stone huts in which escaped convicts and strange visitors might hide, is created upon a scale distinctly larger than life. Like many other Holmes stories, long and short, the tale has a chilly air about it that derives less from the mystery than from the atmosphere surrounding it. The *Hound* has perhaps more of this quality than anything else in the whole saga, except two or three of the short stories, most notably 'The Copper Beeches'.

Apart from such imaginative creepiness the tale offers us three distinct kinds of enjoyment. The first is The Pleasure of the Period Reference. In this category come young Sir Henry's remark about installing a row of electric lamps that will lighten the darkness of the Yew Alley, with a 'thousand candle-power Swan and Edison' in front of the hall door. One is pleased when Laura Lyons, although 'set up in a typewriting business' on her own, and by way of being extremely independent, tells Watson that she could not possibly pay a visit alone at night to a bachelor's house (although she does not flinch at a garden rendezvous). And there must be many readers who, like me, will have had to consult a reference book to find out what kind of stick was called a Penang Lawyer. It is a Malayan stick made of dwarf palm, often confused in England – although one hopes not by Watson – with a malacca cane. The charm of the Period Reference lies partly in the recognition that it is so only for us, and that Edwardian readers will have found such things as much a matter of course as the hansom cab which 'flew madly off down Regent Street' when Holmes spotted its black-bearded occupant as the man following Sir Henry Baskerville.

The Pleasure of the Unsolved Mysteries occurs here more than in the other novels. In the *Hound* Holmes shows an unusual interest in art. His suggestion to Watson that they should drop into a Bond Street picture gallery and fill in the time until they are due to meet Sir Henry at the Northumberland Hotel may sound merely casual, but then we learn that he became 'entirely absorbed in the pictures of the modern Belgian masters'. Who can they have been? The only Belgian painter of the time now remembered is James Ensor, whose macabre masks and skeletons were not being exhibited in London at that time, and would have been unlikely to please Holmes. The detective evidently annoyed the usually placid Watson, who says that his friend had the crudest ideas about art. What sort of ideas? When, in the early days of their acquaintance, Watson made a list of Holmes's accomplishments and limitations, he did not even bother to mention art. In this story, however, Holmes is able to identify a Kneller, and a possible Reynolds. That sounds an orthodox taste enough, so what annoyed Watson? Had Holmes visited one of the Impressionist exhibitions, or seen some of the pictures Monet painted in London? Was he an admirer of Whistler's 'Nocturnes'? The puzzle is minor but insoluble.

One of more importance, directly linked to Holmes's professional skills, is his curious indifference to discoveries in the fields of medical and forensic criminology during the last quarter of the nineteenth century. His own achievements, of course, were immense. In the *Hound* they make it possible for him to date an eighteenth-century manuscript at a mere glance, and instantly to recognize fragments cut from newspapers. There is as much difference between 'the leaded bourgeois type' of a *Times* article and the 'slovenly print' of a halfpenny paper, he tells us, as between a Negro and an 'Esquimaux'. We know from other cases that he was expert in distinguishing cigar, cigarette and pipe ash, had written on tattoo marks, secret writings (he had analysed 160 separate ciphers), the use of dogs in detection – this list of accomplishments is by no means complete, but the omissions are equally surprising.

In this period Alphonse Bertillon was at the height of his fame, yet in the whole Holmes canon there are only two passing references to the great Frenchman, one (in this book) a little huffy. Then there is the question of fingerprints. Francis Galton's *Fingerprints*, with its suggested classification of deltas, arches, loops and whorls, did not appear until 1892, but one might have hoped Holmes could have been working on the same lines. There is, however, not a single case in which he shows any interest in identification through fingerprints. He showed no awareness of current developments in ballistics, nor does he mention Lacassagne's astonishing achievement in forensic medicine, when in 1889 he reconstructed a skeleton so that by comparison of bone sizes, analysis of a deformed knee, examination of teeth, hair colour and thickness, he was able to pronounce with certainty on the skeleton's identity. Well, perhaps it was part of Holmes's genius that he managed without such knowledge.

The Pleasure of Holmes and Watson is something we get in every story, but there is something unusual about it here, the particularity resting in the fact that a little more than a third of the book consists of Watson's solo investigations. He reports back to Holmes in London, where the detective is the only person who can stop a blackmailing scandal involving 'one of the most revered names in England'. Watson behaves with a commonsense intelligence for which he is rarely given credit, and Holmes acknowledges the value of his friend's investigations with much more than usual warmth.

In all of the four novels Conan Doyle seems to have felt that to keep Holmes on the scene throughout, with the consequent need for new mysteries to be posed and fresh deductions made about them, might become monotonous. Many of the short stories turn upon a single ingenious point, but Conan Doyle tried to enlarge the interest of the novels beyond such ingenuity. In the three others he turned back to the past, not altogether satisfactorily, but here the break from Holmes is made by leaving him in the background for a while and turning the spotlight on Watson. We are given the doctor's narrative and can make our own deductions, although the interest of the story is such that generations of readers have been carried along by it, without feeling too much concern about the puzzle. Taken as a puzzle simply it contains some characteristic felicities – reading the story again after a longish

interval I found myself enjoyably baffled once more by the stolen
boots – and some aspects that make one raise a reflective eyebrow.
Among them is the fact that the villain, although no doubt
planning 'refined, cold-blooded, deliberate murder', as Holmes
says, actually does nothing which would have led to conviction in
any court of law or even, as it seems to me, to his arrest. It was
just as well that the great Grimpen Mire claimed another victim.

The fame of Sherlock Holmes has spread far beyond the printed
word. The films about him alone are numbered in hundreds. Many
are ludicrous, a few attempt faithfulness. The German *Der Hund
von Baskervilles* of 1914 seems to have been the Hound's first
screen appearance, the first British production coming in 1921
with the properly hatchet-faced but diminutive Eille Norwood as
the detective. In 1932 Robert Rendel, again a rather short actor,
played Holmes (with dialogue by Edgar Wallace), and in 1939
Basil Rathbone's combination with Nigel Bruce made what many
consider the best Holmes and Watson pairing. There have been
other Sherlocks and Watsons, in plays and musicals, on radio and
TV. Even the best of them, however, like Granada's TV series,
unintentionally emphasize that Sherlock Holmes is essentially a
literary creation. Conan Doyle's dialogue is faithful to its time,
which means that it sounds stilted today, and if the superman
figure of Holmes is played faithfully he may well seem disagreeable
or ridiculous. Inevitably outlines are softened, conversations
changed, the two great characters altered, and although this may
be done intelligently and with good intentions, much of the original
magic is lost. Holmes and Watson are not characters in the ordinary
sense, but mythic figures who belong to the British past. They
cannot be removed from that past and made modern without
having their stature much lessened, or being turned into a joke.
Like Johnson and Boswell they are mythical creatures rather than
three-dimensional living men. They belong not to stage, cinema,
TV or radio, but to the printed page.

(1987)

Erskine Childers:
The Life and the Book

1

In the last quarter of the nineteenth century British governments, both Unionist and Liberal, had frequent spasms of alarm about the possibility of invasion in the event of war. Fortifications were constructed for the defence of London, in Essex on a line from Tilbury to Epping, and along the North Downs. A chain of linking fortresses was built, most of them in Kent and Surrey, and in the event of invasion these were to become mobilization centres, to be manned by more than a hundred thousand volunteer infantrymen and gunners, and more than two hundred guns. As late as 1897 the leading Victorian military theorist Spenser Wilkinson was writing of the need to complete the connecting works between the Kent and Surrey fortresses. The enemy envisaged in this war, the possible invader, was Britain's European rival for most of the past century: France.

All this seems strange, perhaps hardly credible, today: but in a world where France was automatically considered as Britain's likely enemy in time of war, it can be understood that a tremendous shock was caused in 1903 by *The Riddle of the Sands*, in which Germany replaced France as the potential invader. The most prolific writer of spy stories at the time, William Le Queux, was inclined to regard all European nationals as likely plotters against Britain, but his chief villains were French, with Russians a good second, and the Germans a long way behind. *England's Peril* (1899), in which Lord Casterton is the victim of an exploding cigar, concerns an attempt by the head of the French Secret Service to get hold of the plans of Portsmouth Harbour. Casterton had been making speeches about the inadequacy of our military preparations, and had to be got out of the way. *The Great War in*

England in 1897, published in 1894, has the feared invasion taking place, the French having joined hands with the Russians. It is true that *Of Royal Blood* (1900) introduces the German spy Oswald Krauss, but we learn that he has changed from the German to the French Secret Service, and is attempting 'to secure possession of the secrets of the Foreign Office'. Even more important secrets are at risk in *His Majesty's Minister* of 1901 where a French spy, operating from a cottage between Staines and Kingston, has tapped the private wire between Windsor Castle and the Foreign Office. *The Under Secretary* (1902) finds the Italians joining in by inducing Dudley Chisholm, the Foreign Minister's secretary, to copy vital cipher despatches from Constantinople. In *The Man from Downing Street* the French, 'plotting against English supremacy', are prepared to cede the French Riviera to Italy in return for help against the hated British.

Le Queux's books were widely read, even by important politicians. (Arthur Balfour, then Prime Minister, asked, 'Are you criticizing my taste in literature?' when found reading a Le Queux novel.) *The Riddle of the Sands*, however, had the propagandist motive of convincing the military and naval establishments that the chief danger to Britain came from Germany. Soon after he began writing, Erskine Childers told a friend: 'It's a yachting story, with a purpose, suggested by a cruise I once took in German waters. I discovered a scheme of invasion directed against England. I'm finding it terribly difficult as being in the nature of a detective story.'

Childers was not a professional novelist, and did not write the book for fame or profit, but as a warning. He was thirty years old at the turn of the century, a patriotic Englishman, although the family had strong Irish connections on his mother's side, and much of his childhood and youth had been spent in Wicklow. He joined the City Imperial Volunteers in the early weeks of the South African War, and on his return wrote *In the Ranks of the CIV*, which had considerable popular success. Small, neat, and not very articulate in company, Childers was unobtrusively talented. He had passed third highest in the Civil Service examination, and seemed settled in a true civil servant's post, that of committee clerk at the House of Commons.

Behind the unemotional exterior, however, was a powerful

romantic imagination, nurtured on Dumas and Fenimore Cooper and expressed in early manhood chiefly through a passion for sailing. Childers was undeterred by the permanent sciatic limp left with him after some adventurous walking in Ireland, and was known as a sailor even at Haileybury where he spent a lot of time piloting 'strange craft on the local river Lea'. He owned first a 'nice little eight tonner' named *Sheila*, and later the seven-ton *Vixen*, of which he wrote:

No one could call the Vixen beautiful. We grew to love her in the end but never to admire her. A low freeboard, a high coach-house cabin roof, and a certain over-sparred appearance aloft, would unnerve the most honied tongue. In the 'saloon' [the sailor] would find just enough headroom to allow him to sit upright: and before he could well help himself, the observation would escape him that the centreplate case was an inconveniently large piece of furniture . . .

Readers of *The Riddle of The Sands* will find no difficulty in recognizing here some aspects of the *Dulcibella*.

In 1897 Childers crossed the North Sea in the *Vixen* in the company of his elder brother Henry. They explored the Frisian islands and the sandy channels between them, like Davies and Carruthers in the book, and when Henry had to return to England his brother carried on alone. In the following year he repeated the voyage, with some variations, with a hired hand as companion, and made altogether six trips to and around the islands. There is no record of the occasion when he discovered the 'scheme of invasion directed against England', and he later said he had invented the whole plot, although 'I have since had most remarkable confirmation of the ideas in it.' When he sent the manuscript to a publisher, drastic revisions were asked of him, some of which he made. The book's purpose was, as he put it, to offer 'convincing fact', and he complained that the publisher had 'tried to wreck it by advertising it as a "novel"'. He was astonished by the chorus of praise for the book, as indeed was the publisher. It was a success from the day of publication, and has almost never been out of print.

2

The Riddle of the Sands received attention immediately because of its topical importance. Childers was no writer of cheap thrillers but a respectable civil servant, and what he said was taken seriously. The warning of possible German invasion and its surprising nature (the details are part of the book's secret) lent impetus to the reformers who were calling for an increase in the size of the Army and the establishment of a General Staff, and to such naval figures as Admiral Fisher, who insisted that the biggest danger to Britain came from Germany's rapidly increasing naval power. But of course these controversies, in which Childers's book played an important part, are long dead. Indeed, if any part of the story is heavy-going today it is the passages which were most obviously topical. *The Riddle of the Sands* is read now as a tale of adventure.

The book has the charm and gaiety of youth, and succeeds brilliantly, in part because of its lack of calculation. The message about German intentions was serious, but the rest of the story was written for fun, and the author's enjoyment, his zest for sailing, his feeling like that of Davies that 'the "shore" . . . was an inferior element, merely serving as an annexe to the water – a source of necessary supplies' comes through sweet and clear. *Irresponsible* is a word that would have made the serious-minded Childers wince, yet it is a sort of irresponsibility in Davies, a reckless disregard of probabilities communicated in the end to Carruthers, that gives the story its unique flavour. There are many sailing details, and they are important as the technical gimmicks used in some spy stories today are important, yet no knowledge of sailing is needed to enjoy the account of Davies's narrow escape from drowning, or on a mundane level the problems posed by the centreplate. Nor need you be a sailor to understand the most exciting chapter in the book, the fog-bound journey in a dinghy through the narrow waters of the Memmert Balje. The extraordinary character of the Frisian islands, hardly more than sandbanks on which a few people live, is also quite remarkably conveyed.

An adventure story, whether it is *Kidnapped* or *Greenmantle*, doesn't call for great depth of characterization, and it is right that *Dulcibella* should be described with more exactness than either

Davies or Carruthers. Yet they are clear and distinguishable, and
so is the code that leaves them worrying about the ethics of spying
even for their own side, although they are in no doubt that a
Briton who plots with Germans is 'the vilest creature on God's
earth'. Those with a keen eye for comparison between past and
present may notice that the concept of the double agent is vaguely
outlined here, perhaps for the first time in fiction. There is some
mockery of the popular conception of a spy, perhaps with Le
Queux in mind. Davies and Carruthers are certainly a long way
from 'those romantic gentlemen that one reads of in sixpenny
magazines, with a Kodak in his tie-pin, a sketch-book in the lining
of his coat, and a selection of disguises in his hand luggage'.

Nor are the Germans seen as villains. Childers takes pains to
make it clear that he has little but admiration for the German
desire to become the leading nation in Europe. They are already,
Davies says, the greatest military power on the continent:

'But what I'm concerned with is their sea-power. It's a new thing with
them, but it's going strong, and that Emperor of theirs is running it for all
it's worth. He's a splendid chap, and anyone can see he's right ... The
command of the sea is *the* thing nowadays, isn't it?'

At the time such remarks were true and timely, although within
a few years the development of the aeroplane changed the shape
of warfare.

If the book has a weakness it is not, as Childers thought, because
he had been 'weak enough to "spatchcock" a girl into it'. To the
contrary, Clara Dollmann is a perfectly adequate heroine, lively,
personable, and quite well integrated into the story. With her
father, however, the author is distinctly uneasy. It is likely that he
had no taste for drawing villains, and would have found it
impossible to create an attractive scoundrel like Rupert of Hentzau
or Long John Silver. One of the book's attractions, in fact, is that
Childers so often involuntarily proclaims himself an amateur. He
was not by nature a writer of fiction. It was simply that the period
was right, the setting was one he loved, he decided to convey his
message about national defence in fictional terms – and the result
was a classic adventure story.

3

The book made Childers famous, a desired guest at dinner parties, a man whose opinions on military and naval matters were courted. Le Queux briskly changed enemies, so that in *The Invasion of 1910* (published in 1905) and other works, the threat to Britain came from Germany. It might have been expected that Childers would try to repeat the success of *The Riddle of the Sands* in a sequel, but he never attempted another work of fiction. His opinions on national defence, too, made him sometimes an awkward customer. When invited by Leopold Amery to write the final volume of the great *Times History of the War in South Africa* he produced a work often highly critical of military attitudes, and with a concluding chapter so strongly Liberal in tone that Amery, an aggressive Imperial Tory, insisted on making changes that amounted to censorship.

The decisive event in his life, it can be seen in retrospect, was marriage in 1904 to Mary Alden (called Molly) Osgood, daughter of a well-to-do American doctor. Was it part of her attraction that she was much more lame than he – in fact, almost a cripple – as the result of a diseased hip? In spite of the disability she came to share his passion for sailing, and they had two sons, the elder of whom became in 1973 President of Ireland. The extreme happiness of their marriage can be seen in their moving letters. It came in part from Molly's own ardent romanticism, and the way in which she shared her husband's indifference to orthodox opinion and his determination to see a course through to the end. Erskine Childers was a man always looking for a virtuous and difficult cause: and in 1908 he found one in Home Rule for Ireland.

Home Rule had been Liberal policy for more than a quarter of a century, but Childers brought to it the zeal of a convert from Imperialism. He became a propagandist for the cause, writing in 1911 *The Framework of Home Rule*, and in 1914 engaging in a gun-running exploit of considerable daring when he picked up rifles and ammunition off the mouth of the Scheldt, and landed them at Howth. Childers had been moved to the gun-running by his disgust at the feebleness of the Liberal Government in face of the Curragh Mutiny, when Army officers refused to move north to maintain British rule in Ulster in case of trouble, offering their resignations instead. Molly was with him on the gun-running trip and remembered how, when they were outside Howth in weather too bad for a motor boat to put out, 'he turned to me and said, "I am going to risk it".' She herself was in a state of exaltation during the trip, 'so happy and triumphant, so proud of ourselves that we swear we are comfortable', even though they slept, crawled over, sat and ate on guns.

Yet Childers remained a British patriot. He was in uniform within hours of the outbreak of World War I, first as a naval lieutenant, later as an airplane observer who (now Lieutenant Commander) received the DSC for his brilliance and daring. But Ireland was his continual concern, and in 1917 he welcomed the opportunity to act as one of the secretaries to an Irish Convention called by Lloyd George. His experience as a civil servant qualified him for the task, but the Convention was little more than a device for shelving the Irish question on the part of a Prime Minister occupied with winning the war in the rest of Europe. For Childers, however, the experience was decisive. He had hoped for a peaceful settlement in Ireland even after the Easter Rising of 1916, when he wrote to a cousin:

The typical rebel is often half-crazy and half-starved, a neurotic nourished on dreams. We shoot a decent number – again by a venerable convention, probably justified – the wisest then say, 'Yes, but now we must do something.'

But with the inevitable failure of the Convention Childers gave up hope of 'doing something' through Parliament, and allied himself with those he had called neurotics nourished on dreams. He went back to his wartime duties on coastal reconnaissance, but soon after demobilization in March 1919 went to Dublin, and offered his services to Sinn Fein. 'I have been growing more and more to dislike compromise,' he wrote to Molly, 'and to thirst for whole ideals where the creative work is accomplished.' She doubted, but in the end agreed, and went to live in Ireland.

There were no compromises in his last three years. He became one of the leading rebels, using his pen in the cause of an independent Ireland. His articles on 'Military Rule in Ireland', with their detailed descriptions of brutality officially endorsed, caused a stir when they appeared in the Liberal *Daily News*. He was named Chief Secretary to the Irish delegation that came to Britain in 1921 to discuss a Peace Treaty, and returned with a draft which was eventually signed by all the delegates. The Treaty created an Irish Free State, but not the independent Ireland Childers wanted, and it left the problem of Ulster unsolved. Childers had no vote, only a watching brief, but his opposition to the compromise was so outspoken that Arthur Griffith, soon to become President, accused him of having 'caused the European War [by *The Riddle of the Sands*] and now [wanting] to cause another'. It was not long before Griffith was to assert that Childers had spent his life in England's Secret Service, and to hint that he was in Ireland as an English spy.

The treaty led to civil war in Ireland between the newly created Irish Free State and the Irish Republican Army, with de Valera leading the rebels against the treaty. Childers supported him and moved around with a small printing press, producing leaflets and news sheets. But he was isolated and distrusted, and when at length he was captured by the Free State soldiers on a visit to his family home, he was tried by a military court and shot. His last acts were to shake hands with all the riflemen, and say: 'Take a step or two forwards, lads. It will be easier that way.'

Winston Churchill rejoiced at the capture of what he called a murderous renegade, and expressed no regret at his death. 'No man has done more harm or shown more genuine malice or endeavoured to bring a greater curse upon the common people of Ireland than this strange being, actuated by a deadly and malignant hatred for the land of his birth,' he said. Popular British feeling was expressed by the *Morning Post* headline: SOLDIER, WRITER AND TRAITOR, although *The Times* was forgiving enough to call him 'a good man gone wrong'. In prison Childers read Churchill's words, and was deeply upset by them. In the long letter he wrote to Molly while awaiting the result of his trial he said, 'I die loving England,' and this was true, even though the rest of the sentence runs: 'and passionately praying that she may change completely and finally towards Ireland.'

It is easy to understand the distrust of Erskine Childers felt by many Irishmen. His aloofness was taken for typical English disdain, his neat precision for pedantry, and the desire for danger and difficulty mere perversity. Molly rebuked him gently for wanting always to choose 'the less easy course', as he called it:

If Ireland's national freedom is a great enough reward to effort . . . then there could be no question of its being a sacrifice and we should go to it of divine necessity, as a lover goes to his true love, or a mother dies for her child.

As Childers said in reply, he found it hard to be reasonable in that way. This fighter for Ireland was in many respects a typical English figure of his time, able to express the high romanticism of his feeling only in action or on paper, never in speech. What he tried to achieve for Ireland is forgotten now: but the romanticism survives, in a way he would never have expected, through the single splendid adventure story of his young manhood.

(1984)

Agatha Christie

(i) Her Autobiography

Several years ago Agatha Christie reluctantly agreed that we should have a discussion about her life and work for newspaper publication. 'I cannot say that I look forward to it,' she wrote to me. 'But I suppose as it is you it will be all right.' At first, however, it was far from all right. I daresay my questions were awkwardly put. Certainly her answers were brief and uninformative. In addition to this I was afraid that the recorder was not working properly, and was too nervous to play it back in case I should erase what was on the tape. When she understood that I was nervous too, Agatha Christie was delighted. She relaxed, we both relaxed, conversation flowed, she agreed afterwards that the operation had been painless.

The incident has its relevance to her autobiography.* What she calls 'my revulsion against the press, my dislike of journalists' dated from her disappearance in 1926. At that time she vanished for nine days. Her car was found tipped over an embankment with a shoe and scarf nearby, and the case was treated by Scotland Yard as one of suspected murder. When she was found, living at a hotel in a spa, she had changed her hairstyle, was wearing spectacles, and had registered in the name of her husband's lover. The press suspected a publicity stunt. In fact her mother's recent death, the responsibility of clearing up everything in a house filled with memories of her childhood, and her husband's unfaithfulness had combined to cause a mental breakdown. The affair was a central event in her life, but those who look for an account of it here will be disappointed. She writes about the wretchedness she felt in the weeks before the disappearance, but does not say a word about those nine days.

This is not, then, an autobiography in the usual sense. Writing

* *An Autobiography* by Agatha Christie, Collins, 1977.

in the intervals between books, over a period between 1950 and 1965, she set down what she wished to remember, particularly of childhood and youth, and ignored things she did not care to recall. There is not much about her life and skills as a detective story writer. We are nearly halfway through when *The Mysterious Affair at Styles*, her first detective story, is published, and the remarks she makes about her fantastically ingenious plots make them sound haphazardly conceived when their balance and subtle deceptiveness shows that this cannot have been so. We learn that Gaston Leroux's locked room puzzle, *The Mystery of the Yellow Room*, first made her think she might write a detective story, and that Poirot was a Belgian because there was a colony of Belgian refugees living in her parish at home during World War I. Most of what she says about her crime stories has been told, and told often, before. There are no spectacular revelations, personal or literary.

And yet it does tell us a good deal about the kind of woman who wrote her books, and it is a work of considerable unaffected charm. Agatha Mary Clarissa Miller was born in 1891 (a date she omitted from her entry in *Who's Who*), the youngest child of a feckless American father who died when she was eleven, and a characterful mother. The Millers were not rich but well-to-do. There were servants, and 'a wise and patient nanny'. She was not sent to school but educated at home, rather casually as it seems. She grew up an exceedingly innocent girl who remained in many ways a naïve and innocent woman. With the innocence went a strong vein of romantic fantasy. This extended much further than having imaginary friends named the Kittens, inventing families for her dolls, and turning her metal hoop into a white palfrey. She imagined in her Devon garden three railway systems, and made plans of them with all their stations and the points at which they intersected. There are a dozen instances of the intensity with which she played her solitary games, and the intricacies with which she embellished them. The kind of imagination that devised them, and that found so much pleasure in putting them down on paper, was later to play the same sort of games with plots. There is a graphic account here of seeing some of the characters in *Styles* in a tram. 'I took them all off the tram with me to work upon – and walked up Barton Road muttering to myself just as in the days of the Kittens.'

These fantasies were indulged by a middle class and extremely shy woman, one who thought that in another life she might have been a dog because she possessed a dog's simple virtues of faithfulness and sincerity, felt that steam train engines were like personal friends, was shocked by the idea of divorce and always felt guilty because she had agreed to divorce her first husband. In 1933 she was astonished when she met her first anti-Semitic Nazis because she had not known such people existed. The opinions she expresses about life and society are never original, often banal. She was both conservative and Conservative in the most conventional way. Yet there runs through the book a vein of great sweetness, a kindness, lack of malice, and vulnerable diffidence, that are altogether touching. And the middle class conventional English lady endured, and sometimes seems positively to have relished, the inconveniences and discomforts of travel, the bed bugs in trains that made her legs swell like balloons, the nights spent on bare boards in a primitive Persian rest house, car and sea sickness. Travel itself was almost enough compensation, and then 'nowhere in the world is there such a good breakfast as tinned sausages cooked on a primus stove in the desert in the early morning'. She was lucky to find in her second husband, the archaeologist Max Mallowan, a personality tenderly protective, and imbued with a sort of realism that happily complemented her own capacity for fantasy.

Agatha Christie was not, as she says here, a good conversationalist, nor was she a vivid personality. The person one met and talked with was a conventional English lady. The interest of this book is that it shows the struggles and complexities and contradictions that made this English lady the creator of the most cunningly deceptive fictional plots of the half-century in which she reigned.

(1977)

(ii) A Reminiscence

Few people outside her family can claim to have known Agatha Christie well. She was not unfriendly, not would it be right to call her manner distant. It was rather that, once an introduction had been made, she seemed to regard that as the end of a conversation. For this her shyness was partly responsible, but a real lack of interest in people played a part. She says in her autobiography that trains always seemed to her more real than people, and she regretted there were no longer engines one could think of as personal friends. No doubt she was not quite serious, but the feeling was genuine. Perhaps her closest friends were railway engines.

She was also genuinely shy, so much so that when she became President of the Detection Club in succession to Dorothy L. Sayers she not only refused to make speeches, but declined to introduce the speakers at our yearly dinners or even to propose toasts. The crust of shyness could be broken, however. When in 1961 she agreed to a full-scale interview with me, for the *Sunday Times*, she ruled out in advance questions of a personal kind, including any dealing with her famous disappearance in 1926, and the paper may have been disappointed with what they got. They made a big feature out of it, however, long Christie interviews then and later being rare.

Presuming on this comparatively successful meeting I tried to get her to join the Crime Writers Association, founded in 1953, to which almost all the best British writers belonged. Her refusals, more than one for I was persistent, were polite but firm. She was not a joiner, she said, she would be unable to attend meetings, she feared the Association might take on the character of a trade union. (The Detection Club was, and is, a private dining club.) Since the first question asked about the Association by media people and others was always 'Is Agatha Christie a member?' her refusal was an embarrassment. When I said this to her she smiled, and said I was exaggerating.

What impression did she make on me? If I had met her without knowing her fame as a crime writer, the answer must have been: almost none. Like other men who sat next to her at dinner and offered remarks that were answerable by monosyllables I found such occasions hard-going, although I have no doubt that for her they were harder. She was, I might have said, a large middle class Englishwoman, who spoke little and then unremarkably, an almost super-typical version of the kind of Conservative lady who presides over a stall at a party fête, and is perfectly at home pouring China tea into china cups and handing round delicate sandwiches to guests on a neat English lawn.

The picture would not have been untrue, yet that was not the whole of her. There was also the woman who invented and solved in her books puzzles of extreme ingenuity, and whose knowledge of poisons exceeded that of any other crime writer and many doctors. In her novels and short stories there are more than eighty deaths by poison, the means being sometimes as obscure as gelsemium and ricin, derived respectively from yellow jasmine and castor oil seed. Her biographer Janet Morgan said in a recent radio discussion with me that this interest sprang naturally enough from her work in a dispensary during World War I, but the fascination held for her by the use of poison far exceeded anything she would have learned as a dispenser. Her autobiography remains reticent about the puzzle-maker who pondered on the possibilities that one of the guests at those tea parties might be poisoned, in a manner baffling to everybody except Poirot and Miss Marple. *Three Act Tragedy* and *The Mirror Crack'd from Side to Side* are two tricky examples that come to mind, and her first book *The Mysterious Affair at Styles* offers an apparently undetectable poisoning method of dazzling simplicity.

Did this second personality ever put in an appearance? Not when I was in her presence, although it is quite likely that in the company of somebody with professional expertise in something that interested her – a doctor, dentist, lawyer – she might have ventured opinions and asked questions. Ony once did I get what seemed a hint of the other Agatha Christie.

This was at one of the Detection Club dinners held at a long-gone Soho restaurant called the Moulin d'Or. There were rarely more than a dozen writers at the long table which had first Sayers and then Christie sitting at the end of it. Sayers was dogmatic and autocratic, a layer-down of opinions she did not much care to have challenged. Christie by contrast was gentle and quiet, but had an air of enjoying herself. She was certainly more at ease than in larger, more formal gatherings. At one of these dinners I arrived a little late from working at the British Museum or the London Library, and dinner had begun. I went straight in, took my seat beside Agatha Christie, started belatedly on the soup, and found her mild unemphatic gaze directed at me. Was there a mark on my tie, had she observed my expanding waistline, were (as Dylan Thomas has it) my bones unbuttoned to the halfway winds? As conversation lapped about us I became aware that she was looking at my hands, in a speculative rather than censorious way, and that they were not perfectly clean. With the soup finished I got up, washed them, and returned.

That is all. No comment was made, there is no 'story', although she continued occasionally to look at me with curiosity during the evening. I am convinced, though, that the sight of those slightly grubby hands in a place and among people where one would have expected hands to be perfectly clean, had triggered thoughts in her mind about use of this oddity as an element in a plot. *A man comes to table – his hands are grubby – faintly marked with some kind of stain – yet half a dozen people are prepared to say he spent the whole day in his office* – something like that.

Of course this is pure speculation. There is no doubt, though – the books offer dozens of instances – that she was a keen observer of the trivial oddities of life, and amazingly adroit at turning them into puzzles. Behind that ordinary English lady whose values were expressed in the romances she wrote under the name of Mary Westmacott, was a much more interesting personality, somebody I would have liked to know. In everyday life this figure was concealed behind the barriers of convention, its dark imagination and extraordinary ingenuity being expressed only in the plots of her crime fiction.

(1989)

(iii) A Book About Her

There is a missing chapter in the sociology of literary criticism, one that would consider the works of best-selling crime and thriller writers in terms of their audience rather than their talent. Here are a dozen names of recent best-sellers in the genre: Peter Cheyney, Agatha Christie, Len Deighton, Frederick Forsyth, Dick Francis, Erle Stanley Gardner, John le Carré, Robert Ludlum, Dorothy L. Sayers, Mickey Spillane, Edgar Wallace, Dennis Wheatley. What joins these names and what separates them? Why are Forsyth's sales bigger than those of Eric Ambler, whom most people (very likely including Forsyth) would regard as a better writer?

The answers are to be found in the readers rather than the writing. There would certainly be a common readership for Christie and Sayers, and it would be one that strangely enough might include Wallace. Those who open a book by Cheyney, Forsyth, Francis or Ludlum are looking for what may vaguely be called action or excitement rather than detection, and if they wish to add a sadistic element they will read Spillane. A more intellectual and much more complex approach to the tale of action is found in Deighton and le Carré. Wheatley with his emphasis on Satanism and the occult, and Gardner with his intricate plotting and concentration on legal problems, tap other groups in this immense and varied audience.

Of course these categories are not mutually exclusive, as such a rough and ready division may make them appear. I enjoy Christie, Francis, Deighton, le Carré, find Forsyth, Ludlum and Wheatley unreadable, have varied reactions to the rest. Few readers in the genre stick to a single category. Yet it remains true that real devotees of Christie and Sayers do not much care for violent thrillers, that a typical reader of Forsyth or Ludlum will find Poirot or Lord Peter very slow-going, and that your true Wheatley occultist may well find that none of the other writers comes within his black magical circle. There are further interesting distinctions. I have included Cheyney as an example of an immensely popular writer whose vogue collapsed after his death. In the forties his sales were enormous. In 1944 he published an audited sales figure of 1½ million copies for the year, and two years later had added another million. Not long after his death the sales figures withered, and they have had no second blooming.

By contrast, four years after Agatha Christie's death her sales are as high as ever, new editions are constantly called for, and a third major film from one of the books is in production. The vast *Bedside, Bathtub and Armchair Companion* to her works is soon to be joined by a coffee table book about the Christie book covers of Tom Adams, and an Agatha Christie Who's Who, 'a definitive, completely cross-referenced biographical dictionary to the Christie canon'. Cheyney perished because the sadistic violence that attracted many readers to his books (his Lemmy Caution was the first 'good' character in crime fiction to torture for pleasure) was far transcended by the brutality of Spillane's Mike Hammer and others. Christie, however, is equally old-fashioned in her very different way. Why, then, does she survive and triumph?

Robert Barnard's 'appreciation'* is a crisply written survey of the works, particularly good in its detailed examination of what he calls three prize specimens among the stories, *Murder For Christmas, Murder in Retrospect,* and *A Murder is Announced.* These are not my own favourites, but Barnard shows very persuasively the skill with which the stories are plotted and the clues placed. There is a useful list of the books with brief, and by no means starry-eyed comments. 'There are several fruitier candidates for the title of "worst Christie",' he says about *The Mystery of the Blue Train,* and of *N or M?* remarks that it is 'less racist than the earlier thrillers but no more convincing'. A Christie novice wanting to know which books to read and which to avoid will find this book an indispensable guide. Mr Barnard makes an ingenious approach to the question of literary merit, putting the case for the prosecution ('trivial, dated, class-bound') and the defence (readers enjoy filling in her stereotyped Anglo-Indians, country squires, rural clergymen, as individual characters). He doesn't concern himself, and there is no reason why he should, with the question of what her readers are like, or precisely what attracts them about the books.

My own views, or as they might more modestly be called

* *A Talent to Deceive: An Appreciation of Agatha Christie,* Robert Barnard, Dodd, Mead.

guesses, are that several factors operate. I think the Christie readership has always been predominantly feminine, by about two to one, and middle class by about the same percentage. Few feminists or radicals are likely to read her. In other respects different considerations apply in the United States and Britain. For American readers Christie is the archetypal British detective story writer, in her vaguely sketched village or town settings, her outline of a society that remains hierarchical and characters that are basically unchanging, however much Miss Marple says at times that things have altered. American readers may know that Britain is not really like this, but still they wish it were, and they identify Christie with traditional British values. British devotees, on the other hand, know that Christie country has never existed in their lifetimes, and that her people and places are a fairy tale of Edwardian England, when gentlemen had no need to work, servants were plentiful and always smiling, and like other girls Agatha Christie went out to dances and met all kinds of young men, as she says in her autobiography. This world she transplanted into every succeeding decade from the twenties onwards. Even when she made a formal attempt to be up-to-date after World War II, this never-never world was really the one in which her characters moved. For contemporary British readers her books are as much period pieces as the Holmes stories. It is part of their charm.

Another part of the answer to the question about Christie's survival rests in the absence of any need for specialized knowledge in reading the books. No Agatha Christie story depends on ballistics details, blood groups, identification of hair follicles, weight stresses, or any other bit of modern science. The single exception is in her use of poisons, but even this sophistication is more apparent than real. You don't *need* to know about the poisons to identify the guilty party, and often the knowledge won't help you. Christie clues are always verbal or visual tricks, and it is these that must be spotted. If you don't spot them – well, most readers are happy to be carried along on the smooth tide of dialogue that has nothing in it to disturb the emotions or enliven the intellect. What the stories offer, especially those that contain Poirot or Miss Marple, is the pleasure of the familiar. The addict sinks into them as into a warm bath.

Yet intellectual sloth and a liking for self-indulgent fairy tales are not quite enough to explain the permanence of Christie. If it is true, as Robert Graves said, that her English was schoolgirlish, her situations artificial and her detail often faulty, such adverse comments do not touch her prime virtue, which is that of plot. In that single aspect of the crime story this country Scheherazade showed more cleverness and more variety than any of her predecessors, and it is possible to read a Christie story more than once with pleasure because, while remembering the plot's basic elements, one has forgotten just how the trick was turned. Her characterization hardly exists, as a story teller she could not be mentioned in the same breath with Conan Doyle or Wilkie Collins, and was inferior to a dozen of her contemporaries. Yet as a maker of puzzles she was superior to them all, and the propounding and solution of puzzles has a lasting fascination for the human mind. Not to all human minds, obviously, but there are enough addicts of such verbal puzzles to keep Agatha Christie's best books, her most cunningly deceptive problems, popular in any foreseeable future.

(1980)

(iv) A Final Summing Up

1

Agatha Christie would have felt it both unnecessary and unpleasant to describe the physical details of a violent crime, or the mental agony suffered by a victim of rape. Nobody is ever raped in an Agatha Christie story. Her attitude would have been that one knows such things happen, but that they were hardly suitable subjects for detective fiction. It was the plotting of crime that fascinated her, not its often unpleasant end, and it is as a constructor of plots that she stands supreme among modern crime writers. Raymond Chandler once said that plotting was a bore, a necessary piece of journeywork that had to be done, the actual writing was the thing that gave the author pleasure. Agatha Christie's feelings were almost the opposite of these, which is one reason why she didn't care for Chandler's work.

Her most stunningly original plots are those in *The Murder of Roger Ackroyd*, *The A.B.C. Murders* and *Ten Little Niggers* (also evasively called *And Then They Were None* and *Ten Little Indians*), but although these are her major achievements, she showed from the beginning an extraordinary assurance in handling the devices in a detective story plot.

Her first book, *The Mysterious Affair at Styles*, was published in 1920 but written some years earlier, when she was working in a Red Cross dispensary during World War I. It was written in response to a challenge by her sister, and Hercule Poirot was conceived in a determination to create a detective outside the Sherlock Holmes pattern. Physically outside the pattern at least, for Poirot has both his forerunner's mental acuity and his maddening zest for mystification. In general it is true that nothing becomes out-of-date more quickly than an old detective story but *Styles*, which was turned down by several publishers, remains wonderfully readable today. In part this is because of Poirot, but it is chiefly a tribute to the plot.

Most Christie plots are based upon a single and fairly simple circumstance, which is then elaborated and concealed. In *Styles* the plot springs from the fact that in England somebody acquitted of a crime may not be tried for it again. Suppose, then, that a stumbling block against committing a murder is the fact that you are an obvious suspect, you might – if you have that particular kind of tortuously ingenious mind – take advantage of this very situation by laying a trail of clues leading to yourself, which would cause your arrest. Once arrested and tried you produce an alibi, and acquittal follows. This murder plan may seem unlikely, but it was carried through successfully in real life a decade after the publication of *Styles* by a murderer who confessed when there was little evidence against him, withdrew the confession at his trial, was acquitted for lack of other evidence, and then boasted of his crime. The Christie villain is foiled by Poirot, who sees what he is trying to do, manages to prevent his arrest, and even uncovers his alibi so that he is apparently cleared of suspicion. Poirot's manoeuvring also deceives the reader, who sees the detective proving a suspect's innocence, and so crosses him off the list of those who may have committed the crime.

There are other felicities in *Styles*, in particular several of those deductions that trick us by their very simplicity. The two signifi-cant facts, Poirot tells his Watsonic collaborator Captain Hastings, are that the thermometer registered eighty degrees in the shade on the day of the murder, and that the chief suspect wears odd clothes, has a black beard, and uses glasses. We may say with Hastings: 'Poirot, I cannot believe you are serious,' but the points are clear enough. (1) The murdered woman ordered a fire to be lighted in her room on this hot summer day: hence, she meant to burn something. (2) The suspect has been identified by the local chemist as a man who bought poison, but his peculiarities of appearance make him very easy to impersonate.

Styles was a splendid beginning. Not all of the books that succeeded it were on the same level, and the semi-thrillers that used what has been called a 'master Criminal' theme seem to me inferior in almost every way to the orthodox detective stories. But as Agatha Christie's skills developed, a pattern emerged which might be called the typical Christie plot form. It was used by other people too, but by none so well or so variously as in her books. The form consisted of gathering a number of people together in a particular place preliminary to one of them being murdered, and of showing the reasons for their presence. It is a way of creating a totally closed society, and one can see it happening in very different books: *Death in the Clouds* (1935), *Cards on the Table* (1936), *Death on the Nile* (1937), and *Ten Little Niggers* (1939). To look at the way in which these plots are devised and carried through is to see the high skill that was, with almost deceptive casualness, employed in them.

Death in the Clouds gives us eleven passengers but only ten suspects, since the eleventh passenger is Poirot. There they are, *en route* from Le Bourget to Croydon (in relation to air travel the book has a strong period flavour), and we get glimpses of their actions and thoughts. Among these glimpses are the thoughts, deceptively conveyed of course, of the murderer. The victim is Madame Giselle, she has a mark on her neck, and a wasp has been flying about in the cabin. Was the wasp responsible? But below one passenger's seat is a thorn of the kind used by South American tribes for puffing from blowpipes. The thorn is tipped with curare, and a blowpipe is found under the seat of . . . Poirot.

There are two highly characteristic things about this outline of suspects and setting of a scene. The first is that it confines the suspects to the people on board the airplane and then, by a process of elimination, to those who got up and passed Madame Giselle's seat or had the chance to use a blowpipe; the second, that a trick is being used in the apparently simple outline. At an early point Poirot says that a detailed list of the passengers' belongings will help to solve the crime. We are given this list, which covers three pages, and yes, if we interpret it correctly we shall come up with the right answer. But the interpretation is not easy to make.

In *Cards on the Table* the situation is more deliberately artificial. The rich Mr Shaitana 'collects' undiscovered murderers on the ground that 'murder can be art! A murderer can be an artist'. These are, he says 'the ones who have got away with it, the criminals who lead an agreeable life which no breath of suspicion has ever touched'. Shaitana stages a dinner party to which he invites four detectives familiar to Christie readers – Superintendent Battle, Colonel Race, Mrs Ariadne Oliver and Poirot himself – and four murderers, or four people said by him to have committed murder. Some rubbers of bridge are played, and the evening ends with Shaitana's death. The closed circle is perfect. Veteran Christie readers know that the detectives are beyond suspicion. Which of the four bridge players is the killer? The bridge scores are reproduced at the beginning, and by studying them – and the text – it is possible to come up with the right answer.

Death on the Nile, Agatha Christie's own favourite among her books with a foreign setting, is a more subtle and sophisticated affair. In the first twenty-five pages we meet all the principal characters and discover their reasons, that is the reasons they give to each other, for going to Egypt. The murderer is among these characters, and again a careful reader of these opening pages may deduce correctly what is likely to follow. The deception here is one of the most brilliant pieces of Christie conjuring, because at a fairly early stage the intelligent reader may think he sees what is going to happen, only to be confounded when the crime is committed by the fact that what is suspected seems to be impossible. I should be inclined to put this with the very best Christie plots if she had not been so desperately intent to deceive as to strain credulity at times. Her party of travellers down the Nile includes a kleptomaniac, an alcoholic, a thief and a subsidiary would-be murderer whose activities have nothing to do with the main plot. All this is too much, and indeed is far more than was needed to achieve her ends. The true deceptions, those connected with the main plot, are puzzling enough, in particular one that concerns a pistol wrapped up in a cheap handkerchief and a velvet stole and thrown overboard. Why was this done, Poirot asks again and again, saying rightly that it is the crux of the case. In spite of the red herrings, for which she had perhaps rather too strong a liking, Agatha Christie's sense of fair play is always paramount in relation to a significant clue. She shows it to us, teases us with it, almost openly tells us the truth about it through Poirot – and still we are deceived because of her meticulous way with words, which when she is dealing with a clue in a story are to be taken precisely at their literal meaning. In *Death on the Nile* we see a pistol being fired, and we see the result as a crimson stain spreads over a wounded man's trouser leg, but ... but close reading of the passage is advisable.

I shall have something to say about the plotting of *Ten Little Niggers* later on. Here it is enough to point out the skill with which, in the first section, the pattern is developed as the suspects who are also the victims are seen deciding to accept invitations to the island off the Devon coast where after dinner on the first evening all ten of them hear a recording which says that they were guilty of murder and asks: 'Prisoners at the bar, have you anything to say in your defence?' Again a trick, the first in a whole series, is being played on us. We are allowed to see some of the thoughts of the person who has devised this death trap without having much chance of placing a name to him or her. Except, of course, by a knowledge of Agatha Christie's methods, of the kind of trap she sets.

2

The kind of trap she sets – there are people who claim to be able always to tell the villain in any Christie story by such an awareness. I couldn't make this claim myself, and indeed I doubt whether it is possible to be specific about the 'kind of trap'. Even the pattern I have called the typical Christie plot form does not apply to the majority of her books, although it is used in a high percentage of the best ones. But her work is astonishingly varied. There is a whole slew of books that take their settings from the fact that her second husband Sir Max Mallowan was an archaeologist, concerned chiefly with Assyrian culture, and that she often accompanied him and to some extent shared his interests. But although archaeology has a place in several stories her readers are never oppressed by a feeling of ignorance. She had an instinctive awareness of just how far her audience would wish her to go in showing expert knowledge, and no Agatha Christie mystery depends for its solution on a knowledge of ancient artefacts. Even in *Death Comes as the End* (1945), a not very successful experiment set in ancient Egypt, no specialized knowledge is needed to solve the puzzle.

There are several other sets of books which don't fit into any particular pattern of plotting. These include the five Tommy and Tuppence thrillers, books such as *The Mysterious Mr Quin* in which Agatha Christie indulged her interest in the supernatural, and the collections of Poirot and Miss Marple short stories. All of these seem to me not only inferior to her best work, but also as remote from the main stream of it as are the romantic novels she wrote under the name of Mary Westmacott. The main stream of her writing is unquestionably in the thirty-odd Poirot novels and the much smaller number, eleven at my last count, concerned with Miss Marple.

One sees certain things more clearly in looking back at her work than was apparent when reading the books as they were published. One is the supremacy of the best Poirot stories over the rest of what she wrote. She became tired of Poirot herself and preferred Miss Marple, who did not appear in a novel until 1930, with the feeble *Murder at the Vicarage*. Miss Marple, she said, was more fun, and like many aunts and grandmothers was 'a splendid natural detective when it comes to observing human nature'. Only a minority of readers agreed with her. If one prefers Poirot it is not only because he is an altogether livelier character, but also because his insights are more rational and less inspirational than Miss Marple's. A second thing that becomes apparent is her frequent carelessness in leaving deplorably loose ends, and a third is the verbal or visual form of her plotting. It is not just that you don't need to know about ancient artefacts to solve a Christie puzzle, but that you need no specialized knowledge at all. Think of John Dickson Carr's locked room mysteries, of R. Austin Freeman's (and many another writer's) scientific lore, of the learning paraded by Dorothy L. Sayers, of all those crime stories that depend for their solution upon our technical knowledge of the theatre, or of bibliography, or on changes of temperature, or timetable, or tide tables, and the Christie simplicity will seem most welcome. Yet simplicity is not quite the word. The basic difference in plotting between her and most detective story writers is that the central clue in almost all of her best books is either verbal or visual. We are induced to give a meaning to something that has been said, or something that has been seen, which is not the true meaning or not the only possible meaning. A typical instance of the verbal illusion occurs in a story where we are led to believe that a child named Evelyn, born to a woman involved in a murder case, is a girl. But Evelyn may be a boy's name too. Why do we never think of that as a possibility? Because early in the story the mother gives a newspaper interview in the course of which she says: 'My daughter shall grow up happy and innocent. Her life shall not be tainted by the cruel past.' But we are told clearly enough in relation to the interview that the woman who gives it is *expecting* a child, so that she could not have known its sex. The assumption has been planted in our minds, and when the woman's child Evelyn is mentioned, we take the feminine sex for granted.

Visual deceptions are of the kind suggested already in relation to *Death on the Nile*. Sometimes it is hardly possible for us to penetrate them, but many have the marvellous conjurer's quality that leave one gasping with pleasure at the audacity of the deceiver, saying: 'So *that's* how it was done.' Such visual and verbal clues, when they are used with subtlety and fairness, seem to me the finest things in the classical detective story. At her best Dame Agatha Christie was an incomparable deceiver.

That the level of her work varied greatly has to be acknowledged. Most of her finest performances belong to the 1920s and 1930s. The following decade more or less maintained this high level, but after that the decline was steady and near the end it was steep. The books of her last few years were, with only one or two exceptions, no more than faint echoes of her best work. A book like *The Clocks* (1963) opens very promisingly with a body found in a room full of clocks, most of which have no right to be there. The explanation of this anomaly, which would have been the heart of an earlier novel, is both casual and disappointing. And the people have become shadowy too, as inevitably she lost touch with contemporary life and feeling.

A survey of her whole output shows that she was often slapdash from the beginning in dealing with the technical details from which she flinched. *Murder on the Links* (1923), for instance, has been justly praised for its complicated and brilliant plotting, and for the way in which details of a twenty-year-old murder are interwoven with a current one. It contains one of her most characteristically clever touches of deception, and what must be called an almost equally characteristic carelessness in handling an important plot detail. The touch of deception first. The question arises as to how some intruders left a house. Perhaps, Poirot suggests, they might have climbed on to a tree and jumped down to a flower-bed, but it is pointed out to him that the mound is perfectly smooth. A companion flower-bed, he says, shows marks of the gardener's hob-nailed boots, but the official investigator replies scornfully that on this side 'we have no tree, and consequently no means of gaining access to the upper storey.' When Poirot insists that the gardener's footprints are important he is thought ridiculous. What is their importance? Just that the gardener has weeded both beds, and so must have left his footprints on both. The fact that the second bed is smooth means that the intruders *did* escape that way, and that they had time to smooth the mould after them.

And now the piece of carelessness. At an early stage of the case Poirot picks up a piece of lead piping on the scene of a crime, and much later says that it has been used 'to disfigure the victim's face so that it would be unrecognizable'. But Hastings has already looked at the victim, and neither he nor the police investigator mentions the savage blows that would have been necessary to make the face unrecognizable. Hastings says that it was 'terribly convulsed', which is quite a different matter.

3

In the end Agatha Christie's claim to supremacy among the classical detective writers of her time rests on her originality in constructing puzzles. This was her supreme skill, and it is examined here in three books, *The Murder of Roger Ackroyd*, *The A.B.C. Murders* and *Ten Little Niggers*. Some would add to these, which I regard as her most dazzling performances, *Murder on the Orient Express* (1934) or *Peril at End House* (1932) or even the last Poirot story *Curtain* (1975). But the crime writer who relies on a puzzle is like a tight-rope walker. A perfect achievement is a perfect marvel, but anything less, any slight swaying on the line, leaves us sharply critical. Both *Murder on the Orient Express* and *Curtain* are for me too obviously and purely tricks, and although I rate *Peril at End House* much more highly than do most critics, it cannot quite be ranked with Christie's best.

The Murder of Roger Ackroyd was published in 1926, and probably remains its author's most famous single work. She was inclined herself to say that too much fuss had been made about it, but that was at least in part the reaction of any writer who feels that praise of an early book implies denigration of later ones. But in *Roger Ackroyd* Agatha Christie did something absolutely new in the detective story. It was a plot device, and what can be *absolutely* new in that, a sceptical reader might ask? The same reader might go on to point out that she had already used a modified form of this device in a neglected, very engaging story called *The Man in the Brown Suit* (1924), although there it played only a minor part in the tale. Perfectly true: but in *Roger Ackroyd* the device is at the heart of the book, which really could not exist without it. The whole thing is the blandest, most brilliant of deceptions. When we look back to see how it was done – well, as so often with Dame Agatha it is a matter of some assumptions that we are led to make because making them is customary, plus a few carefully chosen phrases intended to deceive without ever being positively untrue.

The trouble with plot devices is that they often obtrude, so that we have all plot and no story. Part of *Roger Ackroyd*'s success rests in the fact that the rest of the story is so perfectly typical of the period. A country squire is murdered, the body is found in the library, there is a butler and a housekeeper both of whom behave suspiciously, the cast of characters includes several with a motive for murder. All this, even in the middle twenties, was far from new. The novelty rests in the fact that the murderer seems to fit so naturally into such a milieu and yet truly does not belong to it at all. The plot device fits into the framework of the story as snugly as the pearl in its oyster.

One might feel that ingenuity in plot construction could hardly be taken further than *Roger Ackroyd*. Rather more than a decade after its publication, Dorothy L. Sayers suggested that the detective story as a pure puzzle was in gentle and painless decline, partly because those devices that had seemed so ingenious in the form's early days – the poisoned toothbrush, the evaporating ice dart, the pistol timed to fire when the grandfather clock in the library struck twelve – were worn out from too much use, and partly because readers' tastes had changed, so that they were increasingly asking for crime stories in which the characters were as important as the plot. She has proved a truthful prophet, although some of the crime story's developments might have surprised and displeased her. Agatha Christie's ingenuity, however, had always been verbal and visual rather than mechanical and scientific, and she responded to the idea that the detective puzzle was worn out by inventing new and still more dazzling conjuring tricks.

Are *The A.B.C. Murders* (1935) and *Ten Little Niggers* (1939) as good as *Roger Ackroyd*? Not quite, because the trick played on the reader is deliberately artificial rather than fitting naturally into the story. In the later books the Christie cleverness again leaves us gasping, but second and third readings show that the plot has been built around the device used, with total disregard for our belief in the story itself. Who can believe that those ten guilty people would in fact have accepted the mysterious invitation to stay on the small island in *Ten Little Niggers*? Who can believe in a murderer so reckless, and in a gull so stupid, as the characters in *The A.B.C. Murders*? Yet the books remain triumphs of ingenuity, and it is worth trying to see just how the tricks are done.

The A.B.C. Murders are apparently motiveless, or at least their motive seems to be purely alphabetical. Ascher is killed at Andover, Barnard at Bexhill and Clarke at Churston. A copy of an A.B.C. Railway Guide is placed beside the body, and each crime is announced beforehand in a taunting letter to Poirot. 'We're up against a homicidal maniac,' says one of the police investigators, but although Poirot agrees at the time, we know that this cannot be the case. There must be a logical answer.

That is the reader's assumption, and of course he is right. The problem is, then, how to maintain his interest through a series of crimes which in their details (I am trying not to give away too much) are for the most part irrelevant to the plot. This is managed by shifts of viewpoint from Hastings's first person narration to a third person view of the actions of a man named Alexander Bonaparte Cust, or A.B.C. Who is A.B.C.? He is always on the scene of the crime, and it seems that he must be the murderer. The presence of A.B.C. links what would otherwise appear disparate crimes in which we might lose interest. And another problem confronted the author, that of bringing together suspects involved in separate crimes and living in different parts of England. This too is managed with unobtrusive skill. The book is a masterwork of carefully concealed artifice.

And so is *Ten Little Niggers*. The way in which characters and plot are introduced has been described. At an early stage, then, we see what is going to happen. Some of these people are going to be killed, there will be a police investigation, and the person responsible will be discovered. But as death after death occurs, and no investigator appears, it is slowly borne in on us that the nursery rhyme ends with the line: 'And then there were none.' When only two people remain, it seems one must be the murderer. It doesn't, however, work out like that. The book's last sentences embody the nature of the puzzle: 'When the sea goes down, there will come from the mainland boats and men. And they will find ten dead bodies and an unsolved problem on Indian Island.' Poirot does not appear in this book. How could he, when it is a problem that remains unsolved?

4

What are Agatha Christie's chances of survival as a writer who will be read a century from now? To a certain extent this depends upon the kind of society we live in. But if we approach the question in literary rather than social terms, will she be read in the year 2100, and if so, why?

To answer yes, as I would do, is not to say that she was a great or even a good writer, but rather to say that although the detective

story is ephemeral literature, the puzzle it embodies has a permanent appeal. Perhaps W. H. Auden was right in identifying the
ideal detective reader as one possessed by a sense of guilt, and in
suggesting that detective stories should not be considered as art
but as a kind of magic. Certainly the association with myth, and
the links with the classical riddle, are strong. Few crime stories
nowadays are detective novels – they belong, to vary what Auden
said a little, to the real and not to an ideal world – and it is
plausible to consider Dame Agatha Christie as the last notable
figure of her kind. If her work survives it will be because she was
the supreme mistress of a magical skill that is a permanent,
although often secret, concern of humanity: the construction and
the solution of puzzles.

(1977)

Margery Allingham

On the crime fiction stock market Allinghams are set for big gains in '89. Several novels have been adapted for TV, reprints from Penguin accompany them, some uncollected short stories have been gathered for publication with an introduction and scholarly notes, and American academia has provided a critical biography which will 'compare her achievement with that of Christie and Sayers'. Critical, or uncritical? Twenty-odd years after her death, how well does Margery Allingham wear?

Between the critic and the assessment falls the shadow: the shadow of the Great Detective, the Superior Amateur taking time off from his study of Transylvanian folk song to solve the series of crimes that have baffled the professionals. Here the shadow is that of Albert Campion, who has perhaps some wrong-side-of-the-sheets relationship to royalty, and is certainly on Christian name terms with half the peerage. Campion was originally conceived as a sort of second cousin once removed to Lord Peter Wimsey (himself, it is rumoured, half-brother to Bertie Wooster). In her later books Allingham became aware of the incongruities between Campion's man-about-town negligence and actual criminal practice, and toned down the portrait, but her taste for titles remained.

The books are drenched in the kind of snobbery that draws attention to its own good taste. The word *vulgar*, for instance, gets a lot of use in *The Fashion in Shrouds* (1938). A famous actress is said to be charming but 'intrinsically vulgar', a true conceit is 'a vulgarity in the right place', the actress apologizes for her own vulgarity in showing distress about the discovery of her late husband's body, and her present husband for his after complaining to Campion about his wife's 'damned low-class blood'. Et cetera. Often the snobbery is even more overt. In *More Work For the Undertaker* (1948) Campion is stopped while walking in the park by 'a dowager with a name to conjure with', riding in 'an elderly limousine with a crested door'. The dowager, for good aristocratic

measure, recalls dancing with young Kaiser Wilhelm. She congratulates Campion on his new job, which is to be Governor of 'the
last remaining civilised place in the world'. We are left wondering
where that might be, for of course Campion turns down the job.

There is also a kind of inverse snobbery, a wholly unreal
mateyness, in Campion's (or his creator's) attitude to working class
characters, who are almost always seen as comic. So Campion is
aware of 'an impending social crisis' when he has to introduce a
friend of his own class to a pickpocket who greets Campion by
saying, 'Wot O! Cor, this is a bit of all right. 'Ow are yer, chum?'
Campion's 'man', Magersfontein Lugg, a conscientious dropper of
every 'h', instructs his master that 'braces is low, except when
worn with a white waistcoat for billiards', and we are meant to be
in stitches at the absurdity of this ex-Army clod instructing his
master. A country policeman asks the detective, 'Now, what have
you been a-doing of?', and he responds with what we are meant to
regard as geniality, 'My good oaf . . .'

Is the Allingham revival to be regarded simply as a very minor
accompaniment to the Thatcherite counter-revolution, a glimpse
of a world where policemen were happy to be called oafs by their
social betters, and a man might say, as Campion does to his sister
Val, that he is pleased to note she has 'sufficient feminine
weaknesses to make you thoroughly inferior' without fear of
contradiction? No doubt the social atmosphere of the eighties has
something to do with the revival, but there was more to Margery
Allingham than Campion. She was an exuberant romantic who
loved the baroque and the odd, her eye for detail was sharp, and
she had a surprising capacity to order and dovetail plots –
surprising because her taste for the outrageous and disorderly, for
apparently incoherent material, masked the real skill with which
she shaped apparent fancies and fantasies into plausible plots.

Examples of the eye for sometimes ironically observed detail can
be found in the picture of the contemporary art scene in *Death of
a Ghost* (1934), the first book in which her talent is really on
display, and in the well-informed look at the snobberies of
women's fashion – all the more effective because it fascinated her
– in *The Fashion in Shrouds*. The baroque element is on display in
the opening of *Coroner's Pidgin* (1945), which finds Lugg and a
marchioness he praises as a game old girl carrying a dead body up

the stairs to Campion's flat (the typically unfazed Campion, on finding it, says, 'You – er – you only have the one?'), in the undertaker named Jas Bowels, the bank manager Henry James, and the convincingly eccentric Palinode family in *More Work For the Undertaker* (1948), and the perhaps rather over-dense fog of *The Tiger in the Smoke* (1952). The last of these is a thriller, but the others are puzzles, worked out with exemplary skill. And there are times when the tendency to floridity is kept in check and Allingham's romanticism is genuinely moving, like the scene at the end of *Coroner's Pidgin* when Campion returns from war service, sees his two-year-old son for the first time, and his wife Amanda greets him with: 'Meet my war work.'

The best of Margery Allingham – that is, the books which combine her talent for organization with a modicum of Lugg and a minimum of snobbery – is to be found in *The Tiger in the Smoke* and *More Work for the Undertaker*. The first, although dismissed by Graham Greene as 'a most absurd unreal story', has been found by many other readers to be a gripping, uncomfortable book about hunter and hunted in a finely realized post-war London. Campion is a very minor figure here, a fact possibly reflecting the author's awareness that the material she dealt with was too serious to accommodate his characteristic frivolity. The second is perhaps the only crime puzzle she wrote perfectly, the baroque manner fitting the odd characters, the teasing problem fairly handled, the high spirits unforced, the whole a classic of its time and place.

(1989)

P. D. James: A Profile

'The bodies were discovered at eight forty-five on the morning of Wednesday 18 September by Miss Emily Wharton, a 65-year-old spinster of the parish of St Matthew's in Paddington, London, and Darren Wilkes, age 10.'

Those are the opening lines of *A Taste For Death*, and they are typical in their factual exactness, the brisk presentation of what we need to know about two characters who are not there just to discover corpses, but will play minor yet important parts later in the story. The bodies, two dead men, are in the Little Vestry of the church. The scene is horrific, the room a shambles, blood everywhere. And it is as brightly lit as a stage act, by the long fluorescent tube that disfigures the Little Vestry's ceiling . . .

That ghastly garish fluorescent tube lighting the scene, brightening the blood, making the figures seem unreal, is the particular P. D. James touch that makes the reader shudder a little, and understand why Miss Wharton collapses outside the church and has to send Darren to fetch Father Barnes. She has a feeling for macabre detail which is all the more effective because it is placed in settings very solidly realized. So the first paragraph of *Unnatural Causes* describes in careful detail the body of a dead man, his hand-made shoes, silk tie, dark pin-striped suit. A dapper little cadaver this but for one thing – the corpse has no hands. In another book, *Innocent Blood*, young Philippa is determined to discover the identities of her unknown parents, and uncovers an appalling truth when she does so. And, one of the most effectively chilling scenes in any crime story, the death of a nurse in *Shroud For a Nightingale* during a demonstration of intra-gastric feeding, when carbolic acid instead of milk is poured down the feeding tube, is made peculiarly horrific by the accumulation of factual detail. We are told of the funnel, the tubing, the kidney bowl, tongue spatula and forceps, the check on the temperature at which the feed will be given. All the ordinary things that should be there emphasize the appalling nature of what happens. W. H. Auden's view that a crime should be something nasty in the wrong place, 'as when the dog makes a mess on the drawing-room carpet', is one with which Phyllis Dorothy James would heartily agree.

This macabre quality is one of James's strengths as a writer, but it would be wrong to overstress it. Her finest books are in the classical tradition of the British detective story as practised by Agatha Christie, Ngaio Marsh, Dorothy L. Sayers. (James is delighted by the comparison with Sayers whom she admires, deprecates the one with Christie – 'Such a bad writer.') Her stories are always clearly and carefully plotted, strongly characterized, with the puzzle taking second place to the characters. You learn the identity of the murderer three-quarters of the way through *A Taste For Death* but this doesn't damage the suspense, may even enhance it.

From 1962, when she published her first crime story, James knew how to pace a plot, and had decided also that she wanted a professional detective, not a Lord Peter Wimseyish amateur. In *Cover Her Face* she invented Adam Dalgliesh, a Chief Inspector now risen to Commander. James gave him some of the qualities she admires in men, one of them being extreme professionalism, absolute mastery of his job. And the others? Well, she has said that no quality in a man seems to her more sexually attractive than intelligence and talent, and Dalgliesh certainly does not lack either. He is the son of a parson, well educated, 'probably could be described as a gentleman', but she deliberately avoided making him the mannered, casual, often snobbish detective of the British tradition. Dalgliesh gives an impression of efficiency combined with a reticence verging on coldness in personal matters. Perhaps as a counter-balance James made him a poet, and one of repute. The portrayal of Dalgliesh on TV by Roy Marsden emphasizes the element of detachment from any relationship likely to get too close. Although Dalgliesh is the kind of man P. D. James admires, she probably realizes that he is not entirely sympathetic. 'I didn't want to over-romanticize him,' she says.

If one were creating a character sketch purely from her books, it would be of a cool collected figure, a little remote, friendly enough, but probably difficult to know and talk to. But that is not the person who opens the door when one goes up the steps and rings the bell of her handsome house in Holland Park. She smiles, arms outstretched in greeting, and when she says, 'How lovely to see you, dear,' the words seem to have genuine meaning. She positively glows with pleasure at a guest's arrival. When I asked friends and fellow crime writers for a word or phrase describing her, they said *hospitable, unpretentious, marvellously extrovert, wonderfully friendly*. They are all on the mark, yet don't quite convey her total lack of pretentiousness or the good nature and pleasure radiating from whatever she is doing, whether it is cooking chicken thighs for a large party ('One of my few dishes, I'm a good plain cook, emphasis on the plain'), talking to fans at a signing session, or discussing intricate points of criminal detail at a conference of mystery writers. She is a little under average height, with a high colour, mobile features and observant eyes, a ready conversationalist and great talker and laugher. She seems an unlikely creator of Adam Dalgliesh, although one can imagine her having a strong fellow-feeling for her second-string detective, the young private investigator Cordelia Gray. She is the kind of person any friend would consult in trouble with the certainty of receiving practical advice and sensible, emotionally sympathetic help.

Does this sound altogether too much like the work of those Victorian painters inclined to make any subject appear to be a picture in a stained-glass window? Certainly there is another P. D. James, a private woman as well as the public one, and it is the private woman whose imagination sparks off the most memorable scenes in the books. Her house is sizeable, with four bedrooms, a handsome drawing room housing her considerable collection of famous trials, a pleasant kitchen leading out to a large patio garden which comfortably offers space for a party of twenty or more people. She lives in this house alone, although her two daughters and their families – she has several grandchildren – often come to stay.

Her habits of work and behaviour, like those of many writers, are slightly obsessive. She gets up at seven, makes a pot of tea, gets down to work. By midday she is exhausted as far as writing goes. Then she shops, goes for an hour's walk, perhaps has a friend to lunch. If her grandchildren are visiting she plays canasta with them in the evening, if not she watches TV. There is no lack of invitations – to give talks, go out to dinner, serve on committees –

more than she would want to accept. Success has made her rich, but many things in her life are unchanged. She has no car, in Britain normally travels by train and arrives much too early at the station. She remains intent, in small and large matters, on neatness and order. One woman interviewer watched in surprise as her hostess, after giving her coffee in the kitchen, washed up the cups wearing rubber gloves, then dried them and put them away.

The same desire for order and tidiness is reflected in the care about details in her books, and the seriousness behind the smiling face she presents to the world is expressed in her approach to the dead body every modern crime story needs. For her it is not just an object, the start of a puzzle, but a person whose life and beliefs have to be known. Like T. S. Eliot's Webster she is much possessed by death, and sees the skull beneath the skin. Writing crime stories fulfils, she says, the need in her personality 'to intellectualize and distance the fear of death'.

Something about being alone in London, alone in a crowd, is evidently deeply attractive to her, but if she wants to get away she goes to East Anglia, where she has a cottage in the small town of Southwold. Her books hardly ever begin with an idea for an unusual method of murder (hence perhaps part of her distaste for Christie, for whom the murder method was generally the heart of the story), but with a particular setting. 'I have always had a claustrophobic fear of mountains,' she says. 'What I love are wide skies, marshlands, the solitude of estuaries, still water fringed with reeds, remote unpretty villages,' and such typical East Anglian settings have been the background of three James novels. It was a recollection of Blythburgh church near Southwold that moved Dalgliesh to the composition of the only poetic fragment from his hand we have been permitted to read, ten lines beginning 'Remember me, you said, at Blythburgh'. It is no surprise that she calls herself quite a religious person, and says her recreations are exploring churches and walking by the sea. No surprise, either, that her favourite novelist is Jane Austen, whom she re-reads every year, nor that she names Trollope and George Eliot among other favourites. She is more likely to be found reading C. P. Snow or Margaret Drabble among contemporary writers than Hemingway, Saul Bellow or Martin Amis. Her taste is for literal realism, not modernism or caricature.

P. D. James is now in her middle sixties, and says with typical cheerful commonsense that she has at most four more books left to write. Her immense success has come in the last decade, with the publication in 1977 of *Death of an Expert Witness* and three years later of *Innocent Blood* which was a runaway best-seller in America. Before that she sold well enough, but not in such numbers that she felt ready to give up her demanding, enjoyable job as a Principal in the Criminal Policy Department of the Home Office. That job itself was a triumphant culmination to a life that had contained more pain, unhappiness and struggle than most. When she says that some things in it were rather appalling, the words are spoken with characteristic matter-of-factness, not self-pity.

She was born in 1920, the eldest of three children (she had a younger brother and sister) in a family that was, she says, not very close. She similarly recalls her own early years as not particularly happy. Her father was an Inland Revenue Officer, a restless discontented man of whom she was sometimes frightened ('When you are young you want someone to love'), although in retrospect she admires his courage and independence, and remembers with pleasure summer holidays when he put up his old Army bell tent on the cliffs outside the East Anglian fishing port of Lowestoft, and parents and children explored the area by bus and on foot. There was not much money, and although Phyllis was sent to the excellent fee-paying Cambridge High School for Girls she left at sixteen, and that was the end of her education. Perhaps her father did not think it necessary to send a girl to university, perhaps he lacked the money. Phyllis James was nineteen when World War II began, and not quite twenty-one when she married Dr Connor Bantry White, who served during the War in the Royal Army Medical Corps. She looked after their two small daughters, born in 1942 and 1944, and waited for her husband to come home.

When Dr White returned from Army service, however, he was a mentally sick man, suffering from what was eventually diagnosed as schizophrenia. The rest of his life, until his death in 1964, was spent in and out of mental hospitals, from which he sometimes discharged himself and then had to be compulsorily readmitted. Like many schizophrenics he was violent at times. When his widow speaks of him it is with affection, even tenderness, about a man temperamentally unlike herself. (His favourite novelist was Dickens, his favourite modern novel *Ulysses*.) He lived long enough to see her first two books published, was delighted by them and proud of her. But the later 1940s are a period Phyllis James doesn't like to talk about. Her husband had no war pension, and the family was poor. She went to evening classes, studied hospital administration, perhaps because her father-in-law was a doctor like her husband, and got a job as a £300-a-year clerk which still left the family near to poverty. For a time she lived with her parents-in-law, her daughters aged five and three went to boarding school, and in the summer holidays her in-laws looked after the children. It must have been a hard and bitter time. She once said to me that success had come twenty years too late.

Yet she must have enjoyed her professional life. One can't be in her company for long without being aware that she is both a determined and a highly intelligent person. Those qualities took her onwards and upwards through Britain's Civil Service, incidentally absorbing knowledge about hospital administration, forensic medicine, the way the law operates and how British police work, later immensely useful to her as a crime writer. In 1968 she made a major step upward, when, unusually late in life, she took an examination to become a Principal. Unlike many high-fliers she was liked by her colleagues.

That is the professional career, but it was never what she wanted, or all she wanted. She was determined to write, and when the stringencies of making a living had eased a little, sat down to do so. She began with a crime story partly because she admired Sayers, but also to get useful practice for the 'real' novel she might begin next year. But *Cover Her Face* was accepted by the first publisher who read it, and by the time she had written a couple more mysteries she had come to think the detective story's restrictions (you must have a puzzle and a plot, the puzzle has to be solved) were really perhaps a useful discipline.

Those first three books are well told and enjoyable, but to use her own term they are formula writing. With the fourth, *Shroud For a Nightingale*, she had the confidence to make full use of a background and the kind of people she knew well. The scene is a general hospital in the National Health Service, the characters its matron, consultants, nurses, administrators. She set out to create

real people with genuine motives for the way they behaved, and
indulged her own intense interest in the appearance and history of
buildings through her account of the hospital itself, 'an immense
Victorian edifice of red brick, castellated and ornate to the point
of fancy, and crowned with four immense turrets'. The book was
a success, and she must have thought that if you could write
realistically about hospital life and people, why not about other
places too? *The Black Tower* is set in a home for the incurably ill
(no woman crime writer of the past would have tackled a setting
so potentially off-putting for readers), *Death of an Expert Witness*
in a forensic science laboratory described in elaborate detail.

In *A Taste For Death* she has invented two buildings, the church
in which the bodies are found, which has 'an extraordinary
Romanesque basilica' designed by the Victorian architect Sir
Arthur Blomfield, and a house designed by the great Sir John
Soane, in which several of the principal characters live. She has
enjoyed herself in writing about them, and her evident pleasure
comes through. If this is her best book it is in part because she has
felt free to create and describe the credible settings that she seems
to need in order to place even minor characters in them. One of
these minor characters lives in a dismal block of modern flats,
brought to life for us by observation of the twin flower beds
outside them filled with white, yellow and red dwarf dahlias that
'glare upwards like a bloodshot eye' at the inhabitants. When
Dalgliesh visits a fashionable private clinic to interview a suspect
he looks at a painting by Frith, admiring the meticulous detail with
which the painter shows military heroes returning from some
colonial adventure, their mantled ladies and pantalooned daughters
waiting to greet them. Such factual detail fascinates her, and
successful use of it gives her books part of their flavour. They are
important to her, just as vital as the total conviction she brings to
forensic details and the seriousness, almost solemnity, with which
she treats death. Dalgliesh, looking down at one of the bodies
in the church vestry, thinks, 'We can vulgarize everything but
not this,' then reflects that even so this corpse will quickly cease
to be a man and become 'an exhibit, tagged, documented,
dehumanized'.

Remarks like these could only be made by a detective story
writer who hopes that her books will be treated as something more

than light entertainment. All the British Golden Age crime writers – Sayers, Christie, Margery Allingham, Ngaio Marsh – felt strongly about supporting the rule of law in their work and seeing that in their books justice was done. James feels this too, but her attitude is deeper and more complex. At the heart of her work is a moral assertion of the individual's responsibility for his or her actions, and the rejection of modern social attitudes that deny this. Ask her about such things and she is likely to turn the question aside with one of her jolly laughs, or say that she writes books to please herself and give pleasure to others, and this giving of pleasure doesn't imply a moral message. No doubt that is literally true, but it is striking how much moral and religious feeling enters her work. Heroin is smuggled in the handles of wheelchairs bringing pilgrims back from Lourdes (*The Black Tower*), assignations are made in a disused chapel and the hymn board used to fix the times (*Death of an Expert Witness*). *Innocent Blood* is full of Christian symbolism about the importance of redemption.

She insists that she is not telling readers what to think, but press her a little and she will agree that she would never write a crime story in which justice was not seen to be done. Isn't that the very function of the detective story, she might ask, to bring order into a disorderly world? 'However unpleasant a character may be, however evil he may be, he still has the right to live his life to the last natural moment.' That is something she insists upon, and if he is murdered then what she calls the forces of morality in the form of Dalgliesh and his cohorts must bring retribution. In conversation with me, and I'm sure with others, she has deprecated strongly any other attitude. I can't imagine her writing a book which in any way extenuated murder, however attractive the killer and however deplorable the victim. Sherlock Holmes watched a woman shoot the man blackmailing her, and decided justice had been done, but such a solution would never do for P. D. James. I can imagine her inventing a crooked policeman, but it would go against the grain with her to let him play an important part in a book. Life may be like that sometimes, but she would feel that in a detective story order and morality must triumph.

This may sound as if she is a specialist in happy endings, but that isn't so at all. It is where she parts company from her Golden Age predecessors. As she has pointed out herself, Dalgliesh uncovers the murderer in *Death of an Expert Witness*, but leaves behind a trail of distress, a family contaminated by murder. In the new novel young Darren, one of the more attractive characters, is at the end of the book abandoned by his mother and taken into a local council home. 'He's fallen into the clutches of the Welfare State with a vengeance,' one of the policemen says. The end of the book also leaves Dalgliesh's woman assistant, Kate Miskin, with a burden of guilt to carry, in a death for which she feels partly responsible. Dalgliesh reflects that Kate is tough, and will 'learn to accept and carry her personal load of guilt, as he himself had learnt to carry his'. For James detectives are the heroes and heroines of society, but also its scapegoats.

Phyllis James is a woman with strongly held opinions, for the most part cautiously voiced. She is friendly with a number of her fellow crime writers, myself included, but although I suppose most of the friendships could be called primarily professional, she rarely discusses her own work or those of other people. She has expressed open disapproval of books that show no concern for justice, or see villains get away with crime, like Patricia Highsmith's novels about Tom Ripley. She admires John le Carré, but doesn't care much for spy thrillers in general, perhaps feeling that they are potentially subversive of established government. American crime stories? She agrees that Americans are much better than the British at writing police procedural stories like Ed McBain's 87th Precinct books, and at writing private eye novels, but I doubt if she would read Hammett, Chandler or Elmore Leonard for pleasure. They are interested in the violence itself, she only in the results of violence, which is not at all the same thing. She would be more likely to enjoy Ross Macdonald because, behind or through the violence, he was concerned like herself with moral issues.

What about her own books?. If admiration for Sayers sparked her off as a crime writer, she has long ago transcended her model in seriousness and subtlety, while staying mercifully free from Sayers's peculiarly English snobbishness, and her love of a lord. Yet she knows very well that there are dangers in her determination to treat crime fiction seriously. When I wrote a long, not favourable review of *Innocent Blood* in the *New York Review of Books*, saying P. D. James had abandoned the puzzle and detective story element, and that the result showed the risks of too much ambition, she never commented directly on the review, but some time later said to me with a laugh that her next book would be a straightforward detective story. (It was *The Skull Beneath the Skin*.) She added: 'I think with *Innocent Blood* I had aspirations beyond my station.'

The problem she faces confronts any crime writer who wants to do something more than provide light entertainment. Edmund Wilson asked long ago in a famous essay 'Who Cares Who Killed Roger Ackroyd?', and although one answer is that Agatha Christie's sales show a great many people have cared about the solution of her famous puzzle, the very asking of the question shows the general critical contempt for the detective story. It is not easy to write a genuine novel in this literary form which has for so long been treated by critics as Cinderella before she turned into the belle of the ball. To do so you must keep the balance perfectly between 'entertainment' and 'seriousness'. In *A Taste For Death* P. D. James did just what she failed to do with *Innocent Blood*. There is a puzzle to be solved, it is the core of the book, and a vital clue is that old standby, a button missing from a jacket. Yet the problems that face the characters are real ones, not just obstacles placed in their paths to make a detective story.

The murder of Sir Paul Berowne, an ex-Minister of State who believes that he has experienced a miracle in St Matthew's Church so that his wrists show the stigmata, affects not only his unfaithful wife and her autocratic dragon of a mother, but a dozen other people confronted through the connection with murder with decisions to make, questions to answer. As Dalgliesh investigates, probing delicately for things relevant to the crime, looking for motive, intention and possibility like a medical specialist searching for the origins of some malignancy, the people react to him, reveal more of themselves, remind us that murder is the end of one life, but only an incident in other lives that go on after it. If the balance is kept, as it is here, we may forget that what we are reading is a detective puzzle, and become absorbed instead with the fates of the people in the story.

As a writer P. D. James is as firmly British as steak and kidney pie, a realistic practical novelist concerned with social morality, in the tradition of her beloved Jane Austen, and Trollope, or to come more nearly up to date C. P. Snow ... But she is not one to encourage such grand comparisons, and as they appear on my typewriter I seem to hear her saying 'My dear, aren't you going on a bit?', and the sound of her hearty laughter.

(1986)

Ruth Rendell

(i) Barbara Vine*

Ruth Rendell, along with P. D. James, is Britain's principal recent gift to crime readers. Rendell writes three different sorts of crime story. The best known are puzzles confronting Chief Inspector Wexford in the country town of Kingsmarkham, orthodox detective stories with a sharp edge of social comment and a fine ear for the nuances of contemporary speech. In the second sort of Ruth Rendell stories some flaw in personality, often with a sexual basis, leads to what may seem on the surface almost purposeless violence. The Wexford books are excellent detective stories, but the best of the studies in abnormal psychology (*A Demon In My View*, *A Judgement In Stone*, *The Killing Doll*) are powerful novels.

The third and most recent face of Ruth Rendell is Barbara Vine. Why use another name when the identity of Barbara Vine is no secret? To emphasize that these are not straight detective stories nor psychological studies, but something different again, densely plotted leisurely mysteries with an almost Victorian flavour about their intricate development. *A Dark-Adapted Eye*, the first Barbara Vine, told us in the opening chapter of a woman being hanged for murder, and *A Fatal Inversion* begins with a couple burying a pet dog in the garden of their big old country house, and finding as they dig in a cemetery for animals 'the bones, the fan play of metatarsals, of a very small foot'. The bodies of a young woman and a tiny child have been buried here, and the woman has been shot. The mystery in the novel, not solved until almost the end of it, is who they are and how they died.

This is a book that calls for a reader's full attention. The crucial events in the story take place in the summer of 1976, the longest and hottest for many years in Britain, and the narrative shifts

* *A Fatal Inversion*, by Barbara Vine, Bantam.

constantly between past and present, showing how the shadow of the awful thing that happened at rambling old Wyvis Hall, in the heart of Suffolk country, has affected the four people who survived it.

In one aspect the story is about the destruction of innocence. Adam Verne-Smith, a footloose nineteen-year-old, is left Wyvis Hall by his uncle Hilbert. He takes his friend Rufus down to look at the place and its twenty acres before selling it, but once there they are seduced by the lake in the grounds, the warmth, the silence, the well-maintained garden, the carefully netted fruit cage with its vermilion strawberries. It is like the garden of Eden, Adam feels, a paradise that can be entered only on the condition of committing 'some frightful sin or crime that must result in expulsion from it'.

The first crime is trivial, hardly one at all. Neither Adam nor Rufus, a medical student, has any money. Why not sell some of Uncle Hilbert's things, his Waterford glasses, little tables and so on, to maintain themselves? They all belong to Adam, even though he is not supposed to sell them before the estate has been valued. And why not start some sort of commune, got rid of a few more things, and stay in this lotus land for ever? They are joined by a young Indian with a Jewish girl friend, and Rufus picks up a girl named Zosie one night in his old banger. Adam, who has a taste for anagrammatic jokes, calls the old banger Goblander and calls Wyvis Hall Ecalpemos, someplace inverted. This tiny commune, like larger ones, has its sexual entanglements.

The telling of the story is less straightforward than such a summary makes it seem. Contrasted with the lost paradise of Ecalpemos is the present, in which Rufus is a smooth successful medical consultant. Adam an anxiety-ridden man with a boring wife and a much-loved daughter, the young Indian submerged in the menacing urban emptiness of a London ghetto where the least offensive graffito says 'Go Home To Pakistan'. They agreed never to meet again after the terrible thing happened that drove them out of paradise, but when the bones are discovered and they learn that the police are treating the woman's death as murder, alarm bells ring . . .

The revelations when they come are not entirely unexpected, although the neatest ironical trick is turned in the last pages. But the greatest compliment one can pay Ruth Rendell as Barbara Vine is that she doesn't depend on tricks. She has the gift of devising an ingenious plot, and of maintaining interest by driving along the narrative with the zest and cunning of Wilkie Collins, marks of an extremely skilful crime writer who is also a very good novelist.

(1987)

(ii) Wexford*

Ruth Rendell must have thought more than once about killing off George Wexford. He first appeared twenty-eight years ago in *From Doon With Death*, named because she was in Ireland's Wexford at the time of his conception, and created casually with no thought that he would become a series character. His sidekick is appropriately named Burden, for over the years Ruth Rendell's talent has developed and spread, especially in her separate literary incarnation as Barbara Vine. One has the impression that Wexford is now as much trouble to her as Sherlock Holmes became to Conan Doyle and Hercule Poirot to Agatha Christie. Might the Chief Inspector go the way of Nicolas Freeling's Van der Valk, killed in action? Fans of the books (and of George Baker, excellent in the TV versions) can breathe again. Wexford is back after a four-year absence, none the worse for being blown up by a car bomb on his last appearance.

The setting is unusual for Wexford and for Rendell, that of a super-typical country house murder. Two women and a man are found shot dead in the very grand Tancred House. The women were killed at the dinner table and have bled over it, one plate drenched with blood 'as if a bottle of sauce had been emptied on to it for some horror meal'. One is Davina Flory who owns the house, and her husband lies spreadeagled at the foot of the staircase

* *Kissing the Gunner's Daughter*, by Ruth Rendell, Hutchinson.

in the galleried hall. Daisy Flory, Davina's granddaughter, has also
been shot but survives.

Wexford finds himself drawn to this seventeen-year-old girl,
attracted by her courage, dismayed by her calm insistence that
she now has nothing to live for. He recognizes that his feeling
for her is prompted partly by the fact that his erratic daughter
Sheila has a new and very dislikeable young man in her life, a
supercilious and condescending novelist recently short-listed for
the Booker . . .

What develops is in part an orthodox Wexford police novel,
concerned with exact moments at which various people arrived at
Tancred House near the time of the massacre, and with intricate
stuff about changing the rifling marks on a revolver. But it is also
in part a study of Wexford's psychology when confronting his
reaction to Sheila's relationship with Gus Casey, and his own
feelings for Daisy. Further than this it is an investigation of the
characters of the three people killed, Daisy's rather null mother
Naomi, her famous and formidable grandmother, and Davina's ex-
MP husband. The result is rather as if several Barbara Vine
characters had been put down in a setting of Gothic strangeness
and involved in a Christie plot.

The result is flawed but absorbing. Ruth Rendell has a disturbing
skill in visualizing violence, so that both the scene of slaughter at
Tancred House and the apparently unconnected murder of a police
sergeant during a bank robbery stay uncomfortably in the mind.
And although she may not care for the compliment, she has
Christie's skill in deceiving the reader and holding together an
intricate plot. Here a sizeable cast of suspects, including the
housekeeper, her husband and the gardener, all living on the large
estate, are not the usual dummies but credible, interesting characters. So are the young man keener on Daisy than she is on him,
and an American student living nearby. The title itself is a pretty
piece of teasing.

Yet the flaws are basic, springing from the grafting of Vine
characters on to an unsuitable setting and plot, so that we never
learn enough about Davina's personality, which is really the spring
of the story. There is some sloppy Kingsmarkham police work, as
when no airports check is made to find out if a missing woman has

gone abroad. Gus Casey is an unsuccessful caricature. And, most important, the solution depends on outrageously unlikely behaviour by not one but two characters.

It's true, of course, that we barely blink at improbable motivations in many crime stories, but Ruth Rendell has set a different standard of psychological faithfulness and must be judged by it. The root of the problem is that she has outgrown Wexford, but that many readers and even more box-watchers still love him. A mercy killing is indicated, but can she bring herself to it? The ghosts of Conan Doyle and Christie, who found the problem insoluble, bow their heads in sympathy.

(1991)

(iii) Talking to Ruth Rendell

Ruth Rendell and her husband Don live in a pink-washed Suffolk house at the bottom of a grassy track, steep enough to make the Land-Rover they've named Goliath a necessary vehicle in hard weather. Some of the house is fifteenth century, other interior bits are much more recent. It is comfortable, unpretentious, with eleven acres of well-wooded land outside.

After lunch Ruth and I settle down to talk while Don takes my wife out in Goliath, on a tour of the district which includes the thatched cottage where the Rendells lived before they moved to their present home six years ago.

I admired, and reviewed, Ruth's first novel *From Doon With Death* a quarter of a century ago, and we've known each other a good many years. We talk about all three Rendells, and about her powerfully sexual new book *The Bridesmaid*. She answers questions readily, laughs a good deal, yet there is about her a tension and watchfulness rather like that of the four cats who stroll about the house. (One stays in the room, curled up, but keeping an eye on me.) I asked about her family.

'Both my parents were teachers. My mother was born in Sweden but was brought up in Denmark, and thought of herself as a Dane. But when she was living here and wanted a passport the Danes refused it and the Swedes gave her one, so then she thought of herself as a Swede. Then she married my father, who was English, and I was born in London.'

She said nothing more at the time, but later on returned to her background and parentage when I asked about her constant presentiment of an imminent disaster in her own life, some disgrace, humiliation or suffering. She traced it back to childhood.

'I think it comes from my father, who looked for sorrow rather than happiness in life. He started from a situation of great poverty, left school at fourteen, and went to work in the dockyard at Plymouth. He served a full apprenticeship and then discovered there would be no work for him. His mother, who must have been a remarkable woman, managed to get him into university, and he became a teacher of science and maths. He was extremely well read in English literature and was quite a good painter, but his struggles, and an unhappy marriage, made him a hard, pessimistic and sorrowful man.'

Hard to her? 'No, not at all. Very good to me, a very good, sweet and caring father, but I don't know that parents should be like that to their children, saying that in life there is more to be endured than enjoyed, and don't expect to be happy. My mother had MS almost from the time I was born. Little was known about it at the time, she was a very vague strange woman, and her illness was misunderstood, she was misunderstood. So I think I was imbued from a very early age with a sense of doom.' A hearty laugh, head thrown back. 'It may come out in the way I write, but I don't think I'm like that myself.'

There is little sign of such feelings in the Wexford books with which she began. She was in her early thirties when the first was published, and had been writing for several years, short stories which were all rejected, then longer fiction. Don was working for the *Daily Mail*, and asked the Book Page editor to look at a manuscript. He offered her a job on the paper, which she didn't want, but said she hadn't a hope of publication.

'But he knew Harold Harris, editorial director at Hutchinson. I'd sent them a novel which wasn't a crime story, a comedy of manners, and they said they might consider it if I was prepared to do a lot of rewriting, and at the same time asked if there was anything else. I had the first Wexford, and sent them that. Again they wanted a lot of rewriting, and I did what they asked. Wexford was based on other people's fictional detectives, a bit of Maigret I suppose, and quite a lot on Fred Fellows, a police chief in books by Hillary Waugh. I'd been on holiday in Ireland, and that's where the name came from – it might easily have been Waterford. Later on Wexford changed and developed a lot, but that was how he began.

'I think George Baker in the TV series is an excellent Wexford, and indeed now when I write about Wexford I think of him. I never really saw Wexford, except in a hazy sort of way, but I try to make him the sort of man I like – I've done that more and more.'

I said I felt she'd moved beyond Wexford, and asked if she would like to get rid of him.

'Well, if I did I'd just stop writing about him, wouldn't I? What I've been contemplating for some years is writing Wexford's death. I want him to die in heroic circumstances, but he won't die in my lifetime because I wouldn't want to have to resurrect him as Conan Doyle did Sherlock Holmes. I think I must still like writing about him. I just don't want to do it so often.'

Feelings of guilt, and an awareness of the ease with which apparently ordinary men and women can turn to violence through a coincidence, an unexpected meeting, some unforeseeable event, are apparent in such fully-fledged horror stories as *A Judgement In Stone*, *A Demon In My View* or *A Killing Doll*. I asked why she began to write this kind of book.

'The early Wexfords are what I wrote when I thought they were the only things I could get published. The others came when I realized I could write what I wanted, and these other books could indeed sell and be successful.' I asked about the coincidences that occur in several books. 'Yes, there are coincidences, probably too many of them, and improbabilities, but I feel very strongly this situation of the fork in the road, whether you take left or right, and I'm conscious of that in my daily life. I choose one day rather than another to fulfil an engagement, and I can't be free of wondering what would have happened if I'd chosen the other.

'Am I extrovert or introvert? I'd have to say introvert. I live inside me, although I've struggled a lot not to do so. I've inevitably had to meet a lot of people and talk to them, and if that hadn't been necessary I think I would have been very turned in on myself.

'Optimistic or pessimistic? I must come down to pessimism. I regard the world in general as pretty grim, and as I grow older think it gets worse. But I strive for a cheerful outlook, and think in myself I'm a cheerful person.'

Introverted or pessimistic perhaps, but she takes a keen interest in things outside herself. She votes Labour ('Though I wouldn't call myself very political'), and for thirty years has been involved with CND as marcher, speaker and fund-raiser. And she rates herself a moderate feminist, though some more fervent ones were annoyed by her book *An Unkindness of Ravens*.

And so to Barbara Vine, a name derived from her own second Christian name and a grandmother's surname. But why use the name at all? 'I had an idea for a novel which I was going to set in World War I, and had several goes at it over fifteen years without success. In the end I decided it should be set in World War II, and that it would be unsuitable as a Ruth Rendell because it would be set back in time. And really, it suits me very well to be divided in this way.'

The Barbara Vine books have been universally praised, and have won prizes in the US, this country and elsewhere. I suggested that as a novelist she had graduated from Wexford to Rendell Mark II and then Barbara Vine, and she agreed. But in keeping these three separate strands going, was she writing too much?

'I think I am. I hope it doesn't sound arrogant to say I don't think my work has suffered, but I think it might if I went on. It's just that I work all the time, and it isn't necessary. It can't go on. And it won't.'

The Bridesmaid (Rendell Mark II, not Vine) is certainly about somebody with a sexual screw loose, and exemplifies a remark she once made about violent sexual attraction leading to disaster rather than happiness. The young lovers, Philip and Senta, are set on a path that leads inexorably to violence. I said the book was more explicitly sexual than anything else she had written, but she wouldn't have that.

'I don't think it's more explicitly sexual than *Live Flesh* or the

Barbara Vine of *A Fatal Inversion,* there's just more of it. If this book seems more sexual, it's probably because I thought it was time I wrote a book about young love and sex. You mentioned Senta's disgusting apartment and its awful smells, well, I used to know a lot of people who lived in squats, and they were like that. Of course, there's an element of imagination too.'

I asked if the effective counterpointing of the reckless love affair against the background of Philip's lower middle class family was deliberate.

'Oh yes, the contrast was intended. I have the feeling most people are like this, these people are what Orwell called upper lower working class, or lower middle class. It's taken for granted now that children don't live at home with their parents, but lots of them do. And neither Philip nor Senta is paying any rent, so they have money so spend.'

As we waved goodbye I wondered whether she would really be able to write less. To do so must demand a great effort of will. The way her day is divided, she said, is that she reads when she wakes (she reads five books a week), works all morning and part of the afternoon, reads in between spells of work and in bed at night. 'I read when I'm not writing. I might almost say "What else is there to do?"' She laughs, it's a joke. She mentions cooking, gardening, social life. But the joke is serious too, reading and writing are what absorb her. I shouldn't be surprised if, as our car vanished up the grassy track, she went straight back to work.

(1989)

Edgar Wallace and Tomorrow Morning's Newspaper

1

There is a certain kind of youthful experience, short on education, long on rough and tough variety, that seems peculiarly American, the seeding ground of writers like Dashiell Hammett and James M. Cain. By his early twenties Cain had been ledger clerk, inspector of roads, village high school principal, singer, record and insurance salesman. Hammett at the age of twenty-five had been a railroad office boy, a stockbroker's chalkboard writer, door-to-door seller of seafood, and Pinkerton detective probably employed on union-busting assignments. Very few British writers have had similarly hard lives in youth and early manhood, but Edgar Wallace was one of them. Like Cain and Hammett he put the places he lived in and the people he met to good use in his fiction.

He was born in 1875, the illegitimate child of a young actress named Marie (but called Polly) Richards, and the fellow-actor with whom she had a brief affair, Richard Horatio Edgar. There was no question of marriage, and indeed Edgar had married a friend of Polly's before the child was born. She gave the boy his father's names, and added to them the surname of Wallace when he was registered. Polly had a living to earn, in the same company as Richard Edgar and his wife, and no means of caring for a baby whose paternity could not be acknowledged. He went to a working class family in Deptford for fostering when he was a week old. For a while Polly paid five shillings a week to the fishporter George Freeman and his wife Lucy, but when she could not keep up the payments they took the child as one of their own, along with their nine others.

Lucy and George Freeman were both semi-literate, able to read, but not write anything more than their names, yet they brought up young Dick (he was called Dick Freeman) with love and good sense. They insisted that he should stay on at school until he was twelve, instead of leaving at ten like their other children. Afterwards they did their best for him, not always with success, although his affection for them never faltered. He moved from job to job, selling papers, working for a printer where he did nothing more interesting than put names on paper bags, taking a job in a shoe shop, another as proofreader's boy, briefly running away to sea and disliking it, getting a job as concrete-mixer for a plasterer and road-maker. He disliked that too, and when he was eighteen enlisted for seven years as a private in the Royal West Kent Regiment.

'I'll be a great man one day,' he told a landlady at a time when he was still a plasterer's labourer, and the first sign that this might be true came when he was sent out to South Africa as a medical orderly. He began to write Kiplingesque verses which appeared in local papers, and his first published book was a collection of poems. He bought his discharge from the Army, found that he had a journalist's quick eye and pen, married a South African girl, returned to England.

From this time onwards he was a writer, but only intermittently a successful one. His speed of mind and facility in writing were remarkable, but he was reckless about facts, careless with money, full of good ideas which might make him a lot of money, but rarely did. He was not satisfied simply to be a reporter on the *Daily Mail*, and in 1906 published *The Four Just Men*, a book that posed a problem which the public was invited to solve, with a handsome first prize of £250. Why should a publisher get the enormous profits? He arranged to publish the book himself, and spent £1000 or more on advertising. There were 1200 big posters in central London and suburbs, 2000 smaller ones for shop windows, big advertisements in newspapers. The result was a sale of 35,000 copies, but financial disaster. Far too many people solved the puzzle of who had killed the Minister, and clamoured for money. His net loss was £1400, and he had to be rescued by the *Mail*'s owner Alfred Harmsworth, not yet Lord Northcliffe. He then sold the book outright for £72, a piece of folly that he was to repeat again and again instead of making an arrangement on a royalty basis.

His casual way with facts cost the *Daily Mail* £5000 in a libel suit, and for a while he became almost unemployable. The bailiffs were in his kitchen, and various treasures like his watch and chain went into pawn. His second wife Violet, whom he called Jim (both his wives called him Richard or Dick, never Edgar), came to work for him as secretary during World War I. His income during the first five years that she was in his employment, before separation from his first wife Ivy, was never more than £2500 a year. It would have been enough for any ordinary family to have lived on comfortably, but his tastes were expensive, and he never refrained from indulging them. 'If I wait to have what I can afford I shall never have anything,' he said, and he had a gambler's optimism about success, in journalism, authorship, and on the race course. In these years he was producing what he later called his best books, the stories about Sanders of the River and other work based on his life in South Africa and his experiences in the Congo as a reporter, but they produced only part of his income. He wrote reviews and sketches, became a racing tipster who at one time had two separate racing sheets of his own, and even joined in launching an unsuccessful cure for rheumatism. His autobiographical book, *People*, gives a vivid, typically lively picture of his youth and early manhood. The last paragraph begins:

There is no end to any story, but here I will make the end of mine; for an autobiography should conclude at some decent interval from Today. I shall be broke again and rich again; but broke or rich, I shall, if the Lord keeps me in good health, be grateful and happy for every new experience.

By the time this was published, in 1926, he was earning enormous sums of money, and spending them as fast as they came in. He had acquired an agent four years earlier, the agent had brought him to the attention of Sir Ernest Hodder-Williams of Hodder and Stoughton, and when five books had appeared with success the publishers began an advertising campaign saying, 'Make This an Edgar Wallace Year'. When it was plain that every year would be an Edgar Wallace year they followed this with another slogan: 'It is Impossible Not To Be Thrilled by Edgar Wallace'. In the decade before his death in 1932 they published forty-six books, and in the words of his biographer Margaret Lane the sales ran literally into millions.

Books were only one source of income. Perhaps he inherited a love of the theatre from his parents: certainly he had saved his pennies to see plays in his early youth, and he gave passionate attention to all the business of the theatre, not only the writing but every detail of the production. After two failures he had success with *The Ringer* in 1926. This lively mystery melodrama ran for twelve months, and was the play of the year in a commercial sense. He had little idea, then or afterwards, of the distinction between his own good and bad work. *The Ringer* was followed by *The Terror*, which I remember seeing as a very small boy. This was a mish-mash of nonsense with a super-villain playing the organ in the hidden dungeons of the old house, a treasure in the secret vault, corpses appearing and disappearing, sudden black-outs, a hooded figure. But *The Terror* also did well, and so did many (not all) of his other plays.

In six years he wrote sixteen of them. He also became chairman of a new film company and directed films made from his stories, something for which he showed considerable flair. By 1928 he was making £50,000 a year. He had two Rolls-Royces (one for Jim), a box at Ascot, acquired a string of mostly unsuccessful racehorses, gave supper parties at the Carlton for 200 guests, and was known as a soft touch. Very often no touch was needed, for he sent cheques at Christmas to friends whom he knew to be hard up. On his first trip to America he went out in the royal suite of the *Berengaria*, and when he died in Hollywood he returned home on the same ship, his body lying alone in the empty saloon under a mass of wreaths. It is hardly surprising that he died in debt, although within a couple of years all the debts had been paid off. The plays look very old-fashioned today, but many of the books move in and out of print, mostly in paperback.

2

Margaret Lane's biography of Edgar Wallace was written some way this side of idolatry, but nobody reading her book, or *People*, or the memoir written by or ghosted for his widow, could doubt his generosity of spirit or his charm. He was delighted by success, never cast down by failure, and was modest about his literary achievement. It is true that this modesty was based on what was almost a contempt for any kind of literary values. He was proud of being a good newspaper man, and took his plays seriously, but he never considered books as more than a way of making money. The difference in his attitude is expressed by the fact that his plays were written in longhand, while his books – once he could afford a secretary – were dictated to his secretary Robert Curtis.

The persistent rumours in his lifetime that many of the books were written by assistants and collaborators, however, were untrue. Curtis polished up details and checked facts and names about which Wallace was notably erratic, but none of the books was ghosted. The rumours arose because of his extreme speed of composition, yet although his production of more than 150 works in twenty-seven years astonished contemporaries in the twenties, it has been greatly exceeded since then. John Creasey, who customarily produced fourteen books a year, is credited with more than 600 titles under twenty names, and one would not be surprised if that was an underestimate. Creasey did not dictate, but worked straight on to a typewriter. He employed two tasters, whose functions were to correct grammatical errors, and check names and avoid obvious errors, so that a flat in Blackheath was not said a few chapters later to have a good view of Big Ben.

There have been many other big producers, perhaps the most notable being Erle Stanley Gardner. But Edgar Wallace was unique among them in having true gifts as a writer. Gardner had legal knowledge which he used skilfully, Creasey often constructed ingenious plots, but Wallace's talents were natural and of a different order. At his best he wrote brilliant dialogue, his humour was lively, his rendering of cockney characters full of sharp insights. These qualities are fully on display in the best plays, *The Ringer*, *On the Spot* and *The Calendar*, but they are seen also in the books. They sprang from his relish for the salty language, the shyster tricks and the comradeship of the working class world of his youth with which he never lost touch, and from the varied experiences of his knockabout life. At the same time it would be pointless to deny that he was a slapdash and often absurdly sensational writer. It is said that when producing a serial he often had no idea of what would happen in the next instalment until he started to dictate, and there seems no reason to doubt this.

Would he have produced better work if he had treated his talent with more respect? Margaret Lane speculates on the possibility that in other circumstances he might have become a serious artist rather than 'a splendid and sensational craftsman'. She concludes that it was not very likely, and there can be no doubt she was right. Wallace expressed his own view of literature in relation to himself when he said: 'The good stuff may be all right for posterity, but I'm not writing for posterity, I'm writing for tomorrow morning's newspaper.' Yet the ability to turn an effective phrase is apparent in that as in many of his remarks, and because of that ability the books have survived a good many tomorrow morning's newspapers.

Which are the best of them? The question is less easy to answer that might be expected, because almost all contain unexpected felicities of phrase and scene, are marred by slapdash writing, and ask at some point for suspension of disbelief. *Sanders of the River* and the later African tales take their strength from his love of the British Empire and his recollection of Africa. The Educated Evans racing tales attract because he is able to communicate the fascination held for him by every aspect of horse racing. They introduce the wide circle of his acquaintances who were by no means honest and yet stopped just short of being crooks. In the field of the crime story the best books are those most cleverly plotted (*The Crimson Circle, The Fellowship of the Frog, The Case of the Frightened Lady* are three examples), and those which give us a memorable character like Mr J. G. Reeder.

Mr Reeder is the best among a large group of innocuous-seeming or apparently foolish Wallace characters who turn out to be something altogether different. The innocent bystander, the slightly foolish clergyman, even the upright judge, turns out to be a criminal, a murderer, or the mastermind behind a gang. Detectives masquerade as drunks, or – as in Reeder's case – somebody who looks like an old fuddy-duddy is the power behind what is vaguely called the Public Prosecutor's office. Reeder's habitat is more firmly established than usual, and so is his appearance. He lives at Daffodil House in Brockley Road, not far from Deptford where Wallace had grown up. He wears square-toed shoes, a high flat-crowned hat, a ready-made Ascot cravat, and carries an old-fashioned black umbrella.

All this, however, is deceptive. Mr Reeder is the greatest expert in the world on forged currency notes (in his early teens Wallace, when asked by a man to change a number of florins, suspected something was wrong, took one to a policeman and asked: 'If you please, sir, is this money snide?'), and the black unmbrella holds a steel blade. He is also seen, as the stories develop, to be a by no means distant relation of the criminal masterminds in other books. He often repeats that his own mind is a criminal one, and he has that awareness of things he cannot possibly know characteristic of the Wallace master crook. He knows that a discharged chauffeur wrote an anonymous letter, and even the man's address; he recognizes a Canadian crook who has never before visited Britain, and is aware of all his associates; he knows the bank in which a crooked police officer keeps his surplus income, and also that the account is in his wife's maiden name. You need not believe in Mr Reeder in order to appreciate him.

There are other stories about Mr Reeder, but *The Mind of Mr J. G. Reeder* is the best collection. Some are ingenious, all are marked by Wallace's slapdash charm, and they show his feeling for the language and tricks of criminals, and even for their personalities. This is true even though he said that criminals were 'a little less interesting than lunatics, a little less romantic than sewermen'. He knew many minor crooks, and obviously enjoyed characters like the Cape Town pickpocket who, with only the faintest brush against him, extracted his wallet and watch. No doubt he was still more amused by the pickpocket's downfall. The man worked for a fence, failed to tell his employer when he had taken £600 from a passenger on a mail boat, and was shopped accordingly. In life as in his fiction Wallace liked to see justice rather obviously done.

George Orwell thought he discovered in Wallace a zest for hanging, but although it is true that he believed in the effectiveness of both corporal and capital punishment, his feelings did not go beyond what was common in the period. He showed none of the anti-Semitism that marks 'Sapper', John Buchan, and minor figures of the period like Sydney Horler. Anybody taking a course in Wallace might be impressed rather by a curious innocence, for instance in his belief that the British criminal differed from those of other countries in being less vicious and brutal. 'Thieving is unaccompanied by violence,' he wrote. 'The professional gunman is unknown, and a burglar of my acquaintance who found his partner carrying a revolver just as they were going on a job, broke off his enterprise to give his reckless companion a good thrashing.' It is part of the attraction of these stories that they take place in such a lost world of happy innocence.

(1983)

John Mair: One of the Lost

1

Each literary generation contains a few figures recognized by their
fellows as distinct, strongly individual, memorable. They are
remembered by those who knew them at school, college or
university rather for what they were than for what they did, a
youthful success based on style more than substance. A tone of
voice is recalled, a turn of rhetoric, a devastating comment after a
dull evening, the way they wore their clothes and the kind of
clothes they wore. Sometimes such youthful heroes go on to
become established literary figures like Cyril Connolly, sometimes
turn into quirky English teachers or become lost in the wilds of
television, but even those who drop into obscurity are not forgotten by those who were their contemporaries in youth. John Mair
was such a figure so that when, more than forty years after his
death, I asked for information about him in the *Times Literary
Supplement*, I had a flurry of replies. The biographical sketch that
follows is based on them, on the help given by Walter Allen, L. W.
Bailey, Brian Pearce, and in particular by Mair's wife, now Joan
Feisenberger.

John Mair was born in London in 1913, the only son of G. H.
Mair, CMG, and his actress wife Maire O'Neill. G. H. Mair was
by turns leader writer, literary editor, and London political corres-
pondent of the *Manchester Guardian* from 1909 until 1914, while
still only in his twenties. He was briefly assistant editor of the
Daily Chronicle, did various Government jobs in the 1914–1918
War, then in 1919 became Assistant Director of the League of
Nations Secretariat. In 1911 he married Maire O'Neill, who had
previously been engaged to J. M. Synge. *The Playboy of the Western
World* had been written for her, and she was the original Pegeen
Mike. G. H. Mair died in 1926 at the early age of thirty-nine,

leaving his son and daughter in the care of their beautiful but erratic mother.

John had been entered for Westminster before his father's death, and went from there to University College, London, where his talent blossomed. He edited the University magazine *Review*, read the modern English poets including Eliot and Auden, and had a sound knowledge of English and classical literature, but made a mark particularly as a conversationalist. Tall and dark with a pale complexion, he was an eloquent debater, although handicapped by what some say was a slight and others a pronounced stammer. One friend remembers him as having a marvellous gift for spontaneous and highly literate conversation, another as a non-stop talker with puns and jokes interspersed between witty comments and entertaining asides. He wore his hair longer than was usual at the time, sported bright or pastel ties in one fashion of the period, and was fashionably aesthetic also in deriding sport, although he had learned to box effectively at Westminster. It was no surprise to learn that his favourite modern novelist was Aldous Huxley.

His political attitude was liberal without dogmatism like that of many of his contemporaries, although his own views may have been affected by the career and beliefs of his father. He took little interest in bread-and-butter British politics but was strongly opposed to Fascism and, when the Spanish Civil War broke out, enthusiastically supported the movement to send arms to Republican Spain. In 1934 he attended the Mosley rally at Olympia as a detached observer, but became involved in the defence of a colleague and got a black eye, which he regarded as a badge of honour. In 1939 he contributed to a collection of essays by young writers called *Major Road Ahead*, writing specifically as a Liberal. His article, rather unhappily headed 'A Young Man's Ultimatum' (to Hitler) was among the more informed and balanced pieces. It was to the credit of the German people, he said, that 'the parties of revenge' had taken so long to gain power in Germany after Versailles, and he remarked perceptively: 'Individual brutality is merely the clumsy method of an as yet inefficient system: the real danger of Nazism is its purposed and utopian end.'

After leaving university he became the joint editor, and probably also joint backer, of a magazine called *Janus* which foundered after two issues, one of which contained an early Dylan Thomas story. Like the writer of this introduction John Mair was almost a born book reviewer. He began in his early twenties with pieces in the *News Chronicle*, and early in 1938 began reviewing also in the *New Statesman*, at that time a kind of reviewer's pinnacle, which he reached before he was twenty-five. In 1938 also, his book *The Fourth Forger* appeared. Any idea that Mair's time was wholly spent in talking and reviewing rather than in serious writing would be dispelled by this book about the career of William Ireland, the forger of the pseudo-Shakespearean play *Vortigern*. This scholarly, readable, altogether admirable book was a remarkable accomplishment, and acknowledged as such at the time in long and laudatory reviews.

Only part of his personality, however, was expressed by days spent in the British Museum Reading Room. He was a keen gambler on horses and dogs, professed to have a dog racing system which produced a steady income, and called his bi-weekly trips to the White City and Haringey going to work. He played poker, and when in funds had a flutter on the Stock Exchange. He also had a temporary job, typical of the time, as a dictionary compiler, and worked part-time for the middlebrow literary paper *John o' London's Weekly*. His wife remembers the days before and immediately after their marriage in 1940 as very happy ones, especially when they stayed in the country.

'He was a great walker, talking all the time of course. Sometimes we walked all night. We used to go to the country most weekends when in London – Kent and Surrey and Buckinghamshire were still so comparatively rural, and there were good inns where you could stay and get food for as little as 6/- b and b.'

After marriage the couple rented a cottage in Hertfordshire. There most of his only novel *Never Come Back* was written while he awaited call-up, and there also he edited a one-volume edition of three books by Thomas Love Peacock, and wrote an introduction in which he compared Peacock to Huxley. When call-up came he chose the RAF, as he told one friend because he liked the colour of the uniform, or in another version because it was the only service where you wore a collar and tie in the ranks. While training he became fascinated by star navigation and the names of stars, and sent to his wife a touching little verse which was printed in the *Spectator* as 'Night Flight' by 'Navigator, RAF':

> Al Fard, Wezen, Hamal, Nath,
> Guide me on my aery path;
> Denebola, Procyon,
> Bless the wings that I fly on;
> Acrux, Altair, Deneb, Shaula,
> Bring me brightness in my dolour;
> Mirfak heed me, Schedar lead me
> Through the darkness of the night;
> Rigel see me, Peacock free me,
> Aldebaran bring me light.

He was commissioned as a Pilot Officer, and killed in a training accident off the Yorkshire coast when two planes collided, in April 1942.

There were two views of John Mair, as there always will be of people now labelled charismatic, but who in a time when that word in its present sense was unknown, might have been called magnetic personalities. He was, perhaps by inheritance, something of an actor, and enjoyed creating an aura of mystification around his activities. An unfriendly view has it that he was used to dominating when in a group, wanted admirers rather than competitors, and did not care for those unprepared to listen to his conversation. There is no doubt that he was a spellbinder, but there will always be a minority on whom spells don't work. I never met Mair, rather oddly since we swam in the same literary goldfish bowl, but I doubt if we would have liked each other. I should not have cared for the constant talk, and would have regarded him as too eager to be in the fashionable literary swim. His verdict on me might have been that of all wizards on the unenchanted, that I was a disagreeable fellow.

This feeling about Mair as a personality does not at all affect, indeed rather enhances, my admiration for *Never Come Back*.

2

Choosing the Best of this or that is a party game made all the more enjoyable because one's choice of the Best English Cricket Team Ever, the Ten Best Lyric Poets, World Dramatists, Roman Emperors, Politicians, et cetera, can only be questioned, never disproved. As I've mentioned earlier, in the late fifties I was responsible for the choice of the Hundred Best Crime Stories. Some were chosen by other people, not always with my whole-hearted approval, but I was delighted when Dilys Powell, already famous as a film critic but also a devoted and knowledgeable reader of crime stories, picked *Never Come Back*, calling it a fantasia on murder and espionage. She went on:

Only those who don't really care for crime entertainment want solid character in a thriller. Too much character clutters up the plot, levelling it with the painful realism of the courts. *Never Come Back* has just enough. Cynical, heartless, an intellectual smart-aleck, the hero makes the story believable by the logic of his responses: vanity, cowardice, incredulous panic hardening into unprincipled counter-action. The ingenious adventure disturbs, but enjoyably.

The book's launching was stormy. One of the characters had been named Whitby, and strongly resembled the editor of *John o' London's*, who was called Whitaker. The first printing was withdrawn under threat of libel, Whitby renamed Poole and the portrait of him marginally changed, and the book reissued. It was recognized at once as something original and excellent in crime fiction. George Orwell, reviewing it in the *New Statesman* alongside Koestler's *Darkness at Noon*, said that Mair dealt with Koestler's world in a spirit of burlesque, and suggested that this might be a new kind of thriller 'in which political events subsequent to 1920 are considered mentionable'. Maurice Richardson said it should on no account be missed, James Agate that 'for excitement, narrative power and sheer brains' it was better than anything he had read for years. The book got the kind of press any first novelist would like to have.

Today *Never Come Back* still seems a remarkable performance, and for its time an astonishing one. Desmond Thane is the first anti-hero in crime fiction. He sees himself acting like an orthodox hero ('a punch on the jaw for one, a kick in the stomach for the other . . . and he was free'), but when he tries to put this into practice gets a right to the jaw which sends him sprawling. He knows that he is not the kind of person to hold out under torture, and admits that he has little or no personal and social conscience. This admission is hardly necessary, since Desmond has already murdered two people without feeling the slightest twinge of guilt. The nearest he gets to such a feeling is when, after dropping a man he has bludgeoned into a ditch full of water and realizing that now his half-murder is complete, he thinks, 'I wonder if I really meant to kill him all the time?' The people Desmond kills are extremely unpleasant, 'a Federal Union of the dispossessed' as their Chairman puts it. They represent 'all the great ideological minorities of Europe', old Bolsheviks exiled by Stalin, Fascists and Nazis who have lost out to Mussolini and Hitler, and their aim is to gain or regain power through simultaneous coups in several capitals. Yet, no matter how unpleasant or dangerous an organization might be, heroes of thrillers in 1941 had no licence to kill its members. That was not the way in which heroes of thrillers behaved: nor is it, with some notable exceptions, how they behave today.

At the heart of the book, then, is a credible human being, a character entirely believable in his vanity (when he turns ostensibly to look round for an acquaintance it is really to show his fine Roman profile), his cowardice alternating with bursts of courage, his blend of recklessness and calculation. The three-dimensional figure of Desmond Thane gives strength and plausibility to what might otherwise occasionally be scenes from conventional thriller-dom, and Thane is a convincing figure because – it will come as no surprise to learn – he was a portrait, by no means flattering, of John Mair himself.

One effect of this self-portraiture is to make the book a curious mixture of realism and fantasy. The brilliant opening, with its account of a very odd love affair, probably had a factual basis, and there are other passages which have a personal flavour and are not demanded by the plot. It is in a technical sense a fault that such passages don't marry easily with the international conspiracy which is the core of the story, but the resultant mixture is so odd, and at times so powerful, that one can't really regret it. And the writing, stylish and elegant without affectation, gives constant pleasure, particularly when Desmond is analysing his own character and motives. There is also an astringent uncertainty about the book which is very attractive. It was written during an interregnum, when what was called the Phoney War had suddenly turned disastrous with the fall of France. What next? Nobody knew. The ambiguous but desperate situation is reflected in something reckless about the book and its treatment of motives.

How much did John Mair know about the thriller, how much did the form interest him? He reviewed several of them, writing a particularly witty piece about *No Orchids For Miss Blandish*, in which he totted up the guys rubbed out, hurt bad, worked over, and the dames laid. He had obviously read Eric Ambler, who seems responsible for a touch here and there. And it seems likely that his unheroic hero was created in opposition to figures like Richard Hannay and Bulldog Drummond, characters of impregnable virtue who never had an unchaste thought or showed a hint of cowardice. Beyond that, however, it is unlikely that John Mair cared much about the technique of what he was doing. This is a young man's book, erratic in tone and flavour. At times it is serious and at others frivolous. It is ingenious, exciting, in places implausible, but borne along always on a wave of high spirits. The unwarranted optimism of the ending, with its assumption that 'the control of power by a few, the state of affairs in which important individuals could struggle amongst themselves for rule over millions, was probably over for good', has a certain poignancy today. In its combination of qualities *Never Come Back* is a book *sui generis*. There is nothing else in its own field that is quite like this remarkable relic of a talent that, in the terms of John Mair's hopes and ambitions, was unfulfilled.

(1986)

John Creasey: A Reminiscence

I first met John Creasey on Guy Fawkes Day, 1953, in the National Liberal Club, where he had invited a number of crime writers to discuss the idea of forming some kind of trade association. A dozen of us turned up, to be greeted by a bulky genial figure who said, 'Good of you to come . . . good to meet you,' and then got down to business over tea and corned beef sandwiches. (John was a hearty eater.) The result was the Crime Writers Association, CWA for short, which now has over four hundred members.

John was our chairman for the first three years, when members were counted in not many dozens, and without his hard work and enthusiasm we should never have survived. He was a constantly whirring dynamo, full of ideas. Why not ask Prince Philip to make a speech at our first yearly dinner, saying crime stories help to make a more lawful community? Why not get one of the big London stores to put on a crime exhibition, man it ourselves, and show a collection of weapons used in famous crimes which he could lay hands on? Why not shut John up in a glass-sided box during the exhibition, a box within which he could be seen beginning a new book which he would complete before the exhibition closed? Of these suggestions, three among many, only the second was carried out. Prince Philip pleaded other commitments, and the idea of showing a book being completed in a week or ten days was thought unwise.

The suggestion gives a hint of John's astonishing output. He wrote under more than twenty names, and his products covered the whole range of popular fiction. Tex Riley and William K. Reilly wrote Westerns, Margaret Cooke and Elise Fecamps love stories, the Toff was a gentleman adventurer with a soft heart for women in trouble, the Inspector West books were straight police investigations, Department Z stories concerned with counter-espionage, and so on. As well as all these books he produced the monthly *John Creasey Magazine*, containing crime short stories. His industry and energy were phenomenal. 'I try to keep myself down to writing twelve books a year,' he said to me once. 'It's no good, I can't do it, I write fourteen.' By the time of his death in 1973 he had produced more than six hundred titles, with a good many more stockpiled for posthumous publication.

What kind of man was he, what sort of books did he write? John had remarkable qualities. An attack of polio in childhood left him with a marked limp, which did not stop him whirling round the dance floor. He went to school in Fulham, and it was some kind of triumph for him that he became a director of Fulham FC. He smoked three packs of cigarettes a day for years, then gave up completely. His determination, and his quick intelligence, would have ensured his success in any occupation. At one time he employed a literary agent, but soon realized that no agent could equal him as a salesman. He was an excellent public speaker, though for my taste too Rotarian, personally generous, often emotionally tactful.

And the books? There was the rub, for although many of them contained clever ideas, the actual writing was on the level that might be expected of work done in a few days. That different levels of writing existed was something John did not understand, and that his books should stay unreviewed, or be reviewed caustically, really upset him. This led, alas, to our falling out, the end of what had been on both sides an unlikely friendship.

In a crime review I praised the second or third of his books about Commander George Gideon of the Yard (these police procedurals, written as J. J. Marric, remain the best of John Creasey). He was delighted, and said so. But then books written by him and other CWA members received sharp notices. John was indignant, began to avoid me, look the other way when we were in a group. Eventually he proposed my expulsion from CWA officially, until such time as I started to write constructive, helpful reviews. At this time Val Gielgud was our chairman and Val, hands shaking, implored John to withdraw his motion. He refused, read out a long account of my critical misdeeds – and received no support. Afterwards he came up to me, shook hands, and said nothing had changed. But of course it had. Within a year he resigned from the board of the Association he had founded.

He slowed down his book production to six or seven a year, and turned his energies to politics. He had been a Liberal candidate in 1950, and now founded the All Party Alliance. In 1967 and 1968 he fought four by-elections within eighteen months. Newspapers praised his speeches, and he must have been a splendid canvasser, but of course he lost his deposits. We last met a few months before his death when we were both on a radio programme, and I was shocked to see him shrunk to what seemed half his size, and in a wheelchair. The voice was as strong as ever, though, the manner as buoyant, the optimism unshaken. He had bought a house in New Mexico, was going out there, the different air and different treatment would do him good. His optimism wasn't justified, but I'm glad he went down with the Creasey flag saying 'Anything is possible' still flying.

(1989)

Dick Francis's Career

A horse discards its jockey, who does a thirty-mile-an-hour somersault plus some tumbling rolls, and reflects: nothing broken, just another fall. 'Time and place: sixteenth fence, three-mile steeplechase, Sandown Park racecourse, Friday, November, in thin, cold, persistent rain.' That first page of *Reflex** shows Dick Francis doing what comes most naturally and what he does best, writing about the thrills, spills and chills of horse racing.

There is a lot about riding for money in this book, which gives us a hero who makes a fair living as professional jockey without being the greatest horseman in the world, and all of it is excellent. Philip Nore's love of the game, his detestation of the times when he is told to lose a race, his reluctant acceptance of such instructions because he has to earn a living, and his final determination that he won't pull a horse whatever the consequences, are entirely convincing. Dick Francis has been writing a thriller every year for nineteen years, all of them connected with horses, and he still has all the verve shown in his first book, *Dead Cert*.

All the verve, and such more knowledge about how to develop a story and make a plot work. Dick Francis came to writing after a very successful career as a rider over the sticks. That career included an incident as extraordinary as any in his books: riding the Queen Mother's Devon Loch in the 1956 Grand National, he had the race virtually won when his horse faltered at an imaginary jump, sank to his knees, and finished unplaced. The author who wrote *Dead Cert* five years after his retirement was a professional rider but an amateur crime writer. It seemed unlikely that his specialized knowledge would provide more than three or four fictional themes. Dick Francis has proved those who nursed such thoughts to be entirely wrong. He has varied his plots intelligently, leaving the racecourse to deal with crooked work in transporting

* *Reflex*, by Dick Francis, Michael Joseph.

horses by air (*Flying Finish*), stolen stallions (*Blood Sport*), a jockey who has vanished in Norway (*Slay-Ride*). He has always been good at describing violent action, but he has learned the thriller writer's lesson that violence is more effective when it is firmly rationed. One or two of the early books were rawly naïve in their dialogue, the later ones are crisply efficient and often amusing.

There are several themes in *Reflex*. One is Philip Nore's realization that his only skill is in riding horses, and that in a few years he will be an unemployed jockey, too old to ride. A second is provided by the search for his sister Amanda, whom he had never known to exist, a search which will bring him a fortune if he is successful. A third is Philip's discovery that a recently dead photographer who specialized in racing pictures kept a collection of scandalous shots in what appeared to be his rubbish box, and used them for blackmail.

Upon the whole, this is the main theme. The candid camera shots have been so ingeniously concealed by the blackmailer that each of them needs a different technique of development to show any picture at all. There is a great deal about the ways in which Philip, himself a skilled amateur photographer, does this. No doubt the procedures are all authentic, but if like this reviewer the reader has an acute lack of interest in detection through photography, he is likely to do some skipping.

One is content to see the prints revealing a variety of villains, most of whom get their comeuppance through Philip. In the process he finds his sister, learns something more about his own lonely childhood, acquires a girl whose publishing ambitions are likely to make him famous as a photographer, and gets very badly beaten up. This last is the fate of almost every Dick Francis hero, and the sado-masochistic element in his books has been so often deprecated that it is enough to say that here as elsewhere it seems unnecessary.

The best things in the book, unless you enjoy the photographic puzzles, are the scenes of racing life, which are as good as anything Dick Francis has done. Philip's relationship with Harold Osborne, the trainer who gives him most of his rides, and with Victor Briggs the owner who orders him occasionally to throw races, are shown with skill and subtlety. The blend of affection and irritation felt by Osborne for Philip is particularly well done.

There are limits to Dick Francis's talent. His heroines are present simply to fill a few pages and sometimes to share a bed, his characterization outside the racing people he knows so well is often perfunctory. *Reflex* contains more interesting characterization than most of his books, in Philip's poignant recollections of his shadowy butterfly mother, who used her charm to dump her small boy on one friend after another over the years. So much has been packed into the plot that there is no space to do this aspect of it full justice. Mr Francis might reply that a writer of his kind of thriller cannot afford psychological intricacies, and very likely he would be right. In the end, action is the name of the Dick Francis game. In writing scenes of action, not all of them violent, and blending them into a mystery adventure, he is now a long way ahead of the rest of the field.

(1980)

Eric Ambler

(i) The Autobiography*

The five books Eric Ambler wrote before World War II were immediately recognized as something new in the spy story, quite remote from John Buchan's flag-waving and Sapper's thuggishness. They justified, in particular *The Mask of Dimitrios* justified, the phrase of a book reviewer in the period: 'Ambler first – the rest nowhere.' Ambler wrote with humour (then and now in short supply among writers of spy stories), a heart beating distinctly on the Left side, and an air of sophistication about current politics and of familiarity with many foreign countries. This last is the more remarkable because Ambler was an advertising executive whose experience of travel was pretty well confined to a short stay with a friend in Positano, a fortnight's holiday on the way to and around Marseilles, and a visit to Tangier.

So where did passages like the convincing account of Istanbul and its police chief Colonel Haki in *The Mask of Dimitrios* come from? If Ambler knew he might not tell us, for his autobiography* is written with the calm detachment that is his writing hallmark. It is not exactly that he lacks candour – several of his own verbal and emotional pratfalls are recorded with amusement – but he knows just how much he wants to say about childhood, parents, love affairs, Army life, writing career. The result is not Montaigne saying, 'I expose myself entire,' but a work of Voltairean geniality, scepticism and logic by a writer looking back from his mid-seventies on his first forty years. The title, which appears on the cover as *Here Lies Eric Ambler* is typically ingenious. Equally cunning is the first chapter, which begins with Ambler suffering concussion after a car accident, and recalling the horrors of an American author's publicity tour, which culminates with the

* *Here Lies*, by Eric Ambler, Weidenfeld & Nicolson.

question posed by a TV writer and director at a Los Angeles
bookstore, about 'the autobiography you're planning to write,
champ'. On the rest of the tour, we're told, he invoked this non-
existent autobiography in reply to awkward questions, and now
here it is.

Thus adroitly we are led into an unusual south London childhood. The Amblers came from Salford, but in 1903 moved to
London. Ambler *père* gave his occupation as advertising manager
when registering the birth of Eric Clifford, first of three children,
but although that was his job his heart was on the stage. As Reg
and Amy Ambrose, he and his wife had a living marionette show,
and when marionettes went out of fashion a concert party called
the Harmoniques and another named the What-Nots. The family
lived in Charlton, then moved to Lee Green where five-year-old
Eric saw a bathroom for the first time, along with electric lighting
and an indoor lavatory. He went to a newish LCC school in
Catford where some children came barefoot, others had heads
shaved against nits or ringworm. Not the easiest place for learning
perhaps, but Eric was a bright boy. When socialist Grandad came
to stay, Eric was able successfully to read and pronounced Me-di-
ter-ra-ne-an. Grandad was delighted, and taught him to read and
pronounce ca-pit-al-ism. The present war, he said, would see its
downfall. Eric was seven years old, and the year was 1916.

After that, a scholarship to Colfe's Grammar School, piano
study at the Blackheath Conservatoire ('For music I had an ear but
no talent'), matric taken and passed, then another scholarship
when fifteen-year-old Eric got 100 per cent for a paper in chemistry, 95 per cent for one in physics (5 per cent knocked off for bad
writing). He went to Northampton Engineering College, based
oddly enough in Islington, which offered BSc degree courses in
engineering. But although upwardly mobile Eric Ambler learned a
lot about various aspects of engineering and physical science, some
of it useful to him as a writer, and was fascinated by problems like:
'How long would a 3-core cable with jute-wrapped bitumen
insulation last under five feet of water?', he hankered after the
theatre. He wrote a couple of one-act plays and was briefly half of
Barclay and Ambrose, 'entertainers at the piano'. He turned out
also to have a gift for thinking of publicity ideas and writing copy.
He told his father he wanted to write plays. 'As an engineer you

could have a safe job,' his father said. 'That would let you be original in your spare time.' The senior Ambler's attempt to be original had ended in 1921, when the What-Nots failed to interest a professional theatre management after giving a series of 'subscription' performances in West End concert halls. Elsie Waters later said that the Ambroses could have made a go of a stage act, but gave it up so that Eric and his brother could have an assured future. Typically, Eric Ambler puts this down without comment.

This early part of the Ambler story has the verve and freshness of the pre-war novels. The second half includes a long affair with the daughter of Australian cartoonist Will Dyson, marriage to an American fashion correspondent and designer, success as a writer, and a wartime Army career in which he ended as Lieutenant-Colonel making propaganda and information films for the Army. It is no less sharply written and has some good stories, including one when Ambler rashly corrected Winston Churchill about the stars of *Bachelor Mother* (Ginger Rogers and David Niven, not as the Prime Minister hoped and expected Deanna Durbin), a correction not warmly welcomed. It is less compelling – unbroken success never being so interesting as struggle.

We leave Eric Ambler in mid-career, the war over, wavering between the beckoning bitch goddess of Hollywood (he calls her a sacred cow) and the silence of the novelist's study. For him, as he says, the issue was never clear cut. Army film experience had taught him that he was a good scriptwriter, and the choice was complicated further by the fact that the plot device of *The Mask of Dimitrios*, in which the central character is seen only through the eyes of others for almost the whole book, was as unrepeatable as the biographical approach of *The Quest For Corvo*. He had also realized, as he wrote to me years ago, that the wicked capitalists and virtuous Soviet agents of the pre-war books would no longer do. In the last thirty years he has tried this approach and attempted to infuse the thriller with the depth of a novel, while scrupulously avoiding explicit sex and the pornography of violence. Along with this volume two of his finest post-war stories are reissued. *The Levanter* has one of Ambler's typical non-heroes with an eye on the main chance confronted by nihilistic Palestine guerrillas. It offers excitement plus appalling plausibility. *Doctor Frigo* is even better. This full-scale novel about an exile's unwilling return to danger and possible death in his homeland is the masterpiece of Ambler's maturity, as surely as *Dimitrios* was of his youth.

(1985)

(ii) Ambler at Eighty

Eric Ambler arrived for lunch on a warm day, looking and sounding extremely cheerful. He had just learned he will be the first recipient of a Golden Dagger award made by the Veterans of the CSS (Office of Strategic Services), the unorthodox wartime American intelligence agency headed by General 'Wild Bill' Donovan. The CSS was later merged in the CIA, and the committee making the award included two former CIA Directors and a dozen other intelligence analysts and experts. What pleased Ambler particularly was that the award was given for the 'credibility, veracity and feasibility' of the writer's handling of intelligence work. Yet unlike John le Carré, Ted Allbeury and other writers in the genre, Ambler had no connection with any intelligence agency. I asked him whether that mattered.

'I don't think so, it's not important to know all the details. When I began I thought they could all be imagined, and mostly they can. I've often suspected people who actually are in the spying business have a need to romanticize it, because it is really fairly dull.' And he had little time for writers of spy stories who spice up their books by introducing real people, Brezhnev, Andropov, Churchill, into the fiction. 'It's specious, an attempt to obtain verisimilitude, and it doesn't work, or at least it doesn't work with me. If you're going to use the real names, write historical fiction.'

Coming up to eighty, Ambler's blue eyes are as sharp, his back as straight, as when he was a wartime Army Colonel. His manner is urbane, slightly mocking and self-mocking, destructive of pretentiousness. The speech is occasionally hesitant, the right word searched for, its arrival sometimes deliberately delayed for effect but always eventually found. To say he is held in high esteem by his writing colleagues would be an understatement. Five years ago Len Deighton arranged a lunch in his honour at the Savoy. The thirteen at table included le Carré, Frederick Forsyth, Gavin Lyall, Lionel Davidson. Graham Greene sent a cable: 'To the master from one of his disciples.' Le Carré said his works were the well into which everybody had dipped.

The political thriller came of age with Eric Ambler, first through the implicitly Left-wing novels he wrote in the thirties, then with the uncommitted books that began in 1951 with *Judgment on Deltchev*, after eleven years' silence as a novelist. We talked about that eleven-year gap.

'The War was partly responsible – I was otherwise engaged, you might say. Then I got into Army films, and from there it was a slippery slope into writing commercial films, feature films. But that wasn't solely responsible. Before the War I was very much an anti-Fascist writer, and after August 1939 and the Nazi–Soviet pact I'd really lost my subject matter. I was of the thirties, and long after the tears had been wiped away there was still a sense of loss, a loss of belief.'

The masterpiece of Ambler Mark I is agreed to be *The Mask of Dimitrios*, in which for three-quarters of the book we see the central character only through the eyes of other people, an unrepeatable device which is astonishingly successful. He laughed when I asked what made him attempt something so difficult.

'To tell the truth, I'm not aware of thinking it out. I'd recently seen Pirandello's *Six Characters*, he was very much in my mind, and this seemed another way of doing what Pirandello had done. When I sold the book for films I told my agent they'd never be able to make it, the problems were too great. But of course they just solved the problems by ignoring them.'

He emerged from those silent years when a film company sent him to Asia. 'I was only incidentally looking for material as a novelist. When you're looking you don't find it, if I want to see something I don't take a camera. I'm reminded of Max Beerbohm, when he said Beau Brummel looked life squarely in the face out of the corner of his eye. That's a writer's view. Things overheard are better understood than when you're asking questions.'

So what did he find in or via the Asian scene? 'Another way of writing about politics. I became very wary of identifying people by the colour of their hats, their political hats particularly.' I reminded him that he had said recently that nobody now seemed to believe socialism was possible. 'Yes. I suppose you could say socialism has never been properly tried, but a lot of the stuff that goes along with it makes it very certain that socialism isn't tried. I don't see any way out of that.' What were his political sympathies now? He said with a smile that they would be hard to characterize.

For several years Ambler worked in Hollywood as a successful screenwriter, and he said once that if a writer found the Hollywood experience deeply satisfying then, as a novelist, his goose was cooked. Had he ever feared his own goose was cooked?

'I was scared at one point, before I found a fresh vein. Screenwriting is bound to have a certain attraction when you feel you're doing it well, but you also know that the medium is a bit second-rate. The first-rate medium is the theatre, and film is a slightly second-rate version of theatre. The third-rate version is TV, of course. It's not true to say TV is just another way of projecting film, it has a different size audience, a different context. It's inevitable it should come number three in the scale of possible achievement.' His book *The Intercom Conspiracy* had recently been shown on TV, in a version with which he had nothing to do, as *The Quiet Conspiracy*. The book has the lucidity that is an Ambler hallmark, the TV version is bafflingly complicated. 'If I'd not known the story I'd have said, "It's like *Tinker, Tailor, Soldier, Spy*, I don't understand it." I'd have stopped watching.'

The dozen Ambler Mark II novels range from the light-hearted tales about would-be wide boy Arthur Abdul Simpson, through books that show Ambler's Kiplingesque fascination with the way technical devices work like *The Night-Comers*, to explicitly political thrillers. I was pleased that he chose one of these, *Doctor Frigo*, as his finest achievement.

Doctor Frigo is about the life of a man whose murdered father was a politician in a Central American state, now again on the edge of revolution, a true Amblerian theme. 'It started out as something different. I wondered how it would feel to be the son of a convicted war criminal, and how you would adapt to it. Then the war criminal became a different sort of criminal, somebody not greatly loved, but a man one could respect. And I wanted to write something about the health of our great men and the way it can affect political events, so that became another important element in the story.' I suggested that the book also took a cool look at some of the political activities Ambler Mark I had seen through rose-tinted spectacles. 'Yes, absolutely. One of the things I'm saying is that political rhetoric of any kind should be looked at, not once or twice but several times, before it's swallowed.' On further thought he said it should never be swallowed.

In the end Eric Ambler is a writer of political thrillers rather than spy stories. As he sketched out an idea for a book I saw how much the mechanics of belief, loyalty, betrayal, continue to fascinate him.

'I can think of the kind of book I might write now, though I won't do it. It would be about the planning of a *coup d'état*, and how difficult it is to recruit for your side. Once the recruiting starts, that's when the fear begins. You're offering hostages to fortune all the time. Every time anyone says, "I'm with you," there is a potential assassin. And the fear enters every kind of relationship, even that of families, so that the planner is always asking himself, "Can I be sure . . ." That's the level at which I'd like to write, to show how the whole apparatus works.'

That was the outline Eric Ambler presented – to me, to anybody – of the book he isn't going to write. In his hands it could be a masterpiece, but who else could do justice to it?

(1989)

Three Looks at le Carré

(i) Smiley's People

The spy story seems now to have reached its Silver Age, one of great subtlety and refinement which conceals the lack of a subject truly involving the writer and shows a failure of verve and nerve. *Smiley's People* is about the 'brilliant last duel' between Smiley and his 'Russian opposite number, codename Karla'. (Quotations courtesy of the blurb.) Is there a faint whiff of 'Sapper' about, of Bulldog Drummond and Carl Petersen? It's not like that, of course, and the duel is not to the death but to the point of defection, yet the fact that such a duel between the top men on either side should be envisaged suggests how far le Carré has come since the days of Leamas and *The Spy Who* . . .

Mr le Carré has not lost his skill in orchestrating a book, in juxtaposing scenes effectively, pacing the narrative, showing characters obliquely through conversation. The opening scene here, in which a Russian woman emigré in Paris is approached by a Soviet agent to make a bargain through which her daughter will be allowed to join her in France, is both sharply expressive in itself and an effective introduction to the book's main theme. The daughter's departure from Russia is something to do with Karla, Smiley gets on to it, and slowly turns the cat's cradle of complications into a meaningful shape. In the process there are scenes as good as anything le Carré has written, in particular the interrogation of a minor Russian bureaucrat near the book's end.

But *slowly* is the word. The story's progress is funereal, and there are times when Smiley appears to have lost not his marbles but his memory. Some of the narrative involves Smiley digging to unearth bits of the past that we know already (as in the long, long revelations of a messenger's activities), and we see him prompting the memory of others with information that he apparently already knows. In a talk with Connie Sachs – we have met her in other books – Smiley induces her to remember things about Karla and the girl. 'And the child? There was a defector report – what was *that* about?' If Smiley knows so much about the defector report, and indeed about most of what Connie has to tell him, what is the point of asking her questions? Much of the tale is conveyed to us in this low-toned retrospective vein with the characters gloomily or exultantly recalling the past.

The convolutions of the cat's cradle cover the absence of an interesting or exciting plot. What mystery it contains shouldn't be revealed, but at the end a reader is likely to say: are these unlikely sentimentalities what it was all about? The difference between early and recent le Carré is one of approach, as well as manner. The author of *The Spy* and *The Looking Glass War* viewed spies and their activities with a cold eyl. George Smiley is at first a background figure, a string-puller rather than an important character, and the sketch of him is ambiguous. Now he is at the front of the stage, and it is difficult not to call him the hero. Indeed, the work of the Centre is now distinctly idealized. It is suggested that these may be inadequate or fallible people who can't manage their own lives – see Smiley's miserable relationship with his promiscuous Ann – but still they are modern patriots, sacrificing their chances of happiness by defending the bad against the worse. If only the bureaucrats like Lacon and Saul Enderby would let the Circus men of action get on with the job, it is suggested that we might all be better off. In early le Carré the security services, both bureaucrats and people in the field, were shown as conscienceless men playing destructive and useless games. The great revelation of *Smiley's People*, a mark of John le Carré's apostasy, is that now even Karla is human.

(1980)

(ii) *The Little Drummer Girl*

Graham Greene called *The Spy Who Came In From The Cold* the finest spy story he had ever read, and twenty years on the praise does not seem exaggerated. *Spy* is a book perfect in its kind, beautifully shaped and paced, so that each turn in the story is evidently logical, yet contains an element of surprise. And its springs are not the automatic violence common to this sort of fiction, but the conflicts and interactions between people dear to a true novelist. *Spy* is not only a masterly spy story but a fine novel.

What could succeed such a book? Le Carré's answer was to move gradually away from the spy story with books less warmly greeted, a course that ended with *The Naive and Sentimental Lover*, a disastrously bad love story received with a unanimity of disapproval. Le Carré is a man upset by hostile criticism. He returned to spying, to George Smiley – now the central character instead of a background figure – and to immense success. The publisher's advance on *Spy* was £175. The sales of the later books have been so great that one doesn't know how many zeroes should be added to that figure in totting up receipts.

Praise from uncritical critics sitting happily on the speeding bandwagon lies on these books thick as whipped cream on Viennese pastry. Yet *Tinker, Tailor, Soldier, Spy*, *The Honourable Schoolboy* and *Smiley's People* are much inferior in style and plotting to *Spy*, or even to le Carré's fine first book *Call For the Dead*. They are books bloated with description and analysis, so that almost every scene is written at twice the length warranted by its place in the story, and there is a deliberate parade or pretence of expertise in the use of names like babysitter, housekeeper, lamplighter, shoemaker. There are no such terms in *Spy*, but in the later books they proliferate. Do they really mean bodyguard, security officer, home-based courier, forger? That doesn't matter. The important and deplorable thing is that in these books the author shows off in a way that the writer of *Spy* would never have done. The trilogy also seems to be moving a long way from the realities of spying as represented, say, by Blunt or George Blake.

Happily, *The Little Drummer Girl* is different and better, perhaps even the equal of *Spy*. We have done with Smiley the somnambulist zombie wandering about the past in search of clues to the present, and not a babysitter or lamplighter is to be seen. Instead we are with Israeli agents trying to catch an Arab terrorist responsible for a series of successful bombings. They are admirably characterized, the breezy outgoing Schulmann, really Marty Kurtz, 'far more European than Hebrew', and his sidekick Litvak, in appearance and character the archetypal Israeli fanatic, 'starved, and in conflict with demons'.

The Israelis need somebody to put inside the terrorist organization, and they choose an unsuccessful English actress called Charlie, a middle class sixties rebel out of her time, high on drugs, sex and world revolution, but still looking for something to take seriously. Charlie is lured into an affair by Kurtz's operative Gadi Becker, and then spirited away into a house in Athens where she is cajoled, persuaded, enticed, into playing her part in 'the theatre of the real'. An Arab lover is invented for her, in fact the brother of the master terrorist, letters and other details are forged, the affair is constructed in great detail. Day after day Becker instructs her in the part she will play. And since this is the theatre of the real it will not be merely a part, she will feel with the Arabs and loathe the Jewish Fascists. Sure enough when, much later, she is in a peaceful Palestinian camp bombed by the Israelis she thinks: 'You rotten, killing Zionist bastards.' She is required to believe this and yet, at another level, to remain faithful to her mission.

The conversion of Charlie into the goat tethered to catch the lion (Kurtz's phrase) is a remarkable piece of writing. It takes a long time to get the goat tethered, and some of the Kurtz–Litvak activities seem drawn out or unlikely, in particular a passage of knockabout comedy with Charlie's agent. Yet when the operation begins, and Charlie moves deeper and deeper into the Palestine terrorist movement, one sees that the preparations were necessary to our full belief and understanding. The balance between the two violent idealisms is finely kept, and there is a glimpse or anticipation of 'the ultimate recourse', the brutal invasion of Lebanon that actually took place. Among a large cast of convincing minor characters the German terrorist Helga and the foxy political middleman Dr Alexis are particularly good.

A few doubts and qualifications exist, connected chiefly with le Carré's romanticism, more evident here than in the best of his work. Erotic feeling plays a large part in Charlie's make-up, but le Carré is a markedly unerotic writer, and we are sometimes told what we should be shown. And although it is reasonable that Charlie should fall for Becker, it seems unlikely that a course of instruction plus going to bed with her should generate love on his side, and that they should walk off together at the end emphasizes that the book's essential seriousness is about politics rather than people. Still and all, it's a fine novel.

(1983)

(iii) *The Night Manager*

Few things are staler than a spy story with last week's background. John le Carré, when planning his new book, had to devise a strategy for writing about a society in which, as one of his characters reflects, there is 'no more Russian bear to fight, no more Reds under the bed at home'. Now that the Soviet Union has ceased to exist, and le Carré's super-spy Karla with it, what can replace them? The writer's answer is to blend international arms dealers and the bosses of drug cartels in a single individual, make him a lazy-voiced arrogant stylish Englishman named Richard Onslow Roper, and give him the verbal persuasiveness of Mephistopheles. The result is a brilliant performance, executed with an exuberance, a richness of detail and a narrative drive absent from le Carré's writing for a decade.

The Gulf War and its immense possibilities for arms dealing is the background of the story, but the heart of it is Roper, his entourage, and his arguments in defence of his activities. Does he help to establish dictatorships? Armed power keeps the peace, he says, 'unarmed power doesn't last five minutes'. Are death and starvation in Africa and South America to be laid at his door? Not so. 'Who are the killers? It's not the chaps who make the guns. It's the chaps who don't open the larder doors.'

Swept along in Roper's wake, as he moves around by plane and helicopter from luxury yacht to luxury hotel to his fantasy palace made real in the Caribbean, are a sleazy but sinister group of acolytes headed by the extravagantly queer but deadly clever Major Corkoran. Opposed to Roper is Jonathan Pine, first met as night manager of Zurich's Hotel Meister Palace, but with a past that includes undercover work in Northern Ireland. Pine is backed by one of those under-financed oddball secret agencies met in other le Carré books. This one is run by the well-named Leonard Burr from dingy offices in London's Victoria Street, and backed by a Whitehall mandarin named Goodhew, whose puritan conscience makes him implacably opposed to Roper as the personal embodiment of all drug-dealing and arms-selling evil. A bigger British agency devoted to Pure Intelligence (which means gathering information, but most often refraining from using it for fear of disturbing the status quo) co-operates with the American cousins in keeping a watchful eye on Burr.

Pine's character is built up with great care. The opening fifty pages, which show him as in effect a super-flunkey at the Zurich hotel, disturbed by Roper and overwhelmed by the beauty of Roper's English mistress Jed, are written with a deliberate panache designed both to emphasize Roper's high style and to show us that Pine is in retreat from tragedy and violence in his own life. He has tried to protect the mistress of an Arab colleague of Roper's, and she has been quite casually killed. In the Meister Palace Pine is really hiding from himself and the effect of his own actions. Locked one day by accident in the hotel's wine cellar with no prospect of being found, Pine decides that if saved he will 'abandon his morbid quest for order and treat himself to a little chaos'. Pine is enlisted by Burr, given a new identity and a background of drug running and apparent murder. Burr then arranges a mock-kidnapping of Roper's son Dan, from which Pine is to save the boy. In the event Pine, seeing the frightened boy, loses his cool and breaks the arm of one Burr agent. He is then badly beaten up by another, and becomes the temporary favourite of a grateful Roper.

This is Operation Limpet. Pine is to be the limpet bomb that will cling to and finally destroy Roper.

Put down so simply, this may sound like the ordinary material of an espionage adventure. That is not at all the effect. Such a plot outline inevitably ignores brilliant set pieces like that when Roper's party arrives at Hunter's Island in the Caribbean before the failed kidnapping. There the gigantic Mama Low has a meal in preparation for the party at which Jonathan, renamed Lamont, is cooking his famous stuffed mussels that Mama Low says will make 'ladies 'n' gentlemen screw their hearts out'. Nor can it convey the subtleties of Jonathan's long interrogations by the suspicious Corkoran when he is recuperating after the beating up that was not in the script.

And no plot outline can do justice to the long description of what is justly described as a madhouse in the Panama jungle, where weapons are demonstrated in the presence of potential buyers, and Roper's friends and agents are gathered, Frenchmen and Germans and an Israeli, men who have 'fought every dirty war from Cuba to Salvador to Guatemala to Nicaragua'. The story is built up with the relentless simplicity of Victorian narrative, but it is elaborated and enriched with what are often terrifying gargoyles.

Roper and his crew are not the only villains. Le Carré's distaste for the intelligence agency game and its most enthusiastic practitioners, which seemed in abeyance in the later Smiley books, has never been shown more clearly than in his depiction of the Pure Intelligence outfit in London and its counterparts in Washington. Both groups are chiefly concerned with discomfiting and outwitting rivals, and are ready to dispose of their own agents when they pose awkward questions.

One scene shows the master manipulator Goodhew threatened with ruin or death by a committee man he has always thought an amiable cipher, unless Goodhew abandons support for Operation Limpet. Meanwhile, across the Atlantic, Deputy Assistant Attorney General Ed Prescott breaks the news to Joe Strelski, another Limpet supporter, that Pine must be left to his fate in Roper's hands. This scene is written with a controlled savagery rare in le Carré's work. Isn't Roper inextricably linked with dope running and illegal arms sales? Strelski asks. Prescott smiles ruefully as he says that can't be proved, and Strelski responds with heavyweight irony:

'Don't change, Ed. America needs you as you are . . . Keep fixing things for us. The decent citizen knows too much already, Ed. Any more knowledge could seriously endanger his health.'

Le Carré is a finely ambitious writer, concerned to write stories that can be considered on the same plane as Conrad's *Under Western Eyes* or the best of Graham Greene and Stevenson. His finest books show that in the architectonics of writing, the construction, shaping and pacing of a plot, he has no superiors and few equals among living novelists. The plot construction of the *Spy* could serve as a model for any novelist concerned with such old-fashioned things as a closely plotted narrative, although it is true that in some of the other novels Conradian complexity too often obscures the storyline.

Is *The Night Manager* up to the best le Carré? The equivocatory answer has to be: yes, but only where it concerns the worlds of Roper and the London/Washington agencies. Their activities are handled with total assurance and an evident and infectious enjoyment. Elsewhere, however, le Carré sometimes surrenders to the inescapably sensational nature of the espionage thriller, and also to a romanticism about women characters that leads to the creation of a pipe-dream fantasy rather than a character in Roper's mistress Jed. The saddest thing is the surrender to conventional thrillerdom of an upbeat ending tacked on to a book which cried out for a tragic one. Perhaps le Carré bent before his publishers' demand for a hero who might defeat enormous odds, perhaps the artistic miscalculation was his own. Whatever the reason, the result is a highly implausible conclusion damaging our belief in what for almost all the way has been a splendidly exciting, finely told story.

(1993)

AMERICA

Poe's Short Stories

1

Edgar Allan Poe's work needs, more than that of any other nineteenth-century writer, a brief biographical note to provide the background for an understanding of his writing.

He was born in Boston in 1809, the son of travelling actors. His father disappeared soon after his birth, his mother died in Richmond, Virginia, before he was three years old, and he was taken into the household of a local merchant named John Allan. He was not adopted, but for a while was treated as a son. Allan took him on a five-year visit to England, sent him to school in London, and on return to America enrolled him as a student in the University of Virginia. There the young man contracted gambling debts, quarrelled with his foster-father, and was removed by Allan from the university after a single year. At the age of eighteen he left home and joined the Army. He remained in it for almost four years, in the latter part of that time as a cadet at West Point, and was then court-martialled and dismissed from the service for his deliberate refusal to obey orders.

By the time he left West Point he had produced two collections of poems, and was set upon a literary career. For the rest of his life he maintained himself by journalism, and by writing stories and poems. He was a hard-working journalist, with a remarkable flair for the writing of a sensational story: but he was also quarrelsome at times, in particular after one of the bouts of drinking in which he engaged intermittently. He did not drink for pleasure, but out of some kind of compulsion, in an attempt to ease or eliminate temporarily his financial and emotional difficulties. When he was twenty-seven years old he married his thirteen-year-old cousin Virginia, and they lived with her mother Maria Clemm in a household that was often desperately short of money.

Virginia's death early in 1847 loosened Poe's grip on reality, and his drinking bouts became more frequent and more serious. It had been his constant desire to found and edit a magazine that would raise the level of American literature, and he planned to do this through a second marriage with a woman who would back the magazine. This marriage was still in prospect as a possibility when he died in Baltimore in October 1849, after a long drinking session about which little is known in detail.

This background of almost permanent financial stress, and of some deep emotional trauma going back to childhood, shaped the work of Edgar Allan Poe.

2

Poe thought of himself first of all as a poet, and only secondarily as a writer of tales. The seventy-odd stories and pieces of imaginative fiction that he produced were written primarily to supplement his income from editorial and critical work. Some of them were jokes or hoaxes, like his detailed account of a balloon crossing the Atlantic written for the New York *Sun*, which was so widely believed that people paid a shilling for the 'extra' containing full details of the flight. Many had their origin in stories he read in newspapers about ballooning, extraordinary voyages, mesmeric trances. Others were derived from British magazines, which contained the Gothic horror stories popular at the time both in Britain and Germany.

In 1840 a first collection of stories, *Tales of the Grotesque and Arabesque*, appeared between book covers, and in accordance with his view that poetry was far more important than prose, Poe's introduction deprecated the idea that he had 'for this species of writing, any inordinate, or indeed any peculiar taste or prepossession'. The 'Grotesque' in the title referred to what we would call comic tales, the 'Arabesque' to stories of a horrific kind. Critics called this second kind of story Germanic, and Poe replied in a memorable phrase that 'If in many of my productions terror has been the thesis, I maintain that terror is not of Germany, but of the soul.' This kind of terror, an emotion springing from the writer's own sufferings and despair, found an immediate echo in the minds of readers, an echo that has rung down the decades. The stories remain memorable in part because they contain no real characters, nothing beyond the fears and agonies of their creator. It is to such fears and agonies that, especially in youth, we respond.

Yet although the response to his stories was immediate and widespread, Poe made little money from them. *Tales of the Grotesque and Arabesque* was followed in 1843 by a pamphlet containing what was advertised as the first, but proved to be the only, instalment of *The Prose Romances of Edgar A. Poe* in what was promised as a uniform serial edition. In 1845 a dozen stories were published in book form as *Tales* (they were not chosen by Poe, who was dissatisfied with the selection), and this collection sold a little better. Poe, in spite of his occasional slighting references to the short story compared to the poem as a literary form, made careful revisions of stories for each new publication. None of the collections published in his lifetime had much success, but when the stories and poems appeared in 1850, after his death, they were reprinted fifteen times in as many years. It is against this background that we must consider the stories. They were written for money, and not very much money, by a man who considered his poetry more important than his prose; yet this was also a man whose itch for perfection was such that he made careful revisions with each new appearance of a story in a trivial magazine.

Poe's skills as a story writer were much more various than is realized by readers who have encountered only a few of the tales of terror. More than a dozen of his stories are comic, and although in person a man of extreme delicacy and politeness, in print Poe was a humorist in the vulgar American tradition of the practical joke or the appalling pun. (One story is supposed to come from the book *Tellmenow Isitsöornot*.) There is a sort of jovial brutality about these stories. The Signora Psyche Zenobia, in the tale with her name for a title, has her head cut off by a clock hand. Is that funny in itself? Poe thought so, and elaborated on the problem of a cut-off head taking snuff. Is it a comic idea to have an asylum run by lunatics, who have tarred, feathered and imprisoned their keepers? Again, Poe thought so, and blended with the comedy a characteristic attack upon the do-goodism that at this time was trying to replace severe restrictions upon lunatics by the 'soothing system' which gave the insane a measure of freedom. Other comic stories, like 'Some Words With a Mummy' and 'Mellonta Tauta' satirized democracy and the idea of progress.

The stories that make fiction seem like fact have already been mentioned – 'MS Found in a Bottle' is full of apparently realistic detail, and 'The Facts in the Case of M. Valdemar', although not specifically meant to fool readers like 'The Balloon-Hoax', deceived many people into thinking it was an authentic experiment. There are wholly fantastic stories dealing with life in the next world, and stories almost equally dreamlike which visualize an ideal existence in this one. It is on the basis of such fantasies and hoaxes that Poe has been called, exaggeratedly in my view, the father of science fiction.

There is no doubt, however, about the justice of the claim made for him as the father of the detective story. Poe wrote five tales of detection, and between them they anticipate almost every later development in the genre. 'The Murders in the Rue Morgue' is the first locked room mystery, 'The Purloined Letter' offers the most unlikely solution to a crime, 'The Mystery of Marie Rogêt' is the progenitor of documentary crime fiction, and 'The Gold-Bug' the first of the many stories that have at their centre the solution of a code or puzzle. His stories also introduce to us the omniscient detective and his less intelligent friend, the first among dozens of couples of the kind. Poe's achievement here becomes more astonishing the longer one looks at it, particularly in view of the fact that no detective departments in police forces existed at the time he wrote, and that the very word *detective* was not in use.

And still the tales that have made him most famous remain unmentioned, those stories of terror deeply rooted in the sufferings of the man who wrote them. Most of them are short, in accordance with Poe's belief that a short story, like a poem, should concentrate upon 'a certain unique or *single* effect', and that the incidents of the story should combine to produce that effect. 'In the whole composition there should be no word written, of which the tendency, direct or indirect, is not to the one pre-established design.' The finest of the stories show this theory in practice: the first paragraph, sometimes the first sentence, conveys the theme and the desired effect, the emphasis on madness in 'The Tell-Tale Heart' and 'The Black Cat', the gloom that pervades the opening of 'The Fall of the House of Usher', the emphasis on being 'keenly alive to a joke' in the first sentence of 'Hop-Frog', and the compelling opening sentence of 'The Masque of the Red Death': 'The "Red Death" had long devastated the country.' These are statements deliberately designed to introduce a theme. The note that has been struck is enlarged and elaborated, but no departure is made from it, no extraneous details are allowed to enter the story. Poe believed that all art aspired to the nature of music, and his beliefs called for a kind of musical conception in the stories, with the stated theme swelling at the end to a diapason of terror.

3

Poe, then, was an artist who carefully calculated his effects. He made no similar calculation of his style which, especially in his early work, is extravagantly and absurdly rhetorical when he is most evidently serious. The poet and critic Allen Tate did not overstate the case when he said that 'Poe's serious style at its most typical worst makes the reading of more than one story at a sitting an almost insuperable task.' Yet, as Tate also observed, by denouncing what is absurd or annoying about Poe (in particular his inflated romanticism and his insistence on an often bogus or borrowed erudition) we do not dispose of him. Very well, the style is often absurd: but then, why do these stories remain burned in the memory when many more suavely written tales by other writers are almost instantly forgotten? In part, as I have suggested, this was because he worked so carefully to a design, and in part because in the serious stories he wrote nothing that he did not feel, and the intensity of his feeling is communicated to us.

That intensity is made more impressive by its vagueness. Poe seems always trying to express something he does not dare to say, and this sense of something unstated in the stories, of a final curtain never pulled aside, adds to their effectiveness. His chief characters suffer, as it seems to us, from some sexual frustration, his bloodless women have the somnambulistic air associated with victims of a vampire, yet no word of sexuality or vampirism stains Poe's pages. It is the essence of the finest stories that no explanation of the mysteries they contain is offered, beyond the suggestion of madness. What were the 'thousand injuries' inflicted by Fortunato in 'The Cask of Amontillado', why was marriage to Berenicë so inevitably disastrous to the narrator of that story? Poe does not tell us, and it is useless to speculate. Such obscurities are necessary to the effect he has designed, they are part of his deep originality. His tales had their origins in newspaper or magazine articles, he borrowed and upon occasion stole like a jackdaw, but the end result was never anything else but a product of the mind and sensibility of Edgar Allan Poe.

It is the originality and the ingenuity that a reader who comes freshly to the stories is likely to notice first. Poe was an extraordinarily clever man. He had had little training in mathematics, yet was able to solve all the cyphers sent in to him when he challenged readers of papers on which he worked to send him such puzzles. The speed with which he was able to absorb ideas in the fields of philosophy and metaphysics was as remarkable as his ability to assimilate theories of grammar, new methods of printing, and recent scientific discoveries. The jumble of notes and opinions called 'Marginalia' that he contributed to magazines in the last six years of his life contain, as recent scholars have shown, many ideas taken over at secondhand, but they are still a tribute to the remarkable range of his reading and the butterfly quickness of his mind.

Yet originality and ingenuity are the lesser part of what Edgar Allan Poe offers to a reader. His finest stories spring without doubt from something psychopathic in his personality, but no other literary psychopath has written like Poe. It is not useful to assess him by the standards we usually apply to literature: he communicates to us what is essentially a personal suffering and terror, and we make to it an essentially personal response, not the kind of response we make to Tolstoy or Trollope. The cleverness was important, because if Poe had been a less clever man the stories might have tipped over the edge of irrationality on which they continually teeter, and become merely absurd. Logic, or the illusion of logic, adds to his terrible effects. Poe's greatest achievement is to communicate his terrors, so that his nightmares haunt us all.

(1980)

Dashiell Hammett

(i) Taking Crime Fiction Seriously*

Lives of crime writers mostly remind us that more lively hours may be spent in reading their books, but there are exceptions, the most conspicuous of them being Dashiell Hammett. According to the legend, Hammett turned his own life into fiction. His years as a Pinkerton detective were the basis of the Continental Op stories, and Hammett himself was the origin first of Sam Spade, and later of the hard-drinking Nick Charles in *The Thin Man*. Lillian Hellman helped to create this legendary Hammett in her romantic accounts of their intermittent life together over thirty years, like the story of their first meeting in a Hollywood restaurant, when he was recovering from a long drinking session. 'The five-day drunk had left the wonderful face looking rumpled, and the very tall thin figure was tired and sagged. We . . . went and sat in his car and talked to each other and over each other until it was daylight.' That is Nick Charles Hammett, who may also be glimpsed in the film *Julia*. Sam Spade Hammett can be found in Joe Gores's *Hammett*, which offers a sometimes ingenious fictional reconstruction of Hammett's life in San Francisco.

This legendary Hammett existed, although he was not the whole man. As his friend the screenwriter Nunnally Johnson wrote to me: 'From the day I met Hammett, in the late twenties, his behaviour could be accounted for only by an assumption that he had no expectation of being alive much beyond Thursday . . . Even allowing for the exuberance of youthfulness and the headiness of the certain approach of success, not to mention the daffiness of the twenties, no one could have spent himself and his money with such recklessness who expected to be alive much longer.' But this

---

* *Shadow Man: The Life of Dashiell Hammett*, by Richard Layman, Harcourt Brace Jovanovich; *Raymond Chandler* by Jerry Spier, Frederick Ungar Publishing.

was a miscalculation by Hammett, akin to Dylan Thomas's belief in his early twenties that he would not live more than a few months. To quote Johnson again: 'Lusty friends sickened and died, and Hammett, for whom we all drew a deep sigh every other day, survived ... When the end approached, it was thirty years later than he had expected it, and Death owed him a genuine apology when eventually it made its tardy appearance.' Yet Johnson's account is romantically exaggerated, as Richard Layman's book makes plain. The merit of this first biography of Hammett (William F. Nolan's *Dashiell Hammett: A Casebook*, published in 1968, was no more in biographical terms than an informative sketch) is its factual quality. It has been written without help or hindrance from Lillian Hellman, and is a disproof of her statement that nothing of value could be written about Hammett without her assistance. Mr Layman does not debunk, but tends to deflate. The thin man's face was wonderful, but he had bad teeth.

The story of Hammett's life is dramatic and tragic enough. He was born in Maryland in 1894, the son of a heavy handsome hard-drinking man who never had much success in life. Richard Hammett was an aspiring politician, and then a street-car conductor, clerk, and apparently door-to-door salesman of seafood. Dashiell, the eldest of three children, left school at fourteen to help with the business, which was soon given up. Father and son got on badly. When his father died many years later, Hammett paid for the funeral but refused to attend it. By the time the young man was twenty he had left or lost half a dozen jobs, started to drink, caught a dose of clap. At twenty-one he took a job as a Pinkerton detective and held it for three years until he joined the Army in 1918. He went back to Pinkerton's after his discharge a year later but was now a sick man, troubled by the tuberculosis that affected him for the rest of his life. In October 1920 he was admitted to a public health hospital weighing no more than 130 lbs, and was immediately classed as 100 per cent disabled. He emerged several months later, patched up but not cured and with his pension cut by half, worked for Pinkerton's San Francisco office, and gave up his job as a detective finally at the end of 1921.

In later years Hammett played up his work as a Pinkerton man, and played down his illness. Mr Layman casts doubt on Hammett's connection with the four big cases he claimed to have worked on, but he must have been good at the job to have been so readily re-engaged by the agency when obviously a sick man. During almost the whole of the twenties he was wretchedly, although intermittently, ill. He had married Jose, a nurse at the hospital, they had a small daughter, and 'lived a simple life punctuated by the struggle to meet their monthly bills'. When their daughter Mary Jane was born, Hammett slept in the hall of their apartment because he had been told that he might infect the baby. It was in these miserable circumstances that he began to write short stories. By 1925 he was selling up to twenty stories a year to the pulp magazines that had become popular in the early years of the decade, but according to Mr Layman was 'barely getting by' financially. He took a job as a copywriter for a San Francisco jewellery firm, but within a few months collapsed at work, and was found lying in a pool of blood. He now had another daughter, his recovery was slow (he was on 100 per cent disability pension again), and Jose took the children to live in the country for the sake of economy. Her departure marked the effective end of their marriage. Success was round the corner, and he was about to enter the world in which Lillian Hellman and Nunnally Johnson knew him.

His first book *Red Harvest*, originally called 'The Cleansing of Poisonville', appeared early in 1929, *The Dain Curse* in July, *The Maltese Falcon* early in the following year. They had been written for serial publication in *Black Mask*, but it was book publication that made Hammett famous. Alexander Woolcott's praise of *The Maltese Falcon* as 'the best detective story America has yet produced' was typical. The chorus was, and to a large extent remains, American. Hammett has never been regarded so highly as Raymond Chandler in Britain.

With fame came the call to Hollywood, the immensely heavy drinking, the long-lasting affair with Hellman (although other women were not neglected), money given away and at times almost thrown away. He wrote two more books, *The Glass Key* (1931) and *The Thin Man* (1934), but afterwards there were only book titles. He provided original stories for some 'Thin Man' films, and had his name on a comic strip for a few months, and that was all. He was given a $1000 dollar-a-week contract by MGM as general editorial adviser, and although three times taken off the payroll for 'simply disappearing while a movie he was involved with was being shot', he was hired again each time. In the mid-thirties his income was about $100,000 a year, yet it did not quite match his expenditure. He lived in a Beverley Wilshire penthouse or in the Harold Lloyd mansion, leased a limousine and hired a chauffeur. He was in great demand at parties, and much praised by intellectuals. Malraux called him the technical link between Dreiser and Hemingway, Gide said that the dialogue of *Red Harvest* gave pointers to Hemingway and Faulkner. The praise did not deceive him. He knew that his last book showed a marked decline, and wrote to Hellman about Nick and Nora Charles: 'Maybe there are better writers in the world, but nobody ever invented a more insufferably smug pair of characters.'

The last phase of his career began with his enrolment in the US Army in September 1942, to serve in the Signal Corps. He was sent to the barren volcanic island of Adak in Alaska, where he edited a camp newspaper and was part-author of a booklet on the war against the Japanese in the Aleutians. He was much liked by the young soldiers, who called him Pop. As Mr Layman says, it is astonishing that he was ever accepted for military service. He was forty-eight years old, tuberculosis still troubled him at times, his teeth were very bad (he was rejected once because of them), and after the Spanish Civil War began he seems to have given public support to almost any Left-wing cause that asked for it, so that he was politically suspect. The FBI started a file on him, and said that his support for Communist or Communist front organizations amounted to $1000 a month. The Bureau's investigations were so inept that for two years they were unable to confirm that he was in the Army, and when they learned he had been seen in uniform considered bringing charges against him for impersonating a US soldier. After his discharge in September 1945 'his primary activites were drinking and reading', but the money kept coming in, now chiefly for radio serials. Late in 1948 his health broke down again, and he was told by the doctor that if he did not give up drinking he would be dead in a few months. On that day he became an abstainer.

In 1951 he was brought before a US court to testify regarding a bail fund instituted by the Civil Rights Congress. Hammett was Chairman of the Congress, four Communist leaders for whom bail had been posted failed to surrender to the authorities, and the court asked Hammett for the names of the contributors to the fund, and about other matters. His testimony, in which he consistently pleaded the Fifth Amendment, and his stonewalling do not justify the heroic gloss put on the episode in Hellman's reminiscences. He was sentenced to six months' imprisonment, served five of them, and said afterwards that going to prison was like going home.

It is far from certain that he understood the ruinous nature of his decision. When he came out of prison he found his radio shows cancelled, and his income attached by the Internal Revenue Service. His books were out of print and remained so, since any money from them would have gone to pay back taxes, so that he refused permission to reprint them. The last ten years of his life were spent in a cottage twenty miles north of Manhattan, lent him rent-free by a politically sympathetic doctor. Here he read a great deal, but wrote nothing. Interviewed in 1957 by the FBI, he told them truthfully that he was 'essentially without income'. To a journalist from the *Washington Post* he said he kept three type-writers in the cottage 'chiefly to remind myself that I was once a writer'. Asked why he had stopped writing he said that he found he was repeating himself. 'It is the beginning of the end when you discover you have style.' In these last years he refused to see even old friends, with the exception of Lillian Hellman. He died in January 1961, killed not by the tuberculosis that had haunted him throughout his adult life, but by cancer. Dorothy Parker, Leonard Bernstein, and Lionel Trilling were among those who attended the funeral sevice, and Hellman delivered a eulogy.

The American crime story (distinct from the detective story) has produced three writers of great talent – Hammett, Chandler and Ross Macdonald – and a comparison between Hammett's and Chandler's lives and talents is prompted by this biography. There are some similarities between the lives. Success came late to both men, to Chandler much later than Hammett. Both went to Hollywood and disliked a lot of what they saw, drank hard and could be quarrelsome or rude. But the differences are much greater than the similarities, and it is difficult not to conclude, after looking again at Frank MacShane's thorough biography of Chandler, that Hammett did what Chandler only wrote about. Jerry Speir, in his useful guide to Chandler's work and ideas, deprecates the view that Chandler 'married his mother', but his interpretation seems reasonable in relation to a man who lived with his mother until she died, and then, at the age of thirty-six, married a woman eighteen years older than himself. Hammett might have seduced a nymphet but he would never have married his mother. He was a hard man, hard particularly on himself and what he had failed to do. Chandler would not have been capable of that remark about the smugness of Nick and Nora Charles. He loved his own creations too much for that.

The differences show in the writing. Hammett's style was, almost from the beginning, original: bone-dry, drained of colour, lacking delicacy but full of power, a perfect style for describing violent action without moral comment. It is true that at the beginning this was pretty well all he could do. As Richard Layman perceptively says, the 'hard-boiled' fiction in *Black Mask* sprang from the naturalistic writing of Dreiser and Frank Norris, but 'departed from naturalism in its lack of sympathy for people in the miserable, pitiful, and horrible circumstances it described'. There is not much sympathy anywhere in Hammett, and most of the early stories are distinctive only in the style that he deprecated near the end of his life. They are as stylistically original as the early Hemingway stories which they precede, but the stories are bare intricate bones of plot, lacking the flesh of human feeling. From *Red Harvest* onwards this is no longer true. All of the novels, even the inferior *The Dain Curse*, have their distinctive felicities, but most unusual are the sexual attractiveness of Dinah Brand in *Red Harvest*, conveyed through her big bloodshot blue eyes, uneven lipstick, coarseness and untidiness, and the emotional relationship between Ned Beaumont and Paul Madvig in *The Glass Key*, given in terms of what remains unsaid between them. Hammett's treatment of sex was also remarkably frank for the time. The most marked example of this is the question Nora asks Nick when he has tangled with Mimi Jorgensen: 'When you were wrestling with Mimi, didn't you have an erection?' The question, and his answer, 'Oh, a little,' were omitted from the English edition.

Chandler began also with short stories interesting chiefly in terms of plot, and like Hammett found his talent flowering when he began to write novels. But the wisecracks (one can't avoid the outdated word) that sparkle in his pages have often the air of backchat replies made after the event, and much of Marlowe's conversation has obviously been concocted at a writer's desk, without much reference to life outside the workroom. 'I don't mind your ritzing me or drinking your lunch out of a Scotch bottle', he says to Mrs Regan. 'I don't mind your showing me your legs. They're very swell legs and it's a pleasure to make their acquaintance. I don't mind if you don't like my manners. They're pretty bad. I grieve over them during the long winter evenings.' This is a writer talking to himself rather than a man talking to a woman, and when Mrs Regan replies with: 'My God, you big dark handsome brute! I ought to throw a Buick at you,' we are in the world of male fantasy.

The treatment of sex is markedly different from Hammett's. It is much less frank, and is often implicitly condemnatory of sexual activity. Mr Speir gives expositions and analyses of all the novels, but fails to mention the fact that in them the female of the species is so frequently deadly. It is a good working rule that any woman who shows great interest in getting Marlowe to bed is not to be trusted. But Mr Speir has fresh and unusual things to say, especially about some of the oddities in the books, like the immediate reaction of the racketeer Menendez to Marlowe in *The Long Goodbye*: 'Tarzan on a big red scooter.' Such unexplained phrases, and some ambiguous attitudes, are among the most interesting aspects of Chandler. But as Ross Macdonald has said – he is quoted by Mr Speir: 'The detective-as-redeemer is a backward step in the direction of sentimental romance, and an over-simplified world of good guys and bad guys.'

In Macdonald's own work the detective-as-redeemer has been replaced by the detective as catalyst. An early book like *Blue City*, written in Macdonald's real name of Kenneth Millar, shows markedly the influence of Hammett, and the first stories in the Macdonald name that of Chandler, but from a time that Macdonald himself puts as the publication of *The Galton Case* (1959) his detective, Lew Archer, is a man whose unstated purpose is to reveal the secrets of the past. He is less an orthodox detective than a man who 'tends to live through other people', as his creator says. Some of these later books are repetitious in theme, because they use variations on what was attempted in *The Galton Case*, 'a story roughly shaped on my own early life, transformed and simplified into a kind of legend', while of course still containing a puzzle to be solved. But the variations are skilfully handled, the writing never less than distinguished, and in recent books a symbolic theme, like a forest fire or an oil spill, gives unity to the book. Such later Macdonald novels as *The Underground Man* and *The Blue Hammer* also have a kind of intensity lacking in both Hammett and Chandler. 'He is the hero, he is everything,' Chandler wrote of Marlowe, but Macdonald's achievement is to decrease Lew Archer's importance, even though he is the central character. It is such qualities that mark off Hammett, Chandler, Macdonald, from lively epigones of the hard-boiled form like Roger Simon (*The Big Fix*), Andrew Bergman (*The Big Kiss-Off of 1944*) and Robert L. Parker.

One returns to the puzzle of Hammett's reasons for giving up writing. Nunnally Johnson, who is mentioned in the biography as a drinking companion, but was apparently not consulted by Mr Layman, is in no doubt about the answer:

Hammett told me that he stopped writing because he saw no more reason to write when he not only had all the money he needed but was assured of all that he would ever need for the remainder of his life. This turned out to be a mistake, but it was a sound enough belief at the time . . .

Apparently there was nothing in writing that interested him but the money . . . He had no impulse to tell any more stories, no ambition to accomplish more as a writer, no interest in keeping his name alive, or any other vanity about himself or his work . . . If there is a precedent for a decision like this in a writer I have never heard of it . . . I can't tell you how awed I was and always have been by such astonishing resolution.

Well, it's an explanation, and one that echoes a remark made by a character in a Hammett screenplay: 'I'm in the game for money. Sure, I'm always on the make.' It is, however, contradicted by much that Hammett himself said and did. He wrote to Blanche Knopf when she accepted *Red Harvest* that he hoped to be the first person to make 'literature' out of the detective story, and the revisions he made in the book from magazine to book publication show how seriously he took what he was doing. In one of his few public critical pronouncements he praised the virtues of directness and literal accuracy: 'The contemporary novelist's job is to take pieces of life and arrange them on paper,' and the less ornament they contained the better. There are several indications that he had a bitter knowledge of his failing talent, like the speech he wrote for a play of Hellman's, where a retired General speaks of the turning point in a life, the moment when you can 'do the work you've never done, think the way you'd never thought, have what you've never had', and says that you either train for that moment or fritter yourself away. 'I've frittered myself away.' He let his publishers announce new books, books which would not be crime stories, but so far as is known never got far beyond providing titles for them. His last attempt at fiction, 'Tulip', is a fragment of 12,500 words, abandoned in 1952 or 1953, and he must have recognized that it was a piece of sub-Hemingway writing. The last words are neatly symbolic: 'If you are tired you ought to rest, I think, and not try to fool yourself and your customers with colored bubbles.'

Hammett was a man who never fooled himself, although he sometimes kidded other people. Probably it would be true to say that he gave up writing partly because he felt his talent had gone, partly because he had a strong impulse towards self-destruction, partly because for a long time he didn't need the money. But while he was writing he recognized, like Chandler and Macdonald, that if you want the crime story to be taken seriously, you must yourself be serious about what you are doing. Given an original talent plus that essential seriousness, you can afford a reasonable ration of guns and gangsters, obscure motives and bloody murders, and still produce something that can stake a claim to be called art.

(1981)

(ii) The Other Thin Man

The Thin Man, published in 1934, was Dashiell Hammett's last full-length work of fiction, and almost the last thing he wrote, although he survived for more than a quarter of a century after it appeared. The story has often been called the poorest of his five full-length novels, 'far and away the weakest' according to Robert

B. Parker, while another critic condemned the villain as the feeblest Hammett created. The disappointed critics were looking for an orthodox murder mystery with a large ration of violence, but *The Thin Man* is basically a comedy of contemporary American manners, with a few elements of mystery and violence loosely attached. All three deaths in the book occur off-stage.

A comedy then, but one whose taste is not sweet but sour. Nick and Nora Charles spend their time moving from bar to bar, party to party, drinking with people they sometimes hardly know and often don't much like. The world they move in is that of the Fitzgeralds and Nathanael West, and of the New Yorkers who are viewed lyrically in Carl Van Vechten's novels, cynically here. The immensely successful series of *Thin Man* films that succeeded the book concentrated on the comedy and ignored the implicit social comment. Hammett became seriously involved with the American Communist Party later in the thirties, but his concern with political and civic corruption is apparent in *Red Harvest* and *The Glass Key*. *The Thin Man* is a portrait of a corrupt society, one not criticized overtly because the writer is part of it, and enjoys the corruption – and the good life it offers him.

But what Hammett enjoyed he also hated. This is apparent from his behaviour in Hollywood, where his earnings far exceeded those of Fitzgerald or Chandler at the height of their popularity in the film world. He spent the money, but set out to bite the hand feeding him. He wrote a script for a film about a private detective not only tough like Sam Spade, but actually crooked. The idea would hardly raise an eyebrow today, but horrified studio bosses in the thirties. Darryl Zanuck turned it down, and after the script had been sold elsewhere, changed and then changed again, it eventually came to the screen as *Mister Dynamite*, a light comedy so titled because the detective was named T. N. Thompson.

That was the last time Hammett attempted to write anything serious in Hollywood, but it seems possible that he was trying to do something similar – or at least different from his early work – in the first version of *The Thin Man*. He wrote ten chapters of this, amounting to around eighteen thousand words. In 1942 Hammett gave the original typescript to be auctioned during a War Bonds drive, with a note saying he had begun the story, put it aside while spending a year in Hollywood, and found it easier afterwards simply to keep the basic plot idea along with the names of two characters, the detective John Guild and the murdered Wynant. The text of this first version has never been published in Britain, and so far as I know has appeared in the US only in a special souvenir edition of a San Francisco magazine.

The first *Thin Man* is very different from the second. It is placed in and around San Francisco like earlier Hammett novels and stories, whereas in the finished version the scene is New York. Unlike the Continental Op short stories and *Red Harvest*, however, it is told in the third person. Like several other stories with San Francisco settings it contains a ration of in-jokes, but the style is deliberately drained of colour, a style that avoids style. It might be an exemplification of Hammett's belief that the novelist's job is to take pieces of life and arrange them on paper . . . This was the only time Hammett wrote consciously in accordance with that severe dictum, the intention presumably being that the stylistic directness and bareness would make the sensationalism of the material seem more realistic. The detective John Guild, frequently called 'the dark man', is made as impersonal as possible, an outsider removed from the violent action and unmoved by it. To emphasize his outsider status it is suggested at one point that he could be a mulatto.

Such may have been the intention: but the effect is different. In the ten terse chapters we learn that Wynant appears to have shot his mistress and then disappeared. Guild, a private investigator, is employed by an insurance company to find him. The trail takes him from Wynant's house outside San Francisco back into the city's Chinatown and to a singer named Elsa Fremont, whose brother Charles is mixed up with Wynant. Elsa is baffled by Guild's remoteness. 'Aren't you ever human?' she asks. 'Are you always like this? Is it a pose? Are you a god-damned corpse?' Guild is mildly puzzled, says he doesn't know what she means. Even when he finds Charles Fremont's body Guild remains imperturbable, so that Elsa says trying to come into contact with him is like trying to hold a handful of smoke.

It is guesswork to say that what Hammett was aiming for in this first version was something similar to the abortive film script, a story that would describe the violence it dealt with quite flatly, offering no view about the behaviour of the people involved and making Guild a law-enforcer without beliefs, opinions or habits, in person just a handful of smoke. As William P. Nolan has said, the cute dog Asta would have had no place in this version, and if the almost equally cute Nora had appeared she would have been just another female suspect or sex-object.

Yet such conjectures may be too high-flown. It is just as possible that the fragment was no more than a stylistic attempt to take the terseness of the Continental Op stories a stage further by eliminating all trace of feeling. Such cold colourless prose, persisted in through the length of a novel, would have exemplified Chandler's complaint that Hammett's style 'had no overtones, left no echo', and that there were things 'he did not know how to say or feel the need of saying'. This is a romantic's complaint about a realist, and of course Chandler would have found inadequate Hammett's credo about taking pieces of life and putting them down directly from street to paper. Perhaps Hammett came to agree with him, and turned deliberately to a novel written almost wholly in the dialogue he handled with such easy mastery, and to the laughter with which Nick and Nora accept the spasmodic trivial enjoyments of their world.

Perhaps: all one can be sure of is that between the original fragment and the published book there was a change in Hammett's ideas reflected in a changed approach to the material. On the evidence we have, the original *Thin Man*, if completed, would have been no more than an efficient mystery story: yet there is a sense of something worthwhile attempted and given up, of a final seriousness Hammett realized he would never achieve.

(1993)

Raymond Chandler

(i) An Aesthete Discovers the Pulps

Fairyland is Everyman's dream of perfection, and changes, dreamlike, with the mood of the dreamer. For one it is a scene of virgin, summery Nature undefiled by even the necessary works of man ... For another it is a champaign, dotted with fine castles, in which live sweet ladies clad in silk, spinning, and singing as they spin, and noble knights who do courteous battle with each other in forest glades; or a region of uncanny magic, haunting music, elves and charmed airs and waters.

That is Raymond Chandler writing in 1912 for *The Academy*.

The man in the powder-blue suit – which wasn't powder-blue under the lights of the Club Bolivar – was tall, with wide-set grey eyes, a thin nose, a jaw of stone. He had a rather sensitive mouth. His hair was crisp and black, ever so faintly touched with grey, as by an almost diffident hand. His clothes fitted him as though they had a soul of their own, not just a doubtful past. His name happened to be Mallory.

That is the opening paragraph of Raymond Chandler's first story for the pulps, 'Blackmailers Don't Shoot', which appeared in *Black Mask*, December 1933.

Between the two pieces lay twenty-one years in time and the Atlantic in distance, but they had a common emotional basis. The Chandler who wrote for the pulps was still a man who dreamed of Fairyland. As I have said elsewhere it is emblematically right that in this first story the detective should be named Mallory, echoing the *Morte D'Arthur*. His carapace of iron (only iron could survive those frequent assaults with cosh and blackjack) conceals a quivering core, and whether his name is Mallory, Carmady, Dalmas or Philip Marlowe, he is truly a knight errant. Chandler's stories about criminals and a detective carried over into an alien field the literary aestheticism of his youth.

Raymond Chandler became a writer for the pulp magazines

because he was broke, not because he wanted to write for the pulps. 'Realism and Fairyland' was one of the last pieces he published in England before he gave up the hope of making a literary living there, and he printed nothing in America until 1933. In between he had a variety of jobs, lived with his mother, married a woman eighteen years older than himself as soon as his mother died (his wife Cissy knocked ten years off her age for the marriage register), became vice president of a group of oil companies, drank hard, had affairs, was eventually sacked. At the age of forty-four he had no money and no prospects. At this point he listed himself as a writer in the Los Angeles Directory, and began to study the pulp magazines. It struck him, as he said, that he might get paid while he was learning.

He was not likely, as he must have known, to get paid very much. The pulp magazines, so called because they were printed on wood pulp, began in the nineteenth century with the publication of the Nick Carter stories. The *Nick Carter Weekly* first appeared in 1891, and like *Sexton Blake* in England was the product of multiple authors. The chief of them, the bearded Frederic Dey (that is, Frederic Marmaduke Van Rensselaer Day) produced a 25,000-word story every week for years, and did not get rich. In 1929 he shot himself in a cheap New York hotel. Nick Carter's fame endured, and indeed endures, so that when *Detective Story Magazine* began publication in 1915 its editor was named as Nicholas Carter. *Black Mask*, in which most of Chandler's early stories appeared, was founded in 1920 by H. L. Mencken and George Jean Nathan, but did not take on its true character until Captain Joseph Shaw became editor in 1926. During the decade of Shaw's reign the magazine published stories that moved sharply away from the conventional detective story aspect of earlier pulp fiction (Edgar Wallace was one of the stars of *Detective Story Magazine*) to reflect the violence of American society and the vivid colloquialisms of American speech.

Chandler's approach, his background and his age made him a very unusual figure among the pulp writers. Most of them were hacks, although they would have called themselves professionals. They were hard-working, sometimes hard-drinking men who wrote fast and wrote for the money. To make a fair living they had to write a great deal, for the basic rate of one cent a word meant that you had to write a million words to make $10,000 a year. Many of them, like Erle Stanley Gardner, used several names, and some wrote romances and Westerns as well as crime stories. Such a literary netherworld exists in England now, although because there are no magazines its inhabitants write books, turning out ten or a dozen a year to make a reasonable living. In America during the Depression years similar writers worked mostly for the pulp magazines. Few of them had the specialized knowledge of Dashiell Hammett, who had been a Pinkerton agent, but most had familiarized themselves with some aspects of the law and crime, and knew a good deal about firearms. Many of them appeared to write with an ink-dipped cosh rather than a pen.

Chandler resembled them very little. He had read only three or four detective stories when he set out to make a living in the field, and he learned the technique of the crime story in the spirit of a young artist copying masters in the Louvre. He read everything he could find, in particular Hammett, but also Gardner and other pulp writers. He made a detailed synopsis of a Gardner story, rewrote it, compared the result with the original, rewrote it again, and then apparently threw it away. He took what he was doing seriously, because if he had not done so he could not have justified doing it. He was writing for *Black Mask* and *Dime Detective Magazine*, and he knew that what he did was hack work, but he gave to this hack work the care he had devoted to the literary pieces produced for English magazines long ago.

He knew little about the technical aspects of crime, and never bothered to learn, relying instead on textbooks. From the beginning he sensed that for a writer like himself such things were not important, and that any success he won would come through sharpness of language and observation rather than expert knowledge. In a battling introduction to a collection of his short stories published in 1950, when he had become famous, he defended the pulp crime story by saying that 'even at its most mannered and artificial [it] made most of the fiction of the time taste like a cup of lukewarm consommé at a spinsterish tea-room'. He said also that he wished the stories being republished were better, but that the distinction of the imprint meant he need not be sickeningly humble, even though 'I have never been able to take myself with that enormous earnestness which is one of the trying characteristics of the craft.' In fact he took himself very seriously indeed, and strongly resented adverse criticism from others, although he was prepared to make it himself. He also made claims for the form in which he was working that must seem overstated. 'The aim is not essentially different from the aim of Greek tragedy, but we are dealing with a public that is semi-literate and we have to make an art of a language they can understand.' The aim may be similar but the results, as he should have seen, are so different that the comparison is absurd.

Chandler remained by temperament a romantic aesthete. His feebly literary early essays and poems are full of either/ors like science and poetry, romance and realism. Are we to be saved 'by the science or by the poetry of life'? That, he said, 'is the typical question of the age', and he came down on the side of poetry as opposed to science and of romance against realism. Or rather, of realism seen romantically, so that 'any man who has walked down a commonplace city street at twilight, just as the lamps are lit' would see that a true view of it must be idealistic, for it would 'exalt the sordid to a vision of magic, and create pure beauty out of plaster and vile dust'. The phrases echo Chesterton, and also look forward to the famous peroration of 'The Simple Art of Murder' which runs: 'Down these mean streets a man must go . . .' It was Chandler's strength, and his weakness, that he brought this basically sentimental aestheticism to the crime stories, so that they had increasingly to be about a romantic hero whose activities gave the novels at least 'a quality of redemption' so that he could think of them as art. That was the weakness. The strength lay in the fact that by treating seriously everything he did Chandler achieved even in his early stories for the pulps more than his fellow practitioners.

To talk about Chandler as a romantic aesthete may make him sound like an intellectual, but in fact he disliked intellectuals and the magazines for which they wrote. In the few meetings I had with him near the end of his life, it was possible to sense his distrust. Was this another of those damned critics trying to get at him? He was fond of using big words like art and redemption, but shied away from such things when they moved from the general to the particular. He could be deeply imperceptive and philistine. 'I read these profound discussions, say in the *Partisan Review*, about art, what is it, literature, what is it, and the good life and liberalism and what is the definitive position of Rilke or Kafka, and the scrap about Ezra Pound getting the Bollingen award, and it all seems so meaningless to me. Who cares?' he wrote to his English publisher Hamish Hamilton. He got on well with fellow pulp writers, partly because they regarded him, as one of them put it, as 'a professorial type, more of an intellectual than most of the other pulp writers I knew'. He was the oldest of them, a year older than Gardner and six years older than Hammett. They respected him, and so made him comparatively at ease. In general he avoided places and people through which he might be involved in literary discussion, preferring to talk to garage men and postal clerks. Other writers, and his opinions of them, he put on paper.

Second only to romantic aestheticism in giving his work its colour and character was his loneliness. He seems to have been from youth a shy person who found it hard to make friends, and this shyness was accentuated by his marriage to a woman so much older than himself. In these years also they were poor. For a decade Chandler scraped a living, writing for the pulps and publishing crime novels that received critical praise but were far from being bestsellers. They moved from place to place, had few friends, went out little. Out of this loneliness, now and later, Chandler created his best work. When he began to write for films and became involved in the social life of the studios he wrote little, and that little was usually not very good. Shut up in an apartment, with Cissy in the next room and with 'life' making no demands, he sparkled on paper.

The third important element in Chandler's writing was its Anglo-American character. He had been brought up in England, he longed to return (and upon the whole was not disappointed when he came), and the delighted disgust with which he saw California came partly from the contrast between its brash newness and English good taste. When he read Max Beerbohm he felt that he too belonged to an age of grace and taste from which he had been exiled. 'So I wrote for *Black Mask*. What a wry joke.' No doubt he would have felt hopelessly out of place in an age of grace (if such an age ever existed) and would have written ironically about it, but that is not the point. The flavour of his stories is individual partly because even though, as he said, all the pulp writers used the same idiom, his is filtered through an English lens.

The very intelligent notes on English and American style which he put down in his notebook end with a striking observation of differences in verbal tone:

The tone quality of English speech is usually overlooked. This tone quality is infinitely variable and contibutes infinite meaning. The American voice is flat, toneless and tiresome. The English tone quality makes a thinner vocabulary and a more formalized use of language capable of infinite meanings. Its tones are of course read into written speech by association. This, of course, makes good English a class language, and that is its fatal defect. The English writer is a gentleman (or not a gentleman) first and a writer second.

Most of these distinctions seem to me very good ones, but in any case they were important to Chandler. Once he began to write, he became absorbed in the verbal problems involved, in particular the problem of giving an English variability to the 'flat, toneless and tiresome' pattern of American speech. The best of his work is witness to his triumphant success.

Chandler was not a prolific writer. He wrote in all twenty stories for the pulps, at the rate of two, three or four a year. It is true that almost all of them were much longer than the usual story, and that they might almost be called short novels, but even so the output was small. It has been said already that he was poor in the decade after he started to write crime stories. His average yearly earnings during the late 1930s and early 1940s were between one and two thousand dollars. In truth, there was no way of making a reasonable living by writing for the pulps unless you published ten or twelve stories a year. It is a mark of Chandler's integrity as a writer that he refused to do this, or was incapable of doing it, as later he refused to do what he was told in Hollywood when he was employed there at a salary gloriously or ludicrously large compared with his earnings at the time from stories and novels.

About the pulp stories considered as stories there is little to say except that they are not very good. 'Everybody imitates in the beginning,' as Chandler said himself, and the writer he imitated most was Hammett. The young blond gunman in 'Blackmailers Don't Shoot' is obviously derived from Wilmer in *The Maltese Falcon*, the sadistic thug in 'Pick-Up on Noon Street' is based on Jeff in *The Glass Key*, and there are other echoes. Standard scenes and characters appear in most of the stories. There will be at least one night club scene, a variety of villains will appear in every story, and some of them will be gangsters or gamblers who own the night clubs. The hard men who hit the detective over the head will be exceptionally stupid, and the gangsters will be only a little smarter beneath their thin veneer of sophistication. The police will be tough, cynical, and occasionally corrupt. There will be a lot of shooting, with an Elizabethan litter of corpses piled up by the end. At the heart of the trouble there will be a girl, and she is almost never to be trusted, although she may have 'the sort of skin an old rake dreams of' (Rhonda Farr in 'Blackmailers Don't Shoot') or hair that is 'like a bush fire at night' (Beulah in 'Try the Girl') or even hair that 'seemed to gather all the light there was and make a soft halo around her coldly beautiful face' (Belle Marr in 'Spanish Blood'). The women in the short stories are not as deadly as they become in the novels, but they are dangerous enough.

These standard properties are used in a standard way. The detective himself is not much more than a man whose head is harder and whose gun is faster than his rivals'. This is true of Marlowe, who appeared first in 1934, as much as of Mallory or Carmady. But the basic defect of the stories is that the length to which they were written did not fit Chandler's talent. The weakness of his plotting is more apparent in the stories than in the novels. The demand of the pulps, he said later, was for constant action, and if you stopped to think you were lost. 'When in doubt, have a man come through a door with a gun in his hand.' The novels gave more space for the development of situations and the creation of an environment. One of Chandler's great merits was his capacity to fix a scene memorably. He sometimes did this in a phrase, but he could do it even better in a paragraph or a page. The stories did not give him time to create anything of this kind. Everything that did not carry forward the action was excised by editors.

If we read the stories today it is for occasional flashes of observation that got by the blue pencil, and for the use of language. Chandler's ear for the rhythms of speech was good from the beginning, but it developed with astonishing speed. The stories written in the later 1930s, like 'Killer in the Rain', 'The Curtain', 'Try the Girl' and 'Mandarin's Jade' are often as well written as the novels, where the early tales are full of clichés. 'Smart-Aleck Kill' (1934) has eyes that get small and tight, eyes with hot lights in them, eyes that show sharp lights of pain. There are cold smiles playing around the corners of mouths, and mirthless laughter. But within a very few years these have almost all disappeared, and we recognize the sharp cleverness of the novels when we are told that the garage of a modernistic new house is 'as easy to drive into as an olive bottle' or that a smart car in a dingy neighbourhood 'sticks out like spats at an Iowa picnic'.

It was these later and better stories that Chandler cannibalized, to use his own word, to make three of the novels. This was an extraordinary process. Other writers have incorporated early material in a later work, but nobody else has done it in quite this way. Most writers who adapt their earlier work take from it a particular theme or character and jettison the rest. Chandler, however, carved out great chunks of the stories, expanded them, and fitted them into an enlarged plot. Where gaps existed, like spaces in a jigsaw, he made pieces to fit them. It meant adapting, fusing and adding characters, blending themes from different stories, combining plots. Much of his first novel, *The Big Sleep*, was taken from two stories, 'Killer in the Rain' and 'The Curtain', plus fragments from two other tales. About a quarter of the book was new material, but the passages from the two principal stories used were much enlarged. There could be no better proof of the limitation Chandler felt in being forced to work within the pulp magazine formula.

Almost all of the enlargements were improvements. They added details of description, vital touches of characterization, or they were simply more elegantly or wittily phrased. They also helped to make the stories more coherent. In 'The Curtain' the detective does not call on General Winslow in his orchid house until chapter three. In the novel Chandler, realizing that this was a splendid starting point, begins with it. (He economically kept chapter one for use years later in *The Long Goodbye*.) The difference in the effectiveness of the two scenes is startling. What was no more than adequate in the story has become memorable in the novel, with the old half-dead General emerging as a genuinely pathetic figure. One would need a variorum text to show exactly how Chandler did it, but here are one or two significant changes. The General is telling Marlowe to take off his coat in the steaming hot orchid house. In 'The Curtain' he says:

'Take your coat off, sir. Dud always did. Orchids require heat, Mr Carmady – like rich old men.'

In *The Big Sleep* this becomes:

'You may take your coat off, sir. It's too hot in here for a man with blood in his veins.'

It is the last sentence that gives real flavour to the bit of dialogue, telling us more about the General than would half a dozen descriptive phrases. And, freed from the blue pencil, Chandler let his love of simile and metaphor run free. The smell of the orchids is not just like boiling alcohol as it was in the story, but like boiling alcohol under a blanket. In the story the General just watches the detective drink, but now 'The old man licked his lips watching me, over and over again, like an undertaker dry-washing his hands.' These are samples from thirty similes or metaphors brought into the scene. Is some of it a little too much? That is obviously partly a matter of taste, but the exuberance of it, the sense of a man using his own talent in his own way for the first time, cannot be anything but enjoyable. This fifty-year-old colt is kicking up his heels in sheer pleasure. And Chandler now is on the look-out for clichés. In 'The Curtain' the General has 'basilisk eyes'. Now they just have a coal-black directness.

The famous, and at the time rather daring, pornographic books passage in *The Big Sleep* appeared first in 'Killer in the Rain'. This too has been transformed. In the story the detective knows in advance of the pornographic book racket, while in the novel suspense is created by our learning with Marlowe the meaning of 'Rare Books'. In the book store he meets a girl with silvered fingernails. A comparison of texts shows the value of Chandler's enlargements.

She got up and came towards me, swinging lean thighs in a tight dress of some black material that didn't reflect any light. She was an ash blonde, with greenish eyes under heavily mascaraed lashes. There were large jet buttons in the lobes of her ears; her hair waved back smoothly from behind them. Her fingernails were silvered.

She gave me what she thought was a smile of welcome, but what I thought was a grimace of strain.

('Killer in the Rain')

She got up slowly and swayed towards me in a tight black dress that didn't reflect any light. She had long thighs and she walked with a certain something I hadn't often seen in bookstores. She was an ash blonde with greenish eyes, beaded lashes, hair waved smoothly back from ears in which large jet buttons glittered. Her fingernails were silvered. In spite of her get-up she looked as if she would have a hall bedroom accent.

She approached me with enough sex appeal to stampede a businessmen's lunch and tilted her head to finger a stray, but not very stray, tendril of softly glowing hair. Her smile was tentative, but it could be persuaded to be nice.

(The Big Sleep)

The hall bedroom accent and the businessmen's lunch are the phrases that principally lift this from the commonplace to something hall-marked Chandler, and the elaboration of the scene from one page to three, with a client coming in to change a book, add a lot to its effectiveness.

The blonde reappears, both in story and novel, as the companion of a gangster named Marty (in the book Joe Brody). In both versions the detective gets a gun away from her, she sinks her teeth into the hand with the gun in it, and he cracks her on the head. A couple of grace notes are added to the novel. 'The blonde was strong with the madness of fear,' it says in the story. The sentence is rhetorical, and somehow inadequate. In the book it becomes: 'The blonde was strong with the madness of love or fear, or a mixture of both, or maybe she was just strong.' The final touch is not in the story at all. After Brody has handed over some compromising photographs from which he was hoping to make money, the blonde complains of her luck. 'A half-smart guy, that's all I ever draw. Never once a guy that's smart all around the course. Never once.'

'Did I hurt your head much?' Marlowe asks.

'You and every other man I ever met.'

It is a perfect pay-off line, marvellously done.

One could go through the whole book, and through the other novels that have a basis in the stories, showing how, passage by passage, Chandler converted the mechanical effects of the stories into something unique in style and delivery. He discovered his own quality as a writer through the freedom given him by the form of the novel.

The pulp magazines had shaped him, but once he had learned the trade they were a restriction. The novels enabled him to burst the bonds and to express the essential Raymond Chandler: a romantic aesthete and a self-conscious artist, an introvert with the power of catching the form, the tone, the rhythm, of American speech supremely well on paper. In its kind Chandler's mature dialogue is perfect. One cannot see how it could be better done. The stories are not much in themselves, but without them perhaps we should never have had the novels.

(1976)

(ii) Chandler Reconsidered

Opening the seven Chandler novels again, something I haven't done for several years, I was dazzled once more by the openings. The Sternwood place with its hallway two storeys high, its trees 'trimmed as carefully as poodle dogs', and the dying General in his hothouse asking Marlowe how he likes his brandy; the enormous Moose Malloy, wearing 'alligator shoes with white explosions in the toes', lifting Marlowe up a step with 'a hand I could have sat in' before wrecking a Negro bar while looking for his Velma; Marlowe swatting a bluebottle in his office while receiving a call from pretty little Orfamay Quest who says forty bucks a day is much more than she can pay: these are openings that stay in the memory.

And the other books start just as well as *The Big Sleep*, *Farewell My Lovely* and *The Little Sister*. They carry you along, take you as irresistibly as Moose Malloy took Marlowe, into stories that delight by their constant turning of ingenious and often memorable phrases. Turn to almost any page in the novels and you find a telling metaphor of simile, and something sharply observed. The eyes of a dead man look expectant 'as if he smelled the morning coffee and would be coming right out', a cop's voice is hard as the blade of a shovel. And the good phrases are never allowed to accumulate in a way that might suggest the writer is showing off. After that cop's hard voice comes some hard and shocking action as Marlowe is beaten up by a couple of policemen who are not even vicious, just ready to slap a charge on the next driver they meet.

Anybody not convinced that Chandler had a fine and delicate ear for language should read his pages of notes on English and American style. Nobody has understood better the qualities of the American language, its superb slang, constant freshness and inventiveness – and the limitation involved in the lack of a clear, accepted culture. Chandler concluded that all the best American writing had been done by cosmopolitans, able to use the richness and novelty of demotic American because they had a background of European taste. This is in part special pleading for Chandler himself, who had spent his first twenty-odd years in Britain, yet it is true that his unmistakably American writing is deepened and enriched by what he calls the tone quality of English speech. As he says, the tone of the standard American PI story is 'flat and tiresome'. Chandler used the American language with more subtlety and charm than any other writer in his field.

But although he was the best writer of American crime stories, Chandler was not the best American crime writer. His inability to construct a convincing, coherent plot worried him, and that old joke about having a man come through a door with a gun when deep in plotting trouble wasn't far from the reality. The elaborate final explanations the early books demand are both complex and implausible, and although in *The Long Goodbye* and *The Little Sister* the plot is much better devised and controlled, it is at the cost of some of the early verve. Chandler knew all this as well as any critic, and said as much of it in letters to other writers and to his agent, letters which look wistfully forwards, backwards and sideways at the novel he would have liked to write. 'To accept a mediocre form and make something like literature out of it is in itself rather an accomplishment', he wrote to his agent Helga Greene with a modesty that had a touch of mock-modesty as well.

Whether or not the form is mediocre, what Raymond Chandler did was done supremely well, but a re-reading does disturbingly reinforce an awareness that the indestructible Marlowe has a faint flavour of absurdity. At a recent International Crime Congress in New York, Roger Simon said it was time for the American crime story to break away from the tough guy with a cigarette in his mouth. Marlowe, he added, was not just indestructible, but showed no sign of ageing or emotional development, and in the eighties that just wouldn't do.

Roger Simon is right. The Chandler style survives triumphantly, a model to envy although not to copy, but the idealized figure of Marlowe has lost its sheen, where characters viewed with more detachment like Hammett's Sam Spade, or in another vein Simenon's Maigret, look still as good as new.

(1986)

(iii) *Selected Letters of Raymond Chandler**

No doubt about it, Raymond Chandler was a splendid letter writer. What could be better than his rebuke to the editor of the *Atlantic Monthly* about a proofreader's improvements: 'When I split an infinitive, God damn it, I split it so it will stay split, and when I interrupt the velvety smoothness of my more or less literate syntax with a few sudden words of bar room vernacular, this is done with the eyes wide open.' Sitting up late at night in the study of his single-storey house at La Jolla, this lonely man spun out long letters – to publishers, editors, agents, casual correspondents – that for him replaced face-to-face relationships. He often read, and presumably wrote, with gloves on, 'like a fading beauty of the stage', because of an allergy to carbon paper and newsprint, and gave as much care to the composition of letters as to his books, so that the words should, in his own phrase, 'get up and walk'.

Many of his letters are funny, some of them are moving: yet nobody reading this book will like Raymond Chandler better at the end of it. Behind the don't-take-myself-seriously whimsicality of many letters was a man who consistently complained because

---

* *Selected Letters of Raymond Chandler*, edited by Frank McShane, Jonathan Cape.

he wasn't taken seriously. 'Poor dear Elizabeth' Bowen is criticized for involuted language ('I used to do this sort of thing myself in my thirties'), 'rarefied intellectuals' in general and Edmund Wilson in particular are written about with condescension, yet time and again Chandler shows his longing to be respected by the world he affects to despise, and insists that there are other things he would much sooner write than a Marlowe story. A general illiberality is also noticeable. He thought Nye Bevan a rabble-rouser in the pattern of Huey Long, and nominated Harold Laski as 'the man you would most like to dunk in a sewer'. He felt uneasy with homosexuals, and jokingly suggested that he might write an article about authors called 'You Too Could Be A Pansy'. He thought at times that 'the Jews ask too much of us', and told Hamish Hamilton that it was only a question of time before a Gentile had to wear an armband in Los Angeles.

Chandler's instincts could be generous, especially in relation to those who asked his advice or were down on their luck, but the generosity did not extend to possible rivals. He slapped down an early book by Ross Macdonald as having 'an effect that is rather repellent'. James M. Cain, he told his American publisher Blanche Knopf, was 'the offal of literature' because he wrote about dirty things in a dirty way. Eighteen months later, however, he is writing to Cain as 'Dear Jim', and hoping that the basic conception of Cain's *Double Indemnity* was not harmed by the screenplay Chandler had written with Billy Wilder. And although Chandler often expressed admiration for Dashiell Hammett, he never had a word to say when Hammett went to jail for his refusal to answer questions about his role as trustee of a Civil Rights bail fund. The prickly individualism of which Chandler was so proud did not go far beyond the immediate concerns of Raymond Chandler.

Yet where his vanity was not touched or his literary credentials questioned, Chandler could be the liveliest and most charming correspondent. Nothing could be more delicately considerate than the letters ending the full-time employment of Juanita Messick because he no longer needed or could afford a secretary. (Mr MacShane, whose editing is in general not very helpful, makes us go back to his biography to discover Ms Messick's occupation.) There are many extremely funny letters or bits of letters. About an interviewer who got things wrong: 'By his standards anyone who noticed how many walls the room had would be observant.' About the mind-rotting qualities of TV: 'You don't have to concentrate. You don't have to react. You don't have to remember. You don't miss your brain because you don't need it.' About himself: 'I live in . . . a fairly small place of forty-eight rooms and fifty-nine baths. I dine off gold plate and prefer to be waited on by naked dancing girls.'

These are necessarily excerpts, and the full quotations are even better. Chandler had a wonderful feeling for the American language, and it is constantly apparent in these letters, especially when he is discussing the details of writing. He would have made a fine teacher of English if he could have found students good enough for him. This often grouchy and discontented man was, in the way he caught the tones and rhythms of speech, and the way he put sentences together, one of the masters of American prose in the twentieth century.

(1981)

Patricia Highsmith:
Criminals in Society

Howard Ingham in Patricia Highsmith's recent novel *The Tremor of Forgery* is, like several of her central characters, suspended in a limbo that he has made for himself and that he seems to desire. Ingham has gone out to Tunisia to gather material for a film script which he is going to write. He expects to hear from the producer John Castlewood, and from his girl friend Ina in New York, but days pass without any message from either of them. When he does hear something, it is to learn that Castlewood has committed suicide.

What then? The assignment, a rather vague affair from the start, is obviously finished. The natural thing would be that Ingham, who is puzzled and even anxious about Ina, should fly back to New York. Instead he lingers in Tunisia working on his novel *The Tremor of Forgery*, having desultory conversations with another American whom he christens OWL (Our Way of Life) and with a homosexual Danish painter, killing (or perhaps not killing – he is never sure and neither are we) an Arab burglar, keeping himself as it seems deliberately removed from Castlewood's death and Ina's silence. No explanation of his inactivity is offered, and it is a tribute to Miss Highsmith's skill that we accept Ingham's behaviour, just as in *The Two Faces of January* we accept the way that emotionally footloose Rydal Keener attaches himself to the petty crook Chester McFarland and his wife after Chester has killed a man, or the relationship between Garrett and Coleman in her Venetian novel *Those Who Walk Away*. These people are not puppets but they have suffered some deep failure of the will, or have come to a crisis in their personal lives of which they are not themselves fully aware. In Rydal's case he feels that Chester looks like his father, and Coleman is the father of Garrett's wife Peggy, who committed suicide. Ingham's problem is a concern with the appropriateness of the whole way he is living.

It is not just a matter of whether or not he wants to marry Ina, although that is involved. The book he is writing is about a business man who for years has been embezzling money by forging cheques so that he can help other people. When his forgery is discovered the beneficiaries, now successful men, repay what he has lent them and the rest of his stolen money has been wisely invested. 'In view of the enormous good Dennison had done in the way of holding families together, starting or helping businesses . . . who could label Dennison a crook?' Put in this way the question seems over-simple, but it is relevant to Ingham's own case. If Dennison need not feel the tremor of guilt, need Ingham feel it in relation to the conjectural death of the Arab? In a key passage he talks about this to Ina, who has flown out to Tunisia after revealing that she had a brief love affair with Castlewood. Ingham says he has a problem to discuss with her. He does not actually mention the disappearance of the Arab, about which she has heard rumours, but says that his problem is

'Essentially whether a person makes his own personality and his own standards within himself, or whether he and his standards are the creation of the society around him. . . . I found that since being here in Tunisia, I think about these things a lot. What I mean is − the opposite of authoritarianism. And I speak mainly of morals − I suppose. My hero Dennison makes his own, you see. But granted he's cracked.'

A failure to understand that the book is about guilt and innocence, with the standards of society as represented by the dismal but well-intentioned OWL and by Ina opposed to those of the possibly criminal individual (the homosexual Jensen and the wavering Ingham) has prompted some obtuse reviews. Very often it appears that Patricia Highsmith's central characters are courting violence because it is a way of escaping from the world of Ina and of OWL. Courting is perhaps too positive a word, but these are people who are waiting for something to happen, and when the happening is something violent they recognize and welcome it. *This* is something real, they unconsciously think, I can attach myself to it as an assurance of my own reality.

Most respectable people who had witnessed an act of violence, as Rydal Keener has done, would either report it to the police or get away from the people involved. Ed Garrett is shot at and wounded by Coleman in the opening scene of *Those Who Walk Away*, and again his reaction is to attach himself to the would-be murderer rather than to attempt escape from him. Such situations are closely paralleled in other books. The relationship between the two young men in her first novel, *Strangers on a Train*, and between the detective and the lawyer in *The Blunderer* shows a similar pattern of hunter and hunted, and often the two change places, offering the implicit questions which are asked outright in the last book: what is guilt, who is innocent?

Some clues to what Patricia Highsmith is trying to do, and an indication of her own attitude towards her characters, are given in her very interesting little book, *Plotting and Writing Suspense Stories*, which has been published so far only in America. The simplicity and candour in her account of the way in which her own novels and short stories are written will surprise those who think of her as a difficult writer and a rarefied personality. She reveals herself rather as a novelist unsure of herself and her own achievement, always ready to believe that a publisher or editor may know best. This is not just a matter of being prepared to accept minor revisions like that in *A Suspension of Mercy* where 'my Doubleday editor made me rewrite the scene in which the hero administers sleeping pills forcibly to the lover of his dead wife' because he took the pills too easily. *The Two Faces of January*, one of her finest novels, appears to have been conceived and written unhesitatingly as a work of art. In fact the book was completely rewritten in obedience to the view of her American publisher who said that 'a book can stand one or even two neurotics, but not three who are the main characters', and was then rejected again out of hand. Her comment on these rejections is characteristically practical and modest: 'These little setbacks, amounting sometimes to thousands of dollars' worth of time wasted, writers must learn to take like Spartans.' She put the book away, went on to another, and it was not published until she mentioned its existence casually while having a drink in a pub with a Heinemann editor.

The book on suspense fiction offers revelations more personal than that of her readiness to go down into the market place. Why does she write so much about criminals or people who wish to be criminals, why do they often go free at the end? What she says about this is again remarkably direct and personal:

I rather like criminals and find them extremely interesting, unless they are monotonously and stupidly brutal.

Criminals are dramatically interesting, because for a time at least they are active, free in spirit, and they do not knuckle down to anyone . . . I find the public passion for justice quite boring and artificial, for neither life or nature cares if justice is ever done or not.

Such comments help to explain why the book of hers that many people like best, *The Talented Mr Ripley*, is about a criminal who, after some narrow escapes from being caught, ends up totally successful. Her feeling of identification became so strong that when the book received a prize award she lettered 'Mr Ripley and' before her own name because 'I often had the feeling Ripley was writing it and I was merely typing.'

'In France and England, I am not particularly categorized as a suspense novelist, just as a novelist, and I fare much better as to prestige, quality of reviewing and – proportionately speaking – in sales than in America.' A backlash against the seriousness with which her work has been treated has been evident recently, however, not merely in the reviews of *The Tremor of Forgery*, rather on the line that she is nothing more than a rather confused crime writer who has been made into a cult by highbrow critics. With this tide at the moment swelling fairly strongly it is worth trying to state some of the qualities that make her such an interesting and unusual novelist.

First, no doubt, must come the power with which her male characters are realized. (Not the women, who often seem to be there as formal objects of masculine passion or dislike.) These characters come, as has been noted already, in couples. The way in which their relationship either triggers off or flows from an act of violence is the theme, and even in *The Tremor of Forgery* Ingham's feeling for both OWL and the homosexual Jensen is much more vivid than his presumed love for Ina. The investigation of what would seem to most people abnormal states of mind and ways of behaviour is carried through with a skill all the more impressive because she seems to understand criminal activity so well and to find it so natural. 'I am so law-abiding, I can tremble before a customs inspector with nothing contraband in my suitcases': but her understanding of criminal feelings and desires is such that she could make crimes like Christie's or those of the Moors murderers appear humdrum rather than horrific. In fact sex plays a small part in her books, which have their origin in some idea like that of *Strangers on a Train*, 'two people agree to murder each other's enemy, thus permitting a perfect alibi to be established', or of *The Blunderer* where a clumsy amateur killer tries to copy a crime committed by a more professional one. These are the kind of trickily ingenious plot devices often used by very inferior writers, but she takes them as starting points for profound and subtle studies of character. There are no more genuine agonies in modern literature than those endured by the couples in her books who are locked together in a dislike and even hatred that often strangely contains love.

The way in which all this is presented can be masterly in its choice of tone and phrase. Her opening sentences are, as she says, 'often more stewed over than they appear to be'; they make a statement that is symbolically meaningful in relation to the whole book. The opening sentence in *The Tremor of Forgery* is: '"You're sure there's no letter for me?" Ingham asked.' There is no letter and, as he spells his name uncertainly and then goes away not knowing quite what to do, the style of the whole book has been set. Ingham is waiting and goes on waiting: literally for letters from Castlewood and Ina, for details of Castlewood's suicide and an explanation of Ina's silence; emotionally for some decisive thing to happen which will change his life and reveal his true nature. The setting is also chosen with great care, whether it is Venice, Crete, or an American suburb. It would be wrong to say that places are often more important than people in her books, but it is certainly true that the drama of pursuit played out in *Those Who Walk Away* is closely linked with the descriptions of Venice. In surroundings that are sufficiently strange, men become uncertain of their personalities and question the reason for their own conduct in society: that is what, basically, she seems to be saying. The Tunisian setting in *The Tremor of Forgery* is another case in point. Only under the influence of a way of life which regards human beings as expendable and where boys and girls are equally objects of sexual desire, could Ingham behave as he does. He would be a different man in London or Rome. And the placing of incidents is done with unobtrusive skill, so that this book really splits into two parts, before and after the arrival of Ina which confronts Ingham with the necessity of making a deliberate choice about the kind of life he wants to lead.

The quality that takes her books beyond the run of intelligent fiction is not, however, this professional ability to order a plot and create a significant environment, but rather the intensity of feeling that she brings to the problems of her central figures. The sparking point of a story may be merely sensational, but the development is something different. From original ideas that are sometimes far-fetched or even trivial she proceeds with an imaginative power that makes the whole thing terrifyingly real. This quality of feeling is apparent in the opening prison scenes of *The Glass Cell*, which sprang from a fan letter received from a convict and a book she afterwards read about a man who became a morphine addict after being strung up by his thumbs in prison. She transformed this material into the appalling opening chapters of the book with their description of Carter's sufferings, scenes which are horrifying because of the detailed and calm literalness with which they are set down.

In her last novels she has tried to get away from sensationalism, not always with success. On a crude level it is I suppose fair to say that nothing much happens in *A Tremor of Forgery*. The return of Mr Ripley, which she is contemplating at the moment, may provide a solution to the problem posed for her by the avoidance of sensationalism, of fitting violent events to the things she wants to say about social morality and personal behaviour. Violence is necessary, because the threat or actuality of it produces her best writing, and she has to find a way of using it realistically. The deadly games of pursuit played in her best novels dig down very deeply into the roots of personality. Whatever the results of her rather hesitant new approach to the problems of writing about criminals in society, she has already produced work as serious in its implications and as subtle in its approach as anything being done in the novel today.

(1969)

The Bardin Case

Denis Healey was the guest of honour at a Crime Writers Association dinner a few years ago, one of those years when he was no more than a shadow Minister, and so had time for criminal frivolity. In the course of his speech Mr Healey showed a considerable, almost a dazzling, knowledge of crime fiction. It was an impressive performance, one nearly too much for some of the audience. People who write crime stories are often not great readers of them, feeling perhaps that anything they read will be inferior to what they have written. And when, near the end of his peroration, Mr Healey picked out for special praise the crime novels of John Franklin Bardin, they looked at each other in astonishment. Who was John Franklin Bardin? One is safe in saying that no more than a dozen of the hundred and fifty people at dinner that night had ever heard of him.

Our present Chancellor of the Exchequer is not Bardin's only English admirer. Kingsley Amis, Edmund Crispin and Roy Fuller are among those who have been enthusiastic about his work, but only *The Deadly Percheron* had considerable success. And he has been much more appreciated in Britain than in his native America, where ignorance about him is greater. I have yet to find an American writer or critic who knows his work at all.

It proved difficult, indeed, to discover whether he was still alive, for he had disappeared from literary life rather like one of the characters in his books. Neither his publishers nor his agents had heard of him for years, and stories in papers about a 'Quest for Bardin' produced no response. He was eventually found through the *Third Degree*, the journal of Mystery Writers of America, alive, well, and living in Chicago, where he was editing a magazine for the American Bar Association. He was ready, and indeed eager, to see his three early books republished.*

* *The John Franklin Bardin Omnibus*, Penguin, 1978.

They are all distinguished by an extraordinary intensity of feeling, and by an absorption in morbid psychology remarkable for the period. The crime story immediately after the Second World War was still mostly in the hands of writers who constructed ingenious puzzles, which neither they nor their readers took more seriously than one takes any other game. Bardin was ahead of his time. He belongs not to the world of Agatha Christie and John Dickson Carr, but to that of Patricia Highsmith or even that of Poe. The mental agonies of his heroes and heroines communicate a distress that makes the reader feel uncomfortable. Are they going mad, as they fear, or is there some reasonable explanation for the terrible things that are happening to them? There is a visionary lucidity about Bardin's nightmares that makes his surrealist logic both convincing and disturbing.

The opening of his first book, *The Deadly Percheron*, shows this quality. A young man wearing a scarlet hibiscus in his hair comes into a psychiatrist's office and says that Joe told him to wear the flower. Who is Joe? 'Oh, he's one of my little men. The one in the purple suit. He gives me ten dollars a day for wearing a flower in my hair.' And who are the other little men? Harry, 'who wears green suits and pays me to whistle at Carnegie Hall', and Eustace, who 'pays me to give quarters away'. We think with George Matthews, the psychiatrist, that this is a fantasy spun out of whole cloth – until Matthews meets one of the little men. *The Last of Philip Banter* begins with what seems an impossibility when Philip, an advertising man with a difficult marriage and a drink problem, finds a typed manuscript on his office desk, apparently written by himself, which confuses past and future. It describes what is going to happen as though it has happened already, and Philip, to his horror, sees the predictions coming true. The device is one that would have delighted Poe, and it is used rather as Poe might have used it, to express the course of mental breakdown, personal disintegration.

These are powerful, not perfect, novels. They suggest more than they ever say about the incestuous feelings of parents and children, and the solutions demanded by the problems of the characters seem to be rooted in psychology rather than in reason. Bardin, however, obviously felt the need to provide answers that made sense in terms of an orthodox detective story, and the details of these are not always convincing. One has to admit this, yet on reading the books again recently I found that their power to shock and terrify remained untouched by the not quite satisfactory solutions. And such a criticism does not apply at all to Bardin's masterpiece, *Devil Take the Blue-Tail Fly*, a book whose problems and solutions are conceived wholly in terms of the psychology of its heroine, Ellen. The book was written in six weeks as a first draft, taken away by Victor Gollancz from an agent's office, and never revised. Nor does it need revision, moving as it does with increasing pace and a perfect natural rhythm.

The opening is unforgettable in its blend of the commonplace and the sinister. Ellen is leaving the mental home; she is the patient whose recovery they are all proud of; her longing to see her husband Basil is natural and real. Then, as if a nail were intrusively scraped across a window pane, Ellen does something unexpected and 'wrong', in asking the nurses to turn their backs, and from that moment onwards we know she is not well. The other moments in this opening chapter that convey the ripple of disquiet are also beautifully muted: Ellen's reluctance on leaving the home to go away from the doctor, and her desire to say good-bye to the mountainous Ella, whose Buddha-like placidity apparently 'expressing a god-like peace' contradicts her actual violence. What happens afterwards, the disintegration of Ellen through a mixture of bad luck, self-deceit, and stupidity on the part of the other people (some incidents remain properly mysterious, like what actually did happen to the key), is finely judged and developed. The book is unusual also in its suggestions of the way in which creative ability can be thwarted, and even destroyed. One can believe in Ellen as a musician, and the torments she suffers are partly those of the frustrated artist, 'the agony of flame that cannot singe a sleeve'.

'My basic literary influences have been Graham Greene, Henry Green and Henry James,' Bardin says, but although traces of James and Greene can be seen, the moving power behind these stories is his own life. Without, perhaps, being exactly autobiographical, they are clearly a reworking of events in a stormy, painful childhood and adolescence. Bardin was born in 1916 in Cincinnati. His father was a well-to-do coal merchant, his mother the child of a groom, a girl who came to Cincinnati to work in an office. Misfortune pursued the family. An elder sister died of septicaemia, and a year later Bardin's father died of a coronary. He left very little money, and John had to leave the University of Cincinnati in his first year to find a full-time job. He became a ticket-taker and bouncer in a roller-skating rink. 'Mother had become a paranoid schizophrenic by then. It was on visits to her that I first had an insight into the "going home" hallucinations.' There followed that process of self-education ('I worked at night and read, clerked in a bookstore') undertaken by many American writers.

The biographical details are interesting because they fill in the background of the books and show the pressures that helped to produce them, but of course they do not explain their quality. They were published over a period of eighteen months, the result of an almost continuous surge of creative energy. Their lack of success in America must have been discouraging. *Devil Take the Blue-Tail Fly* was not published there until the late sixties, and then only in paperback. Bardin turned to writing slick, readable, unadventurous crime stories under the pseudonym of Gregory Tree. In his own name he published at least two more novels, one an interesting but unsuccessful experiment, the other disastrously sentimental. He has not published a book for more than a decade, although he has recently started writing again.

The novels sprang out of nightmare experiences, and it does not seem likely that Bardin will be impelled to write anything like them again. They are unlike anything else in modern crime literature. The first two are erratic and exotic, but they are never plodding or dull, and *Devil Take the Blue-Tail Fly* is one of the most convincing and frightening 'psychological' crime stories ever written. It is a pleasure to bring all three books to a new and wider public.

(1978)

PS, 1994. The republication of his work in an omnibus volume brought Bardin temporary celebrity, especially in the US where he was rightly hailed as a previously unknown master of the psychological thriller, but his own story had no happy ending. He gave up his Chicago job, returned to life in Greenwich Village, and wrote one more book, a disappointing would-be chiller called *Purloining Tiny*. He died in 1981.

Ross Macdonald:
A Transatlantic Friendship

'So you've met Ross Macdonald twenty times,' somebody said to me once. 'Did you get twenty words out of him?' I said truthfully that I'd got many more words than that, but it's true that Ken (it seems right to shift gear into the name by which everybody called him) had no small talk. When something was said to him he would consider it, almost visibly turning over the possible implications of his reply, and when the slow-spoken reply came it would be a genuine expression of feeling about the subject in hand. Such a reaction may sound ponderous, but that wasn't at all the effect. His verbally well-shaped response might be light or serious, but it by-passed the ordinary banalities of conversation. He was quite capable of saying that he had no opinion about the subject, or knew too little about it for anything he said to be worth uttering. Even with people he liked, conversation with Ken Millar could be difficult, but it was never unrewarding. Looking back, I'm doubtful if our meetings numbered twenty but still our friendship, much of it conducted by letters across the Atlantic, was a warm one.

We met first in 1965, at the annual dinner of The Mystery Writers of America. His book *The Chill* had won an award from British crime writers which took the form of a dagger, and I had been delegated to hand it over. Ken accepted it, held it aloft, asked: 'Is this a dagger that I see before me?' and made a downward plunge in the air. Afterwards he and I found ourselves having drinks at an apartment in the company of Victor and Ruth Gollancz. 'Isn't she the most beautiful lady you've ever seen?' he asked when we were walking back to our hotels. Ruth was then I suppose in her mid-sixties, and although her features and colouring were delicate I didn't endorse his remark. He had, as I learned later, a special feeling for beauty and dignity in those who had passed middle age. I was struck at this first meeting by his own good looks, the sweetness of his smile, and by a natural courtesy much beyond the ordinary.

We had arranged, as I thought rather casually, to meet on the following day. At nine o'clock the telephone rang. 'That will be Julian,' Ken said in his gentle voice, and surprised me by asking how I felt, with the implication that our half-dozen drinks represented a real night out together. Perhaps they may have done for him, since his use of alcohol was very modest. We walked through Central Park, went to the Guggenheim and saw an exhibition that fairly bowled Ken over (German expressionists? Shamefully, infuriatingly, I can't remember), walked downtown talking about modern poetry. In this connection I perpetrated a considerable gaffe when I said something like: 'The most important English poetry publishers – I don't suppose you know of them – are Faber and Faber.' A pause, a long pause, and then the gentle voice was raised in just indignation. 'Not *know* of Faber and Faber? At Ann Arbor, Julian, I took a course with Auden, I made a special study of Imagism. I used to *buy* Faber poetry when I was in college . . .' I apologized and was forgiven, although the rash assumption rankled for a while. Ken's knowledge of poetry was extensive, especially of the nineteenth-century romantics who had influenced him in youth. Among modern poets he admired particularly Lowell and Berryman.

From that brief time in New York I carry away also the recollection of his amazement when, at lunch with him and the crime novelist Jean Potts after our Guggenheim visit, I ordered calves' brains. Brains – for lunch – after an evening of excess like ours – Ken did not withhold his wonder, and his admiration of such stamina, such intrepidity.

We met again four years later when Kathleen and Sarah, wife and daughter, came with me on a holiday interspersed with lectures that ordered and shaped our movements. I talked about Wyndham Lewis at the University of California at Santa Barbara, and Ken called to collect us from our motel and take us to their house on Via Esperanza. I knew and admired the crime stories of his wife Margaret Millar, and now met her for the first time. She was breezy where Ken was quiet, apparently as bluffly extrovert as he was inward-looking: yet Margaret had her private demons, expressed by the asthma that made it impossible for her to stay in a smoke-filled room, and the eye trouble that made her reluctant to go out at night. As he played with the dogs in and around the pool, Ken said that I should not be deceived by what might look like luxury. 'I make about as much money every year as a good plumber.' He had already embarked on the attempt to re-create and understand his own past that increasingly preoccupied him as a novelist, but the immense critical and popular success in America of his later books still lay a year or two ahead. He was less concerned with such things than any writer I have known, taking little interest in sales and promotion, almost none in the films made from his stories.

It turned out that he knew a lot about Wyndham Lewis (I had not repeated my Faberian mistake), and had been friendly with Hugh Kenner who arranged the lecture. This turned out disastrously, thanks to the fact that the room in which it was given had been changed, and the new room number not made public. The audience was even smaller than it might otherwise have been and Ken, who set out to attend the lecture, spent the evening wandering down corridors and through empty classrooms.

A couple of years later the Millars made what was for them the momentous decision in favour of a trip to Europe. Ken had not been in Britain for more than thirty years, and Margaret I think had never crossed the Atlantic. Kathleen and I wanted to give a dinner party for them, and there was also a plan for a radio discussion with them both. Ken wrote:

If I was dubious, when you were here, about our being able to come to England, it had to do with Margaret's difficulty in traveling and doing the things that people ordinarily and quite easily do. Well, I have got her to the point of abandoning, for a week or two, this continent. But there are still some limitations on our movements. I am being perfectly frank with you and Kathleen because you will understand me. It would be difficult for Margaret to meet any number of people at your house, and indeed it is many years (I think since the inception of her glaucoma, now happily arrested) since she has gone anywhere after dark, even in her own familiar territory. She asks if we could have lunch together, perhaps at a pub, instead? M thrives on informality, as you may have noticed.

The question of coming or not coming to dinner involved a flurry of correspondence, Ken feeling quite mistakenly that what he had said above had been impolite. 'This self-disinvited guest doesn't seem to know how to handle his social mistake without making the further gaffe of reinviting himself,' he wrote. 'Conceivably – I blunder on – we might manage to meet at your house and eat somewhere afterward, with or without dear M.' He had called Donald Davie at Stanford, asked whom he should see in London, and I had been recommended with 'the most outright endorsement of anybody that I ever heard from Davie'. But perhaps, he feared, Kathleen and I had given up on the Millars. 'That would *really* make me feel badly.'

More letters followed, expressing alarm at one moment, eager expectancy the next. All this may sound exaggerated or slightly absurd, but that isn't so. The trip in prospect was both exciting and alarming, with the first true for Ken, the second for Margaret. In the end Ken came alone to dinner with us in Battersea, I later took them both out to lunch, and although the husband-and-wife radio discussion didn't come off, Ken took part in a radio programme in which I talked to him about his books. I can't remember much about the dinner, except that he got on extremely well with the crime critic and political commentator Matthew Coady, but otherwise seemed faintly uneasy. I should perhaps have realized that he flourished in a very small group, with more direct and meaningful conversation than a dinner party encourages.

Our lunch date a couple of days later had some touches of comedy about it. I had booked a table at a French restaurant, but the Millars had been in France, and almost the first thing Margaret said (of course in ignorance of my table booking) was that French food had upset her stomach, and she'd had quite enough of it. Abandoning the French restaurant, I took them to my favourite pub, the Salisbury in St Martin's Lane. There, settled on the red plush, I diverted Margaret from the idea that she could order a cup of tea. She settled for cider, but what was she to eat? Looking around with great interest at the people around us and the food being handed over the bar counter, she asked suddenly: 'Is it shepherd's pie I see over there? *That's* what I'd like.' The shepherd's pie was pronounced the best food she'd had since leaving the States, and on a trip they took afterwards they asked for it whenever they stopped at a pub for lunch. We ended a successful afternoon by walking round various bits of the West End, during which Margaret tried on and rejected several pairs of boots. She was very much a visitor to a strange country, Ken sweetly protective of her.

The radio programme revealed a side of him I hadn't seen before. It was about crime and psychology, and included two or three interviews, including the one with Ken, which took place in his hotel. He talked with characteristic gentle candour about the background of his own books, and their quality for him as an attempt to come to terms with his own childhood. The producer Robin Brightwell intervened once, twice, three times, suggesting questions of a more direct kind that he thought I might put. At length Ken broke off and, without raising his voice or showing any sign of annoyance, said – I am giving the gist of what was said, not exact words – 'Mr Brightwell, I understand I was being interviewed by Mr Symons. I should have been told in advance if I was to be interviewed by you, and perhaps I might not have agreed to it.' It was one of the most effective put-downs I have heard, the more so because of its perfect politeness. When the programme was transmitted I sent him a copy, and he expressed astonishment at the way Brightwell and I had put it together. 'The level of civility was high, though I fear I didn't contribute to that aspect.' He was surprised and amused to be paid a small fee for taking part, and gave the morsel of money to charity.

In conversation Ken was so withdrawn a person that it was hard to know what experiences were important to him, and what touched him only superficially, but it was plain from his letters that the visit to England lingered in his mind. He felt strongly the contrast between the crowded life of London and the 'immense slow calm' of the Millars' life in Santa Barbara, recalled nostalgically the London Library, 'full of peace and light', and of course lunch at the Salisbury. 'So vivid were our recollections of that great pub in St Martin's Lane that the first thing Margaret made when she got home was shepherd's pie.' He was a little surprised to have attracted so much attention from newspaper interviewers, and particularly pleased that in the *Sunday Times* Philip Oakes had mentioned his 'tip of the hat' to Auden, 'without whose cheerful encouragement I might never have made it into print'. A little later, reading a book of mine about the thirties, he remembered – something he never talked about to me – 'the London of my youth when I took part in the anti-Fascist demonstrations and was chased by policemen on horseback'. He went on to other things never expressed verbally:

I value the book above all as an expression of my dear friend Julian, for I know how much you were a man of the thirties – a desperate time when it was after all, at least in the democracies, remarkably good to be alive. I'm a man of the thirties, too, and if I hadn't been a Canadian I might have stayed in London and had a quite different life. But I had other fields to plough.

He returned to the theme in later letters: 'I was tempted to stay there and go to the University where I had friends. But a Canadian-American with an education in English has to be careful in his choices. In the thirties, at least, it was regressive for a Canadian to go English, or so it seemed to me. That's probably no longer true. Canadians are finding themselves in Canada *via* England. But I was pulled back and processed through the giant American route, ending as that combination of qualities, a Californian, or perhaps just a Canadian after all.' And again, years later: 'If I had London available, I'd find it hard to stay out of it, and possibly even harder to live in it.' He consoled himself with the thought that Santa Barbara was about the same size as Periclean Athens. 'We live almost in the country, in effect, but five minutes from a shopping center. That doesn't *sound* too much like Athens, does it?'

Reading Edmund Wilson's *Upstate* he pondered on the possibility of writing something of the same kind. 'As I get older and look forward and back, I wonder if I can undertake the kind of family and personal history that I could, and probably should, write. . . . It's too soon yet, though, to embrace all that old sadness, the substance of my mother, the shadow of my father.' The outline of such a book can be glimpsed in some of the pieces collected together by Ralph Sipper and titled *Self-Portrait*, but it is no more than an outline. The inwardness of those youthful feelings was expressed only at one remove, in the novels.

Our correspondence, not constant but without many breaks in it, dealt very little with crime stories. It marked the wide range of Ken's reading, from a new life of Ibsen to Gogol to John Berryman's last poems. He valued poetry above prose, and noted wistfully that 'we prose writers secretly write for the poets and secretly yearn to be noticed by you'. Reading the transcript of a discussion about his work that I did with Al Alvarez (I committed another gaffe by suggesting that he might not know of Alvarez, and was told that Ken had *The Savage God* on his shelves, and was a charter subscriber to the *New York Review of Books* for which at that time Alvarez often wrote), he said that he felt as if he had been buried in Westminster Abbey, then moved from joke to seriousness. 'Actually I plan to have my ashes scattered in the Santa Barbara Channel where, in the destructive element immersed, I have spent the best hours of my best days.' By this time he was famous in his own country, but praise from British literati seemed to hold special importance for him.

There is little more to say that wouldn't be repetitious. In 1974 I suggested Lew Archer might have fulfilled his catalytic function, and that Ken would perhaps feel freer in his absence, and was told: 'That is precisely what I am working towards – just between you and me,' and that although 'Archer hasn't hampered me much it's time I essayed something new, with the option of returning to him later.' There was little sign, however, that his last book, *The Blue Hammer* of 1976, might have been the final Archer novel. In that year Kathleen and I visited Santa Barbara, and were greeted as warmly as ever. Ken had discovered the likely time of our arrival and suddenly appeared outside our motel, we had lunch at their splendid beach club, followed by an afternoon of swimming and talk.

We next met at the world crime writers' conference of 1978 in New York, where Ken made a speech, the early part of which was uttered rather as though he were talking to himself, with no audience in mind. The effect was odd, but seemed attributable to his public shyness. Later we agreed to meet for breakfast, and he came across from the Algonquin to where we stayed at what was then its poor cousin the Royalton, a good hour earlier than we expected. Disturbing? We thought he had simply mistaken the time, but it seems likely now that these were advance warnings of his illness. Our last visit to Santa Barbara in 1981 was a sad one. When I telephoned and said we had arrived, there was a pause. Then Ken said: 'Hello, Mr Symons, I'll call Margaret to speak to you.' At lunch the next day he smiled with his usual sweetness but said very little, and neither Kathleen nor I could be sure that he knew who we were.

One writes with regret at the failure to know better a man who was less withdrawn towards me than to the most of the world. Expressing, on another occasion, regret for a failure to meet, he wrote: 'I value your friendship above that of any transatlantic man, or cis-Atlantic either, for that matter. And the pull of Europe, which I have kept narcotized since 1938, is beginning to stir again.' The shelf of novels remains but, good as the best of them are, they are not quite what he hoped to write. It is a sadness that he will not write the autobiographical book about his youth that he contemplated for so long, or visit England again as he hoped and meant to do (the pull of Europe would never have taken him away permanently from Santa Barbara, but was still powerful), and that his writing life has been so abruptly terminated, with what might have been the finest things unachieved.

(1984)

James M. Cain*

James M. Cain wrote one excellent short thriller, *The Postman Always Rings Twice*, a good long short story that made a better film in 'Double Indemnity', an interesting but sentimental Hemingwayesque novel called *Serenade*. Is there much else that rises above the level of competent popular fiction? Can there be any possible justification for a biography of Cain running to more than 700 pages? Well, no, there can't. Mr Hoopes's book is interesting, however, in the sense that Cain is a super-typical example of a sort of writing that might be called American demotic, sired by Hollywood out of everyday journalism. American demotic is fluent, energetic, readable, but sentimental in approach and feeling, eminently forgettable.

Cain was born in 1892, and fulfilled a requirement of the American demotic writer by running through a number of jobs when young. Ledger clerk with Consolidated Light and Gas of Baltimore, inspector of roads, high school principal in a Maryland village, would-be singer, insurance and then record salesman – it is almost a standard apprenticeship, in Cain's case ending when in his mid-twenties he landed a job on the Baltimore *Sun*. Mr Hoopes spends dozens of pages in showing us that Cain was an alert journalist, quick in the uptake, writer of 1300 editorials and 90 pieces under his own by-line in seven years. He learned to talk out of the side of his mouth, was pockmarked, he drank hard, but within this traditional toughness was an equally traditional marshmallow heart.

The standards of biographer and subject are very similar. Mr Hoopes considers that Allan Nevins 'wrote beautifully', and that Cain like Walter Lippmann was a perfectionist. (Cain was by now on the New York *World*.) Certainly he rewrote a great many of his editorials and had, his biographer assures us, an obsession with

* *James M. Cain*, by Roy Hoopes Holt, Rinehart and Winston.

style. His 'use of realistic, colloquial speech' had been developed through journalism, and by pieces he wrote for Menchken's *American Mercury*. Mr Hoopes insists that Cain was not stylistically influenced by Hemingway. Perhaps not, but it is worth remarking that this tart, taut style was being used by Dashiell Hammett before Hemingway started publishing short stories. Cain claimed never to have read more of Hammett than a few dips into *The Glass Key* ('I said forget this goddam book'), but the point is that American demotic was developing fast in the twenties. There is no need to suggest that Cain copied any other writer, but equally he was not the originator of the style he used.

In 1931, after a few unhappy months as managing editor of the *New Yorker* (when, after the success of *The Postman*, Wolcott Gibbs asked Cain to consider writing something for the magazine, he received the reply: 'On the whole, I would rather be dead'), Cain went to Hollywood as a scriptwriter for Paramount. He stayed there for seventeen years, worked on dozens of scripts, but got only three shared screen credits. His failure in Hollywood, if somebody who made a living out of the place for so long can be called a failure, was attributed by Raymond Chandler, who worked on *Double Indemnity* as a film, to the fact that Cain's dialogue read splendidly on the page, but wouldn't play on the screen. This is an interesting idea, which I should like to have seen explored more fully. Mr Hoopes tells us that Cain always disliked the cinema, and viewed it with contempt. He compared it with working in a whorehouse, but few work voluntarily for seventeen years in a brothel when they have a good job waiting outside, as Cain had in the form of writing novels – unless, of course, they secretly like it.

Cain was in his early forties when *The Postman*, his first novel, was published, and made him a celebrity overnight. The plot came, we are told, from the drives he took through California canyons and valleys with his second wife Elina. At one filling station a 'bosomy-looking thing . . . the kind you have ideas about' always filled up the tank. One day Cain read that this 'appetizing but utterly commonplace woman' had killed her husband. So 'what about a novel in which a woman and a typical California automobile tramp kill the woman's husband . . .?'

In 1948 Cain, by this time with his fourth wife, left Hollywood for Hyattsville, Maryland, where they passed the rest of their lives.

She became an invalid, and much of his time was spent nursing her.
He wrote a dozen more novels, all assiduously researched, and
although none repeated the success of the first, most were reviewed
favourably even though some of the praise was ambiguous, like the
New Yorker's comment that Cain was 'the best comic-strip artist in
the country'. He died at the age of eighty-five, not ignored, but no
longer highly regarded by many. His own uncertainty about his
achievement worried him. 'How you write 'em is write 'em,' he
once observed, but this homespun wisdom did not altogether sat-
isfy him. Why did some books turn out badly, why did he write
better in the first person than the third? 'What have I done?
Nothing that gives me the slightest lift. I work, I sell something
occasionally, I make a living. That's about all there is to tell.' That
was Cain in old age. If Hoopes had paid attention to such remarks,
we might have had something better than this overblown work.

Cain's chief limitation as a writer was coarseness, not of language
for which he was much reproved at the time, but of feeling. His
imaginative standards were those of American cinema in the
thirties and forties. The outspoken manner of *The Postman* was
shocking in its decade ('From then on I began to smell her again
. . . She was down there, and the breath was roaring in the back of
my throat like I was some kind of an animal'), but has been
overtaken by changed social attitudes, and nowadays looks commonplace or even slightly comic. This is one of the risks run by
any writer very much in tune with a particular period, and *The
Postman*'s merits survive such passages. The coarseness of feeling
is typified in the climactic scene conceived by Cain for his historical
novel, *Past All Dishonor*. Roger Duval, who kills a man for the sake
of a Virginia City prostitute, is heading for Mexico with her, when
Duval hears dogs barking and thinks they are being pursued. 'Then
he hears a twig snap and whirls to see Morina standing there,
dressed in all the jewels they had stolen. But it is too late; he fired
as he turned. She sinks down, bleeding in the white snow.'

He was very proud of this ending, of which it may be said, as
Oscar Wilde remarked of Little Nell's death, that only a man with
a heart of stone could read it without laughing. Cain worked hard
on the book, learned 'every last detail about mining in Nevada in
the 1850s' spent 'countless hours' in libraries, refused to make
Morina a good girl and insisted that she must be a prostitute. He

was indignant when after the book's publication Malcolm Cowley said that he was tethered in celluloid, and Edmund Wilson that he had been eaten alive by the movies. He could not understand that a story conceived in such terms must be worthless, no matter how faithful the research. It is no surprise that when working on a movie version of *The Great Gatsby* (he thought the book 'clap-trap') he suggested that Gatsby, thought to have been killed in the car accident, should attend his own funeral, meet there a gum-chewing former girlfriend from the mid-West who really loves him, and be led away by her into a new life. It suggests Mr Hoopes's own critical standards that he calls this ending, 'A little too tricky, perhaps.'

The greatest skill Cain possessed was just such trickiness. Both *The Postman* and 'Double Indemnity' are plotted with cunning. Cain could construct ingenious plots and write excellent dialogue, and there his serious merits end. If he hated the moving picture industry it was because he subconsciously knew that the imagina-tive conventions they obeyed were also his own, so that even when he wrote a 'daring' novel about incest in *The Butterfly*, he flinched from the actual relationship. His incestuous father is so by inten-tion but not, as it turns out, in fact. The book's quality as a shocker has vanished today, and the plot of this short novel is, again, the most impressive thing about it.

But the last thing Cain wanted was praise merely for his plots. His refusal to read Hammett and Chandler no doubt sprang from the feeling that he was a real novelist, and they mere writers of hard-boiled crime stories. In fact, as a writer he was inferior to both of them. His protest against *Mildred Pierce* being turned into a crime story on the screen by the addition of a murder mystery was no doubt genuine enough, but it did not stop him from anxiously considering every book he wrote as a potential money-spinner on the screen. It is not really true to say that Cain was eaten alive by Hollywood, since from the moment of his first success as a novelist he was always primarily a man who thought and wrote in terms of the movies.

(1982)

Cameron McCabe: A Curiosity*

This book, one of the most extraordinary in the annals of the crime story, also has a very unusual publishing history. It was first published in England in 1937, when the author was twenty-two years old, a refugee from Hitler's Germany whose English was fluent but erratic. French and German translations appeared, as well as English reprints, but this is the book's first publication in the United States. Even now it comes, with appropriate unorthodoxy, through a direct mail house, and not an ordinary trade publisher.

The story is told in the first person by Cameron McCabe, and the title refers to an actor being eliminated from a picture by scissor-work in the cutting-room. McCabe is told by the producer to delete a girl named Estella, one of the three principal players in a just completed film. On the following morning Estella is found murdered in the Special Effects studio, which contains an automatic camera rigged up by Robertson, head of the department. Robertson's Silent Automatic-Infra shows everything that happens in the room, and should reveal Estella's death. The film, however, has been removed.

This sounds like the opening of an orthodox detective story, but there is a hallucinatory air about the book from the beginning. The style is that of American crime films, circa 1937, chatty and energetic. Expressions and phrases, however, are often slightly wrong, something that makes the dialogue curiously exotic. This exoticism extends to the characters, who are vividly described, but seem oddly motivated. What are we to make of Detective Inspector Smith, 'nice and quiet and gentlemanly, very much like Oscar Wilde's idea of a gentleman', who takes McCabe with him to interview witnesses, follows the film man about, and engages in knockabout comic back-chat with him? Or of McCabe's dalliance

---

* *The Face on the Cutting-Room Floor*, Cameron McCabe, Gregg Press.

with his secretary Dinah Lee, and his passion for the actress Maria Ray? Or of the gathering of suspects and reconstruction of the crime by Smith, something typical of the period, which here comes less than halfway through the book instead of at the end as is usual, and finishes with the detective walking out, saying that McCabe had better take charge of the reconstruction? All the ordinary elements of a thirties detective story are seen as in a distorting mirror, with a lunatic logic ordering the actions of detective and suspects alike. We are hardly surprised when, at the end of a long explanatory speech, Smith thunders: 'The murderer, Mr McCabe, is you.' McCabe is arrested.

But we are still only two-thirds of the way through the book, which loops round and round in surrealist spirals, with McCabe's trial succeeded by an epilogue written by a minor character named A. B. C. Muller 'as epitaph for Cameron McCabe' who has written a posthumously published book called *The Face on The Cutting-Room Floor*. Muller quotes long extracts from reviews of the book written by a dozen English critics of the time, W. H. Auden, Cyril Connolly and C. Day Lewis among them, reviews which praise and discuss McCabe's work. And there is still a further coil to the spiral, as Muller meets Maria Ray and says 'Poor Mr McCabe', to which she responds in the Americanese used by many of the characters: 'Well, honest to God, you are a crazy feller.' And as they talk, as Maria offers a solution of what happened that has never occurred to anybody, Muller is moved to the action that ends the book. Ends it, that is, apart from an apology which admits that the reviews, although real enough, all have McCabe's name and the title of his book substituted for those of genuine books and authors.

The Face on the Cutting-Room Floor is a box of tricks, a book that outrages all the conventions of the detective story, and pushes the artificiality of the form as practised at the time to ultimate absurdities. It is a spectacular performance, a book that survives through its constant ingenuity and engaging youthful high spirits. To this edition the author has appended a long postscript, in some aspects much in key with the book.

His name is Ernest Wilhelm Julius Borneman, and he now lives in a large farm in Upper Austria. He is a University professor who teaches Libido Theory at Salzburg University and Sexual

Psychology at Marburg. In the past he has been a film-maker who worked at various times with John Grierson, Bertolt Brecht and Orson Welles. The Welles–Borneman film of the *Odyssey* and the *Iliad* ran out of money, but was finally shot by a different director with Kirk Douglas as Odysseus and Silvano Mangano as Penelope. Borneman has also been at one time or another jazz musician, journalist, playwright, novelist and controller of a projected German Federal TV network. His most successful novel, *The Man Who Loved Women* was, he says, sold for $50,000 to a paperback house, but still 'it's my experience that you can't live by writing books'. Nevertheless, he is now ensconced in a thirty-roomed house, with a library that contains between 20,000 and 30,000 books.

So far Mr Borneman's career. But what about *The Face on the Cutting-Room Floor*? This was the first and last work with Cameron McCabe's name on the title page and sprang, Mr Borneman says, from the fascination held for him by Proust, Joyce, dos Passos, Hammett and Aldous Huxley. It was 'no more than a finger exercise on the keyboard of a new language', and seems to him now 'mannered and puerile'. In spite of this uncharacteristic touch of modesty on the author's part, the book is required reading for anybody interested in the history, the construction or the mores of the detective story.

(1981)

Martin Cruz Smith: Gorky Park*

If, as Auden suggested, the ideal detective story reader desires an unchanging fictional world in which the same problem is endlessly repeated with minor variations, the ideal thriller reader demands almost the opposite, a fix of novelty. The agent becomes over the years double, triple, multiple; he is numbered 007 and licensed to kill; history is invoked and turned on its head as Churchill meets Hitler secretly in Len Deighton, a whole mythology of agency terms is invented to add verisimilitude to John le Carré's Circus. Such novelty is provided in *Gorky Park* by offering a Russian criminal investigator as hero, and Moscow as principal setting. A not very helpful map of the city is used as a frontispiece.

The novelty of this approach, and the well-publicized fact that the author spent only two weeks in the Soviet Union, are in part no doubt responsible for the book's success. Is it also a 'powerful, compassionate and original work . . . a strange and marvellous book . . . a panoramic view of Russian society today,' as readers exultantly quoted on the cover say? Not so. *Gorky Park* is much above the average thriller, but almost equally far below the best of Ambler, Deighton and le Carré. Its outstanding virtue is the conviction with which the Moscow settings are rendered, and the assurance with which they are given us in detail, its particular weaknesses feeble characterization and a vast over-indulgence in violence. The hero is stabbed (the knife penetrates colon, stomach and diaphragm), thrown on to the rails of Moscow Underground, spends months under interrogation in a Soviet psychiatric hospital, and in the final shoot-out which disposes of most of the other characters gets bullets in chest and thigh. I may have omitted one or two of his other escapes from death, but those are enough to show his near-immortality. A correction should be made also about 'most of the other characters'. The shoot-out takes place on

* *Gorky Park*, by Martin Cruz Smith, Random House.

Staten Island, but a good many minor characters have already been disposed of in Moscow.

The near-immortal hero is Arkady Renko, 'chief investigator' in the police arm of the MVD, which 'directs traffic, chases drunks and picks up everyday corpses'. The story would be more plausible if Renko were a pillar of Soviet orthodoxy, but instead he is that traditional figure, a good guy in a bad organization, with many people ready to deceive him, most hands against him. Renko has no belief in Communism, and is at odds with his wife who sets divorce proceedings going during the course of the book. We realize, long before Renko does, that he is being used as a tool by those above him, but it still seems unlikely that he would have kept his position as long as he has done.

Accept Renko if you can, accept what I found the jarring convention by which the Russians speak demotic American ('You going to puke?... We haven't screwed in months ... You'd be a cinch to be a Central Committee Inspector'), and there is a good deal to enjoy. The narration is crisp, lively, at times amusing. There are occasional similarities to Ed McBain's 87th Precinct stories in the mass of detail about police work, but that adds to the feeling of authenticity, which is enhanced by such bits of information as the news that Arkady and his wife Zoya together make 300 roubles a month, half as much as a factory foreman. There are details about hotels, prostitutes, the Moscow Underground, the gradations of rank in the Soviet Union and much else, and whether or not the details are accurate they sound right, and are skilfully embodied in naturalistic conversations.

Many of the descriptive passages are equally good. A train is leaving from Savelovsky Station (not to be found on the map). The station is normally used by commuters, but this train is special, for it is taking labourers to work in the northern mines. Arkady, who is on the run after at last discovering how fully he has been tricked, joins them:

On the train he moved with the flow into a compartment already filled with men and the stink of sweat and onions. A dozen faces studied him. They were the same tough and homely faces as on the Politburo, but roughed up and down the street a bit. They sported bruises and unusual scars, their knuckles and collars were dirty, and they carried their possessions in bundles. Basically they were criminals, men wanted for violence or theft in one town instead of the whole country. Little fish who thought they were escaping through the holes of the great socialist net, only to be funneled into socialist mines in the north. Tough fish, urkas, brothers, hard cases, men with tattoos and knives.

There is an excellent scene in a bath house, where Soviet apparatchiks discuss the heresy of 'Vronskyism' or individualism, while swallowing masses of caviar. Mr Smith is very good at catching the tone of Soviet officialdom in, for example, a psychiatrist's outline of the 'pathoheterodoxy sydrome', from which Arkady is found to be suffering. There are other convincing scenes, like a visit paid by Arkady to his old father, General Renko.

Return to the main plot and the all-too-plentiful action, however, and we are back in a very conventional thrillerland. The book's opening is promising, with three bodies found frozen and mutilated in the deep snow of Gorky Park, and a struggle between Arkady's MVD and the KGB for possession of them, but the interdepartmental battle soon moves into the background with the entry of a sinister American named Osborne, lean and dark, with 'straight white hair and black eyes, a long nose and an almost feminine mouth . . . an extraordinary combination, equine and handsome'. Osborne played a heroic (or was it treacherous?) role at Leningrad during the War, he is an informer for the KGB (or is he perhaps informing *on* the KGB?). Either way, he is the mainspring of the plot, and plays an important and consistently villainous role right up to the end.

But no sooner has that phrase been put down on paper than one doubts its validity, because the plot requires every important figure except Arkady to be playing at least a double game. The New York cop Kirwill who attacks Arkady in Gorky Park, prosecutor Iamskoy who keeps him on the case against KGB wishes, Wesley the FBI man who looks after Arkady when he is sent to the United States, even Irina with whom the investigator falls in love, are not exactly what they seem. On several occasions Arkady expects to be killed. 'Were they going to kill him in the park?' he wonders as he drives around Central Park with Osborne in a limousine, and indeed why isn't he killed, why does Osborne instead simply go on talking, and giving Arkady information? Why haven't 'they' already disposed of him in the psychiatric hospital, why didn't the doctor who handed a KGB man 'a needle the size used for horses' containing poison that would have killed Arkady, make sure the needle was used? For that matter, why is he released from hospital, and sent with his Irina to the States? The general answer is that Arkady is thought still to have his uses, but he has caused so much trouble that the decision to treat him once more as a tool seems outrageously improbable.

Is a critic bearing down very hard on *Gorky Park* by treating its deficiencies so stringently? Yes, or at least perhaps. Yet although belief is often strained in spy stories and thrillers, the strains nowadays are rarely of this unsophisticated kind. *Gorky Park* has been acclaimed as a work of exceptional merit in the genre, and it is not that. Below its excellent realistic surface lie crudities of approach that the best thriller writers have long since abandoned. The book is not in the same league as Ambler's masterly *Doctor Frigo*, Deighton's inventive yet finely restrained *SS: GB* or le Carré's early work. There are good things in it, the writing is brisk and intelligent, no doubt it will be one of the best dozen thrillers of the year. The rest is the roll, the rise, the carol, the creation, of publicity boys and girls, and of those deceived by their wiles.

(1982)

ELSEWHERE

Chekhov's Only Novel:
The Shooting Party

The general view of Anton Chekhov's work held in the West is a misleading one. We think of him as the author of four great plays who also wrote some interesting but comparatively minor short stories – 'The Lady with the Little Dog' is sure to be mentioned, and also perhaps 'The Duel', 'The Kiss' and 'The Party' (the titles vary with the translator). The view is misleading because it gives no sense of the way in which Chekhov's art developed. Chekhov became famous as a short story writer, and when in 1888 he was awarded the Pushkin Prize it was for a collection of stories, *In the Twilight*. The first of the great plays, *The Seagull*, was not written until 1895, and was a disastrous failure when performed in St Petersburg in the following year. Success did not come until the play's production in 1898 by the Moscow Arts Theatre under the guidance of Stanislavsky and the playwright's old friend Nemirovich-Danchenko. The triumphs of the later plays, all produced at the Moscow Arts Theatre, were compressed into the last six years of his life.

Chekhov was not a playwright who produced short stories on the side, but a professional writer who found that he could make a living most easily from writing short narratives, many of them fictional. In part he earned his living as a doctor, but his tendency to treat patients for nothing if they were poor meant that from the beginning he relied on writing as a major source of income. He once said medicine was his lawful wife and literature his mistress, and that when bored with one he spent the night with the other, but as the years passed most nights in the week were spent with the mistress, and that mistress was the short story. The inclination that Chekhov undoubtedly felt towards the theatre was checked by his inability to get his youthful melodrama *Platonov* performed, and by the irritation he felt with actors and actresses even after the critical praise given to *Ivanov* on its performance in 1889 at St Petersburg. Varying the wife and mistress metaphor, he called prose narrative his wife, drama the mistress.

Again it should be emphasized that in the English-speaking world we have read almost nothing Chekhov wrote in his first five years as an author, because so little of it has been translated. By way of explaining this, the often-told story of his early years needs brief repetition. Anton Chekhov was born in 1860 and brought up in Taganrog, a small port six hundred miles south of Moscow. His grandfather was a serf known simply as Chekh, who managed to buy the family's freedom. This was not well used by his son Pavel, who combined a severe upbringing of his six children with grandiose ambitions to have not one but two grocer's shops, and to build his own house. Deep in debt and trouble Pavel Chekhov fled to Moscow and there, after finishing his education at Taganrog, Anton joined the rest of the family. He enrolled at the Medical Faculty of the University for the five years of study necessary before he could become a doctor, and set out to help maintain the rest of the family by his pen. Some of the other children worked too, but Anton soon became their principal financial support. From the age of twenty until he qualified as a doctor in 1884, Chekhov was a punctilious medical student who in his spare time wrote dozens – indeed, hundreds – of sketches and stories, mostly for St Petersburg comic papers.

From the description given by Chekhov's English biographer Ronald Hingley, it would seem that *Oskolki*, the magazine to which Chekhov most frequently contributed, was a kind of Russian equivalent of the contemporary *Punch*. Its staple sources of comedy included mothers-in-law, drunks, foreigners and Russian citizens unable to speak good Russian, bureaucratic officials, young men and women awkwardly courting before marriage, husbands and wives quarrelling after marriage ... Yes, very reminiscent of *Punch*, and resembling the English magazine also in a relentless insistence on brevity. A thousand words was the limit imposed by the editor, and within this length Chekhov had to be amusing, light-hearted, whimsical, never for a moment serious. He wrote notes and sketches, provided captions to pictures or comic mock-advertisements, and produced similar trivia. It is no wonder that all this was done under assumed names, most often that of A. or

Antosha Chekhonte. Not until 1886, in a contribution to the St Petersburg daily *Novoye vremya*, did Chekhov use his own name.

The ability to do such hackwork speedily and successfully indicates his extreme flexibility as a writer. He often referred to what he was doing as excrement, he often railed against Leykin, the editor of *Oskolki*, but still he conformed without much trouble to what was needed. He was in practice the reverse of the long-fingered aesthete we might expect to have written the plays, a man distinctly robust in expression, and at times coarse in his treatment of sexual matters. The man and what he produced were not identical. In 'The Kiss' the shy bespectacled lieutenant Ryabovich is overwhelmed by the kiss mistakenly given him in the dark and feels on his left cheek a faint delicious tingling sensation as from peppermint drops, but this was not the view of his creator who called actresses cows, and said of ballerinas that they all smelt like horses after their performances. If one asks what kind of man Chekhov was, and what beliefs he held, the questions are difficult to answer. He certainly had opinions, powerfully expressed, but they were often contradictory. He might say in letters that Leykin was a cheat and a villain, but when Chekhov moved in 1892 from Moscow to Melikhovo in Moscow province, the editor of *Oskolki* was a welcome visitor. He insisted that he must leave Moscow because as a doctor he needed patients (in a year he treated without payment hundreds of peasants), and as a writer found it essential to have a permanent home away from city life, but when he got to Melikhovo he filled the house with friends so that he had to build a small cottage away from the house as a place of work.

It is a mistake, then, to take any expression of opinion by Chekhov as final, especially in relation to serious subjects. He was much more nearly a mirror of his times than a moralist pronouncing on them, hence his uneasy relationship with the ideas of Tolstoy, which Chekhov at first tried to absorb in some not very successful stories and then rejected almost completely. He admired the novelist but criticized the philosopher, often in sharp practical detail. And it is a particular mistake, common in the last half-century, to claim Chekhov as a political progressive, consciously and deliberately charting the decay of Imperial Russia in his plays. No doubt it is true that Lopakhin is the most significant character in *The Cherry Orchard*, and certainly Chekhov conceived the play

as very funny and quarrelled with Stanislavsky because the producer insisted on treating it as heavy drama, but when Chekhov
called the play a comedy (a term he never defined) he did not have
in mind the kind of crude social criticism that would see in the
chopping down of the orchard a prophecy of the fall of the Tsarist
régime. Edmund Wilson, watching the play performed in Moscow
during the thirties, noted with apparent surprise that it seemed
just as usual, without any special socialist interpretation. Chekhov
was never dogmatic, and his political views were not partisan. In
1900, along with Tolstoy, he was elected an honorary member of
the newly created section of Belles Lettres in the Academy of
Sciences, but a couple of years later he resigned because Gorky
had been expelled from the Academy by personal order of the
Tsar. An ardent liberal, then? Yet probably Chekhov's closest
literary friend was the renegade liberal and anti-Semite Alexey
Suvorin, owner and editor of *Novoye vremya*, although their
relations cooled over the Dreyfus affair, Suvorin being an ardent
anti-Dreyfusard.

But although Chekhov often changed his tune about what he
believed and what he wished to do, he never had any doubt that
most of what he had written was rubbish, up to that time in 1886
when he signed his name to an article for the first time. He said
this often and variously, perhaps most memorably to the novelist
Dmitry Grigorovich, remembered now principally because of his
early perceptiveness in seeing Dostoievsky's genius and his much
later appreciation of Chekhov, but then an established and greatly
respected novelist. Grigorovich, almost forty years Chekhov's
senior, wrote in 1886 what might be called a fan letter to the
young man, but one which urged him to take his own talent
seriously, deprecated the use of a pseudonym, and said that
Chekhov must not sin against his own genius by flippancy, or by
the use of erotic material. Chekhov's reply was fulsome. He was,
after all, a young man in his middle twenties being praised by
a respected elder, and it is not surprising that he should say
Grigorovich's letter had struck him like a thunderbolt and had left
a deep mark on his soul. He continued:

If I have a gift that should be respected, I confess before the purity of your
heart that hitherto I have not respected it . . . Up till now my attitude

towards my literary work has been extremely frivolous, casual, thoughtless . . . I cannot think of a *single* story at which I worked for more than a day, and 'The Huntsman', which you liked, I wrote in a bathing cabin. I wrote my stories the way reporters write notices of fires: mechanically, half-consciously, without caring a pin either about the reader or myself.

He ends by promising to do better, and asks for a photograph of Grigorovich. The fulsomeness of this letter receives a typically Chekhovian corrective, in a note about it sent to the assistant editor of *Oskolki* saying that the old boy had rather laid it on with a trowel.

In 1899 Chekhov sold the rights to his collected works for 75,000 roubles, and a ten-volume edition was published between that year and 1901. He made the selection himself, and used a ruthless hand in dealing with the work written by A. Chekhonte, although retaining the majority of his contributions to *Novoye vremya*. Among the work omitted was *The Shooting Party*.

The Shooting Party appeared in 1884 as a serial in the daily paper *Novosti dnya* ('News of the Day'), published in thirty-two more or less weekly instalments (although with one considerable gap) between August 1884 and April of the following year. It has been generally ignored or dismissed as juvenilia by writers about Chekhov. One of the few to have considered it in any detail, Ronald Hingley, changed his mind about the story between his book about Chekhov published in 1950 and his full-scale biography of 1976. In the first book he remarked on the ingenuity of the plot and commended the tale as 'excellent light reading', although 'not a completely homogeneous work', but later he called it a juvenile thriller, a semi-absurdity. Chekhov himself never referred to the story in his correspondence.

It is surprising that *The Shooting Party* should have been so briskly dismissed or simply ignored. It has several points of interest: as the longest piece of fiction Chekhov ever wrote, a work far removed in tone and style from the flippant stuff he was turning out for the comic papers; as a novel of considerable atmospheric power; and as a rare example of the nineteenth-century detective puzzle, not a thriller but a precursor of the tale that sets out deliberately to deceive.

The first half of the book renders the sights and sounds of rural

Russia with a sort of desolate romanticism Chekhov rarely evoked so directly. The walk beside the lake in the opening chapter, the Count's gardens with their pavilions, grottoes, foreign fruit trees and avenue of limes, the vivid picture of the forester's cottage, all this is descriptive writing of a high order. And the relationship between the principal characters is both curious and convincing. The examining magistrate, handsome, conceited and egotistical, both envies and despises the drunken lecherous Count who has drowned in alcohol any notion of decent behaviour. The Count on his side shows the fawning affection for the magistrate often felt by the weak for the strong. Although the Count is the magistrate's social superior he cannot bring himself to use this as a way of bringing the magistrate to heel, so that when Kamyshev insults the Count's mysterious Polish friend out of sheer ill-will, the Count does not show the outrage one might expect, but merely pleads that Kamyshev should restrain himself, and changes the subject by talking about the rational management of his estate.

Within this subtle picture of a dominant personality and a weak one, both bent on self-destruction, are set scenes of drunkenness and debauchery which are presumably the kind of thing deprecated by Grigorovich. And certainly there are distinctly outspoken passages, like the Count's casual mention of his two planned seductions, and Kamyshev's reluctant acknowledgement that one ought not to touch married women. There is, however, a change of gear at the end of Chapter XII when we are told that 'the introduction is finished and the drama begins'. From this point onwards we are less concerned with rural Russia and social relationships, more with a murder story.

There is no doubt that the second half of the book does not fit easily with the first. Ronald Hingley suggests that Chekhov's editor insisted on excisions and changes designed to speed up the story, and to emphasize melodrama at the expense of style and tone. There is no direct evidence of this, although some of the comments in the 'Postscript' about material omitted suggest it, and one can imagine an editor who had commissioned a melodramatic mystery becoming impatient with the leisureliness of the early chapters. Whatever the reason the emphasis changes, and we are confronted with an ingenious murder mystery.

That Chekhov had an interest in crime and crime stories is shown by the early short story 'The Swedish Match', in which a trail of false clues leads to the conclusion that a man has been murdered, when he turns out to have been kidnapped by his mistress. In the novel Chekhov offers the kind of deception used by Agatha Christie in what is probably her most famous story *The Murder of Roger Ackroyd*. In the context of time and place this was a stroke of extraordinary ingenuity, and there is nothing else at all like it in crime stories of the period. The actual use of the device, however, is comparatively unsophisticated. The footnotes appended by Chekhov in the role of editor make clear his scepticism about the magistrate's story, and this is true particularly of the footnote about Kamyshev's insistence to the dying Olga that she must name her murderer, who will be sent to penal servitude. Such a use of footnotes to make editorial comment on what is supposed to be authentic narrative is, again, a strikingly original device, and would be so even today, but for twentieth-century readers Chekhov gives too much away. Did he mean to show us the identity of the murderer? It is hard to think anything else, but those who bought *Novosti dnya* were undoubtedly more innocent about the devious ways of crime writers, so perhaps they were deceived. A suggestion that the story is in part a parody, rather on the lines of 'The Swedish Match', does not seem to me to have any firm basis.

One should not make extravagant claims for *The Shooting Party*. It is a landmark in the history of the crime story, not in the work of Chekhov. Yet it is a continuously interesting although uneven novel, far from mere juvenilia, a diamond among the trivia and rubbish of the early work. In its melodramatic manner, its outspokenness and deliberate gloom, it represents a kind of writing recognizably Russian, although very unlike what we think of as Chekovian. Dostoievsky was a writer Chekhov found uncongenial in the fervency of his beliefs and the extravagance of his temperament, but there is something Dostoievskian about the early part of *The Shooting Party*. Perhaps Chekhov rejected the story less for any lack of literary merit than because he knew the path of melodrama and violence taken by such a tale was one that did not suit him, the expression of an attitude alien to his natural genius.

(1986)

Georges Simenon

(i) A Profile

Behind the 400-odd books, each of them written in a few days, Georges Simenon is an enigmatic figure, a man lonely and obsessed. He lives in a Swiss village ten miles east of Lausanne, in a house built to his own design. It has an indoor swimming pool and its own electric plant, and one of his admirers has remarked that it would be ideal for some kind of clinic.

The loneliness and the obsession came through clearly in a TV interview Simenon gave a few years ago, an interview which turned into a psychiatric self-examination. The books were written in seven days, Simenon said, because physically he couldn't stand being in such a highly wrought mental state for any longer time. At the beginning he knows the important characters, their names and ages, even their telephone numbers. He knows the location, Paris or New York or a French provincial town. And in writing he becomes the characters, so that his children know that his book is about an old man because of his speech and behaviour. You have a man inside you, Simenon believes, and you have to discover everything about him.

Everything?

Yes, and he added: 'Sometimes it is disgusting, because you discover that you have a little – not much – the same tendency as the man you write of.' In a discussion with Charlie Chaplin, actor and writer agreed that they were both psychopaths. 'The difference is,' Chaplin said, 'that other psychopaths pay to be cured, and on the contrary we are paid to cure ourselves.' They may cure themselves, but living with them is still difficult. At the time that Simenon gave his remarkable TV interview, his wife and one of his children were in hospital psychiatric wards.

All this sounds a long way from the creator of Maigret, and of course Simenon is much more than that. In the orthodox sense he is not a detective story writer at all, and as he once told me he has read only half a dozen detective stories in his life. (Three of them were by Agatha Christie.) Those looking for such features of the classic detective story as the locked room, the alibi constructed and then broken, the body in the library, the parade of suspects all trailing red herrings behind them, will be disappointed by Simenon, for he has no interest in these things.

It is the logic of events that passionately concerns him, and he is more interested in the criminal and his motives than in the solution of the crime. This is true both of the Maigret stories, and of the other books which Simenon calls his 'hard' novels. Just as Sherlock Holmes became a kind of Old Man of the Sea to Conan Doyle, so Maigret is often an irritant to Simenon. He deprecates the fact that the Maigret books are much more popular than his other work, and along with most critics I would feel his finest stories are those which ignore police work, concentrating on the motive for a crime, the committing of it, and the result. My own favourites would include *The Stain on the Snow*, with its central character who becomes a killer out of disgust with his own background in prostitution and crime, and *Monsieur Monde Vanishes* which exploits one of Simenon's most frequent themes, showing a middle-aged rich Parisian's attempt to escape from the boredom of his business and family life.

Both of these books were written in the 1940s. Add to them *Sunday*, a much later book about the owner of a good fish restaurant whose life is controlled by his appalling wife Berthe (the emotional or financial power exerted by one person over another is another frequent theme), and you have a trio of extraordinarily powerful novels which reflect Simenon's feeling that such lives and situations might have been possible for him. 'I was always tempted by what I call complete liberty,' he has said about himself, and many of his central figures are moved by a desperate need to break free of the bonds of family, sex or money that hold them. They hardly ever manage it. At the end of *The Stain on the Snow* the pimp and murderer Frank asks to see Holst, whose daughter he seduced and then had raped by another man. Holst's comment sums up Simenon's philosophy: 'It is a difficult trade to be a man.'

But although the finest stories are among the hard novels, the creation of Maigret is Simenon's greatest achievement. We know him as well as we know Sherlock Holmes, certainly better than any other modern detective, through his screen, TV and radio incarnations. For me the British Rupert Davies is the nearest thing to a perfect Maigret, but there have been French, German, Dutch and other Maigrets. On the screen he has been played by Charles Laughton and Harry Baur, among others. A radio Maigret series used the ingenious device of a discussion between Maigret and his creator at the start of each story.

The remarkable thing about Maigret is that he defies the law that makes all other fictional detectives two-dimensional. Holmes is a deerstalker, a magnifying glass and a capacity for reasoning, not a human being. Lord Peter Wimsey is a Bertie Wooster endowed with intelligence but still ridiculous, Hercule Poirot a stock version of the comic foreigner, Nero Wolfe hardly exists except in relation to food, beer and orchids. They all come out of fairy tales of classical detection, and we are never under the impression that they bleed or suffer.

Maigret is different. He is more than a pipe and a liking for aperitifs, although such things help to fix our understanding of him. Maigret, seen all the way round, emerges as the ideal French bourgeois, married to a solid reliable woman who is also a good cook, sometimes pedantic and fussy, humane and decent but limited in his views like any other member of his class. We know that Maigret would think modern art incomprehensible, distrust liberal education, be uneasy in the presence of the aristocracy and resent his own feeling of discomfort. He is much affected by weather, capable of doing distinctly scatty things on a fine spring morning, and made gloomy or irritable by persistent rain. We know how he talks to his wife in unbuttoned moments (although we never see him literally unbuttoned in bed), and that he is sexually susceptible to other women. He has no obvious politics, but we are pretty sure how he would vote.

And Simenon has created for him a background absolutely right for his class and personality. His father was bailiff at a Château in the Auvergne. He met Louise, who became Madame Maigret, when taken by a former student friend to a party at which she provided the reassurance the awkward young man needed. He gave up his medical studies and became a policeman almost by accident, but perhaps basically because he felt himself to be a man 'who would at first glance understand the destinies of others'. Only in this important respect is Maigret a superior version of the Average French Bourgeois Man – or perhaps in this and in the occasional flashes of intuitive understanding about motives and actions that make him a great detective.

A witty and delightful view of the detective is provided in *Maigret's Memoirs*, which shows us this background and also describes Maigret's relationship with his creator. The detective complains that Simenon put a bowler hat on his head when he never wears one, and said he wears habitually an overcoat with a velvet collar when in reality this is an old coat which almost always hangs in the wardrobe. All this is excellent – and for Simenon very unusual – light-hearted fooling, but what were the real origins of Maigret?

They can be found in *Pedigree*, the long book that Simenon wrote about his youth and adolescence. The narrator in it is named Roger, but he is unmistakably Simenon. *Pedigree* was written in 1942, and in recent years Simenon has spoken more openly about his early life. He was brought up in Liège, the child of an easy-going quiet father who was happy in his dull job as a clerk, and a forceful pushing mother who sent her son to a Catholic school – 'everything was taboo – I hate taboos' – and took in lodgers, so that 'my father didn't have the right to sit in his own armchair'.

The young Simenon rebelled against the strict conventions of his life. He had had by his own account many mistresses by the time he was sixteen, while his mother was still praying daily that he might be kept virgin until he married. He thought of his father as a kind of god, but when his mother died in the late 1960s at the age of ninety-one, he was very little moved. It comes as no surprise that his father provided the model for Maigret, his mother for the many overbearing power-loving women in his books. 'Some people tell me that I am too severe with women. I think that the man believes he is the chief of the family, but in fact he is almost nothing. It is the woman who is the chief of the family . . .' Such feelings clearly go back to his childhood, and Maigret is in some ways a compensation for an unhappy family life. Like Simenon's father Désiré, Maigret is a happy man, but he has better reasons for happiness since he has been given an interesting and important job and an immensely tolerant wife.

The young man left home in his teens and became a journalist.
His first novel was published in 1921 when he was eighteen years
old, and in his twenties he wrote a thousand short stories. A few
of them are reprinted occasionally in magazines, but Simenon does
not encourage this, and calls them frankly hackwork. He used for
them the name of Georges Sim. He bought a boat to tour the
rivers and canals that play a prominent part in many of the books,
and a year later sold it for a larger one, a 35-foot craft named the
Ostrogoth. Reality and fiction blend together when, in *Maigret's
Memoirs*, the detective receives an invitation:

Georges Sim has the honour of inviting you to the christening of his boat,
the 'Ostrogoth', which will be performed by the *Curé* of Notre-Dame on
Tuesday next.

The invitation was real enough, and the party is said to have
gone on for three days and nights. Maigret, however, was not
present, and indeed had not been born. He arrived a year later,
with a collection of eight books published together. Now Georges
Sim was abandoned, and the author used his own name: Georges
Simenon.

From the beginning the Maigret books bore as little relation to
ordinary detective novels as they do to the horror stories of Edgar
Allan Poe. There is a point in many stories when Maigret is
becalmed, as other detectives have been from Holmes onwards
and downwards. Instead of attempting to use logic or assess clues
(there are rarely any clues to assess) the Superintendent sits
smoking his pipe, drinking one aperitif after another in a bar, or
eating one of Madame Maigret's dishes of *morue à la crème*, and
considering the relationship and characters of the people in the
case until he arrives at an intuitive solution. It is magnificent, but
it is not detection. The interest lies in the situations Maigret
encounters, in the way that he approaches them, and often in the
personality of the criminal.

Partly for these reasons, the stories are remarkably even in
manner. The early ones are highly sensational, like *The Madman of
Bergerac* in 1932, which involves a psychopathic murderer and his
doctor son, who first burns down part of a hospital to save his
father, and years later kills him when he discovers that the old man
is still a psychopath and is still murdering women. The terrific verve

of these early books is perhaps linked with their sensationalism, and upon the whole I prefer them to the more plausible but often ramblingly philosophical later stories. One of the pleasures of the books is Maigret's very strongly individualized team of assistants, young Lapointe, the aggressive and occasionally brutal Torrence, Janvier, the miserable Lognon who is a principal character in one story, and of course the ever-reliable Lucas. Sometimes Maigret behaves preposterously, but always his observation of people is acute, and his role as an impersonal Nemesis, what C. Day Lewis called a bloodhound of heaven, is particularly impressive. Simenon himself thinks that too much fuss is made about both Maigret and the stories. He has said that there is no mortality or immortality in the detective, that he is simply a functionary who does what he has to do. That is not how most readers see it.

(1977)

(ii) The Memoirs and the Late Novels

It would be unwise to regard any of Georges Simenon's three approaches to autobiography as literally accurate. *Pedigree* (1948) began with the writer drawing a genealogical tree of the Simenon family, but became a book which although obviously based on the writer's childhood and adolescence in Liège, has a protagonist named Roger. Twenty years later Simenon called it 'not really accurate . . . in spite of what people think and what, out of laziness, I have let them think'. *When I Was Old* is a notebook record kept from June 1960 until early in 1963, when Simenon was nearing sixty. It appeared in 1969, published because 'I have not felt old for a long time' and 'no longer feel the need to write in notebooks'. The notebook contains tender pictures of family life, Easter eggs for the children hidden in Denise Simenon's boudoir, chocolate bunnies bought for everybody by ten-year-old Marie-Jo. It gives an affectionate picture of Denise, called D throughout, 'who wants so much to make us all happy' but is often unwell, struggling to regain her joy in living. 'What did I say to provoke a painful crisis? I don't know at all. I search in vain . . . Words are like drops of acid on a burn.' This, we are now told, is a book that should never have appeared, much of it having been written 'to try to keep a woman, my wife, from slipping into the abyss' of alcoholism.

If *When I Was Old* is not to be trusted, what can one say about *Intimate Memoirs*? Three times during the building of their twenty-six-room villa in the hills outside Lausanne, D took refuge in psychiatric clinics, and in 1964, soon after its completion, the couple parted. In May 1978 Marie-Jo shot herself. Her relationship with her father had been from childhood emotionally, although not physically, incestuous. In her last messages she wrote of 'yearning for your arms' and asked that when she was cremated the 'wedding ring' he had bought her when she was eight years old should be buried with her. Since her death Simenon, the villa abandoned, his five cars sold, living now in a small Swiss farmhouse in retreat from the world, has been working on these memoirs. They are of little interest as the account of a public life, although Simenon trudges again over ground already much covered, including his early successes, and the occasion in 1940 when he was given no more than two years to live. Famous names are mentioned – Pagnol, Duvivier, Cocteau, Gide, Vlaminck, Derain, Picasso, many others – but they have nothing interesting to say, nor is their work discussed, they are merely names on pages. 'A great writer, Thornton Wilder', introduces Simenon as a lecturer at Yale, and disappears thereafter. Simenon kept no diary, but congratulates himself more than once on an 'almost stereoscopic memory for events in their tiniest details, for facial expressions, gestures, nd the spoken word'. Yet the pages of conversation which fill much of the book read like the most banal fiction. A fragment, one of dozens, runs:

I phoned her, and the phone rang and rang before she answered.
    'Who's this?'
    'Me.'
    'Georges?'
    'Yes.'
    Her contralto voice seemed to move me more than ever on the telephone.
    'You're lucky. I'm just washing my hair. That's why I couldn't go out.'

Such conversations are often effectively used in Simenon novels
to show the dull course of a life. They have no place in a memoir.

Intimate Memoirs has two purposes. The first is to take revenge
on D, who has already published her own scurrilous account of
the marriage, the second to emphasize Simenon's love for all his
children, in particular for Marie-Jo. The last 140 pages of the book
are given to her letters, stories and poems, some of the latter
recorded on cassettes. They show much sensibility but little talent,
and express again and again passionate love of her father. Occasionally they are unexpectedly reminiscent of Sylvia Plath's last poems,
in their passion and incoherence.

The rebuttal here of D's account of her relationship with
Simenon is a succession of 'So are yous' and 'You did it firsts',
occasionally unintentionally amusing, but in the end wearisome.
Did he penetrate ten thousand women as he claims, or is the
number a mere twelve hundred as D asserts? When they had a
joint encounter with a 'little countess' on a transatlantic liner, did
he penetrate her at once as described here or was the progress
more leisurely as in D's account? Did he persuade D to take part
in orgies, or was she keen for the experience? Is it he or she who is
an alcoholic, is his indignant denial of her statement that he
'worked on whiskey' accurate, and does it much matter since he
never drank less than three bottles of wine a day? Did he rant and
rave, did her illness include a passion for disinfecting everything,
so intense that her first act in any hotel was to replace the paper in
drawers and closets and vacuum the furniture? What seems certain
is that the hard-drinking randomly sexual life led by these two,
combined with his obsessive insistence on neatness and order,
must have had an effect on the four children, the eldest born to
Simenon's first wife, the others to D. It says much for the three
boys that they survived a life of constant stress. Only Marie-Jo was
destroyed.

No regrets about his own conduct are voiced by Simenon, who
portrays himself always as one driven by forces it would be
pointless to try to resist. By implication he identifies himself as he
has done before with the perfectly natural man, seen elsewhere as
the tramp free to sleep under bridges (it was Anatole France who
remarked that rich and poor are equally free to sleep under bridges,
but only the poor do so) and here as 'the black shiny-skinned man

I was able to meet in his tribal home in the heart of the bush country, who . . . had no idea of what the word "money" meant.' This myth of the noble savage sprang from Simenon's early days as a reporter, foreseeing very intelligently as early as the thirties the end of white rule in Africa.

On the whole one is glad that the memoirs make no apologies. Unhappily they are addressed to the children with a sentimentality that revolts because it is so untrue to what is revealed of the writer's character. Each of them is apostrophized before or at birth, and in many later passages, in terms like: 'Greetings! My Johnny to be! In a month I will be advised of your existence . . . Are you happy, Marie-Jo? You who already have papers that make you officially a member of the human race. Was it selfish of me to give you that name, and will you someday hold it against me?. . . My real life, children, revolves around you, especially you, Marie-Jo.' The treacle is spread thicker elsewhere, perhaps to cover unadmitted guilt. As the colours of Marie-Jo's life darken and she enters a home for 'difficult' children, takes up classical dancing, learns to play the guitar, has one-night stands, tries to write poems and stories, becomes convinced of her own hopeless instability, the contrast between her agonized letters and his conventionally affectionate responses makes painful reading. He seems unaware of any dereliction. Did he not, after all, buy her a large Paris apartment and give her the money to furnish it? Perhaps it would have been impossible for him to have participated more closely in her life, but she seems to have understood that something not merely sexual was lacking in the relationship. In spite of her inability to make contact with other human beings, her unordered romanticism, her awareness of doom, Marie-Jo retained a certain sceptical shrewdness that made her not just one of the lost, but a distinct and interesting personality. The postscript to her last message suggests that perhaps a few of her ashes might be scattered in the open, 'so as not to remain imprisoned *completely* in something "closed" but to join with the wind and . . .' She breaks off and adds, surely with irony or self-contempt, 'Poetry! no doubt . . .'

Simenon continued to write letters to Marie-Jo after her death, as he went through her papers. 'Unfortunately, I don't have the detachment of a professional confessor,' he says at one point, but this is just the quality he does possess. The self-absorption that made him an unsatisfactory human being gave strength and character to the novels, and *Intimate Memoirs* has value in showing the way in which he transformed bits of life into fiction. Of course such a process is not unusual, but it is rare to see it so clearly in operation. It is apparent in the 'hard' novels, not the Maigret stories, which become more casual over the years in conception and execution, providing evident justification for their creator's frequent assertion that they are minor works, even though Maigret is a major character. Simenon makes typical comparison between the Maigret stories and his 'real' novels, when he says that the difference is like that between going sexually with a professional and making 'real' love which 'has always something serious, even dramatic, about it'. The division between the two kinds of book is less apparent in the thirties and forties when the best Maigrets were written, but by the sixties Simenon's need to express the difficulties of his life by putting them into print made the inevitable artificialities of the Maigret books irritating to him, although he continued to write them. Most of the 'real' novels in his final decade as a writer of fiction (the last, *The Innocents*, appeared in 1972) are far more immediately linked to his life than the early stories.

Not that he would admit much of this. *The Disappearance of Odile (La Disparition d'Odile*, 1971) will, he says, 'mistakenly be taken as a reflection of my private life', and it is true that although Simenon's daughter left home as Odile does in the book, she did so five months after its publication. The central character, however, is without doubt Marie-Jo who is seen clearly in her brief bursts of enthusiasm (Odile takes up the guitar), her frequent threats of suicide, her confessional letters, her feeling that she does not belong to ordinary humanity and cannot communicate with other human beings. Odile's father becomes a minor figure for the purposes of the fiction, her confidant being her brother Bob, but her mother shows the indifference to her daughter ascribed by Simenon to D. The book is not a success because the incestuous love that ordered Marie-Jo's life is omitted, so that Odile lacks motivation and becomes simply a sixties case history, demanding freedom without knowing what to do with it. Yet she is shown with great sympathy, and with a depth of understanding that excludes the banality and sickly sentiment of the *Memoirs*. In *November* (*Novembre*, 1969) the Marie-Jo figure is named Laura, and the theme parallels the divisions within the Simenon family. Laura's mother is an alcoholic, her father takes refuge from emotional problems in his study, her younger brother Olivier has replaced her father as lover of the Spanish maid. (Simenon bedded any willing maid as a matter of course.) Laura herself is in love with a fifty-year-old professor at the hospital where she works, a man with a daughter not much younger than Laura. She speculates about her parents, as the Simenon children must have done about their father and D, who for some years seemed happy. 'What went wrong? Or have things always been like this? Were my father and mother never in love, were they never a proper couple? I incline to lay the blame on Mother, who must always have been somewhat unbalanced.' These late Simenons are most convincing where they stick closest to reality, least when the plot demands fictional invention. In *November* the mother, beside herself with jealousy and drink, kills the maid who is assumed to have gone home to Spain, and Laura later discovering the truth acts as her mother's accomplice. It is a denouement which we do not believe, because nothing has prepared us for it.

Other stories in this last decade of undoubted decline explore the connection between ordinary people and violence. Simenon insisted that he was himself an ordinary man (which was true in minor matters like dress, pipe-smoking, and conventional behaviour in public, but is absurd when one considers his career and character) and at the same time, in the interviews with psychiatrists to which he eagerly submitted, proclaimed himself a psychopath kept within the bounds of legally permitted conduct only by the act of writing. *The Man with the Little Dog* (*L'Homme au Petit Chien* 1964), *The Neighbours* (*Le Déménagement*, 1967), *The Cat* (*Le Chat*, 1967) and *The Glass Cage* (*La Cage de Verre*, 1971) all seem to be books by a man at the end of his emotional tether. Simenon says with unusual restraint that *The Man with the Little Dog* is not a happy novel. Like the others it could be called a desperate one.

The four books are uneven in quality (*The Cat* is the only one on the level of Simenon's best work), but show similarities far beyond the fact that in three of them the protagonist is named

Emile. All are studies in obsessional hatred and frustration. A husband and wife communicate only by notes, buy and cook their food separately, keep it in different cupboards; a man who has killed his wife's lover and done time for manslaughter lives alone with a little dog and constantly contemplates suicide; a man who has never kissed his wife on the lips or slept in the same bed with her becomes obsessed by a sexually provocative neighbour and strangles her; another man whose wife still locks the bedroom door after fifteen years of marriage hears through a partition wall a couple saying and doing things almost unknown to him, and tries to enter their world with fatal results. These people are all middle-aged or old, most live by routine actions which they repeat even though they dislike them, all regard themselves as ordinary or normal but have deliberately raised barriers between themselves and the rest of humanity. The man in *The Glass Cage* feels secure only in the glass-partitioned office where he is shut away working on the mechanical job of proofreading; the central figure of *The Neighbours* moves to a new district and to a recently built block of flats, in a useless attempt to improve his relationship with wife and son; their feelings are summed up by the man with the little dog. 'We are all robbers. We all steal lives, or parts of lives, to feed our own lives with.' There are many links with Simenon's own life in these books. Most concern his love-hate relationship with D, some reach back into his youth, there is even a 'charlatan with a diploma' who tells one character, as a doctor told Simenon, that he has only two years to live. All the tales have his characteristic intensity, but it springs from the personal feelings behind him and not from the writer's imagination. Only *The Cat* shows any real inventiveness. Elsewhere a printing works, a travel agency, a new high-rise block, are sketched perfunctorily where in the past they would have been vividly realized.

When one looks back at the total achievement, Simenon seems to be the most extraordinray literary phenomenon of the age rather than a great creator. To have produced so many books on such a high level (and here one would include the Maigrets) is remarkable, yet the more one reads the more apparent variety turns into repetition. All the books are short, but it frequently seems that this is not the result of insistent compression as has often been said, but springs rather from the expansion of an idea fit for a short story into a novel. The awareness of contemporary life is remarkable, the observation of detail more exact than that of any other living writer, particularly in relation to travel, weather, lodgings, food and drink, but this mass of detail covers large omissions. A French critic has pointed out that not merely World War II but almost all current history is absent from Simenon's work. This might not be worth mentioning in relation to another kind of novelist, but must be a limitation in one who has often proclaimed the importance of reality, and stressed his desire 'to simplify, to suppress, to make my style as natural as possible' so that the facts of a situation and truths about the people involved in it should come through unhampered by 'literature'. Simenon has very little interest in any kind of history, almost none in day-to-day politics ('current events repeat themselves – the same winners, the same losers', he said dismissively to a journalist). His vague ideas about society are embodied in frequently expressed admiration for the free life of the tramp or the savage, which he has no wish to live.

It is not accidental that writing about Simenon's work so often merges into discussion of his personality, for psychological analysis offers more clues to the nature of his writing than literary criticism. He has often agreed that if he had not been a writer he might have been a criminal. We may be glad that the production of books has been not only successful therapy but a source of pleasure to millions, yet in the end they are not so much about life as about Simenon's own life. They are what his astonishing memory has retained, often for years, and then reflected in situations which he feels that he might have experienced if . . . if he had not become a famous writer, Georges Simenon. Many imaginary toads inhabit these real gardens, but they all have Simenon's face.

(1982)

REAL LIFE

The Hiss Affair*

In August 1948 Whittaker Chambers, a senior editor of *Time*, testified to the House Committee on Un-American Activities (HUAC) that in the 1930s Alger Hiss had been a member of an underground Communist Party group, along with others working for the Roosevelt Government. Three months later Chambers enlarged this accusation. He now said that Hiss had engaged in espionage, and produced documents to support this.

Alger Hiss was in his forties. He had been for several years in the State Department, a figure important enough to play a part in organizing the American side of the Yalta Conference. He was now President of the Carnegie Endowment. From his days as a law graduate onwards Hiss seemed the model of a handsome patriotic American. He had distinction even in youth. As one friend said, if Hiss were standing at the bar with the British Ambassador, and you were told to give a package to the Ambassador's valet, 'you would give it to the Ambassador before you gave it to Alger'. Chambers, by contrast, was shabby, unkempt, overweight, an ex-Communist who had passed secrets to Moscow before World War II. But with the enthusiastic help of a freshman Congressman on HUAC named Richard Nixon, and of J. Edgar Hoover, Chambers prevailed. After one trial with a hung jury, Hiss was found guilty at a second trial and received a five-year sentence for perjury.

All this was long ago. Americans have returned different answers at different times to the question: was Hiss guilty? In the full flush of McCarthyism during the fifties he found few defenders. With Watergate and the fall of Nixon, popular feeling went into reverse. In 1975 Hiss became the first lawyer ever readmitted to the Massachusetts Bar after a major criminal conviction. Chambers is dead long since, but Hiss is still campaigning, as he has done since his release, for full vindication.

* *Perjury: The Hiss–Chambers Case*, by Allen Weinstein, Hutchinson.

Was Alger Hiss innocent? Allen Weinstein's book on the case is much the most complete view of it. He has been involved in research for eight years, and has used much new material. By suing the FBI he forced the release of their 30,000 pages of classified files on the case. He found fresh information in dozens of public archives and in the files of Hiss defence attorneys. He examined the CIA and Department of Justice files. He talked to everybody still alive and remotely connected with the case – everybody, that is, who would talk to him – including Alger Hiss and his wife Priscilla. And his conclusion, stated unequivocally, is that Alger Hiss was guilty.

The book is on any terms – that is, whether one agrees with all its conclusions or not – an astonishing achievement, masterly in its smooth handling of a great mass of material, going into minute detail yet bringing out the full drama of this extraordinary conflict between what at first seemed a knight in shining armour and an obsessed neurotic ex-Communist. Mr Weinstein's case against Hiss is made from dozens of points, none decisive in itself. Hiss is shown to have evaded and lied about one thing after another, from the first confrontation in a hotel room – stage managed by Nixon – when Hiss eventually identified Chambers as a freelance writer named Crosley whom he had met 'ten or eleven times' in 1935. This was a man, it turned out, who had lived in the Hiss house (and was able to describe it in detail although with some errors), had been loaned money and given a car by the Hisses.

By industrious digging Allen Weinstein also shows that there were doubts in the State Department about Hiss long before the Chambers revelations. Most of these were prompted by Hoover, who obtained agreement before the end of 1945 to put phone taps on Hiss, examine his mail and provide an agent to keep tabs on his movements. The move from State to the less sensitive Carnegie Endowment post sprang from the uncorroborated rumours about him.

The strongest single piece of evidence against Hiss was that of the typewritten material produced by Chambers from a dusty envelope in a dumbwaiter shaft, material which he said he had kept since the thirties. These sixty-five typed sheets summarized or copied State Department cables that had passed through Hiss's hands. They had been typed on a machine which showed characteristics identical with letters typed by Priscilla Hiss during the same period. From the type, experts identified the machine as a Woodstock.

What had happened to it? The Hisses said that they could not remember. In fact it had been given by them to the Catlett family, Clytie Catlett having worked for them at the time. In the Hiss defence files Weinstein's researches turned up what seems to him a damning item. In December 1948 Hiss asked one of his lawyers to 'check on an old machine which he gave to Pat, the son of Claudia Catlett'. Testifying to the Grand Jury a few days later, however, Hiss said again and again that he could not remember what had happened to the typewriter, and he has repeated this since then. The lawyer's note directly contradicts his story. This, Weinstein says, was a calculated cover-up. 'Hiss understood the dangers of allowing the Government to retrieve the Woodstock. For over five months he . . . tried to keep the FBI from finding his old typewriter', and it was produced only when the FBI were hot on its track.

The typewriter itself was not so important, except that tracing it through the Catletts proved that it had not been stolen by Chambers. The crucial identification, as the author says, 'came from comparison of the standards of Hiss typing during the 1930s with Chambers documents, not from Woodstock N 230099'. Mr Weinstein's remarks here about a calculated cover-up suggest a basic hostility to Hiss. What kind of cover up is it that actually raises, as Hiss did, the question of an old machine given to the Catletts? It was, after all, the defence that produced the Woodstock. The awful defence problem was that, as even their own experts agreed, the Chambers documents and the Hiss standards (that is ordinary letters sent by Priscilla) had been typed on the same machine. How could this possibly have happened unless Alger or Priscilla had typed them? To counter this, the defence tried to forge a typewriter – that is, build one that would reproduce the Woodstock's characteristics exactly. It took them a long time, and they failed. Hiss, however, still maintains that he was the victim of 'forgery by typewriter'.

Innocent or guilty? The case against Hiss as a man prepared to lie to preserve his social and political standing is made out completely. The case against him as a spy is strong, yet residual doubts remain. Much of the evidence against him has an air of being manufactured, even though one can't see how it was done. Chambers called the documents his 'life preservers', but they wouldn't have preserved him much in 1938, when he broke with Moscow, for at this time Hiss was only a man of promise. Isn't it strange that such a large proportion of the documents he kept should have concerned young Alger? And then why didn't the Hisses, either personally or through an agent, toss the Woodstock into the Potomac? That, as Allen Weinstein says himself, remains a mystery.

This is the only case of its kind known to me in which typewriter characteristics play a major part, and that is only an element in its fascination. Hiss has said that by the time he is eighty, in 1984, the truth will be known and he will be 'respected and venerated'. It is more likely that, as in other great criminal puzzles – the death of Charles Bravo, the conjectural guilt of Nicola Sacco – the debate will go on for ever.

(1978)

The Lindbergh Kidnapping*

On the evening of 1 March 1932 the twenty-month-old Charles Lindbergh, whose father had become a national hero when he made the first solo flight across the Atlantic, was kidnapped from his home at Hopewell, New Jersey. Ransom money was paid, the serial numbers of the notes being recorded, but the boat where the kidnappers' note said he would be found did not exist. Ten weeks after the kidnapping the child's body was found. He had died on the night he was kidnapped.

A number of the ransom notes were passed in the following two and a half years, but none was traced until September 1934, when a carpenter named Bruno Richard Hauptmann passed one at a Bronx filling station. More than 14,000 dollars of the 50,000 dollars ransom money was found in his garage. A crudely made ladder had been left near the Lindbergh house, and a wood identification expert named Koehler testified that one of its rails fitted into a section of plank missing from Hauptmann's attic. Handwriting experts said that the carpenter had undoubtedly written the ransom letters. At the end of what was called 'The Trial of the Century' Hauptmann was found guilty, and after various delays was electrocuted in April 1936.

Ludovic Kennedy, who has an astonishing and splendid record of working successfully to set right legal injustice, most successfully in the cases of Timothy Evans and Patrick Meehan, here seeks to show that Hauptmann was an innocent man deliberately framed by the police, with the tacit and sometimes active complicity of the prosecution. His book developed from a TV documentary, *Who Killed The Lindbergh Baby?*, but an hour-length programme necessarily limited the scope of commentary and argument. Actually, the present long book doesn't try to answer that original

---

* *The Airman and the Carpenter*, by Ludovic Kennedy, Collins.

question, its slightly different subject being described in the sub-
title: 'The Framing of Richard Hauptmann'.

In elaborate and convincing detail Kennedy shows the framing
being carried out. It was preceded by a severe beating from the
police after Hauptmann's arrest, in an attempt to make the
carpenter confess. When the beating failed the frame-up began.
Hauptmann worked on the day of the kidnapping, something
sworn to by his supervisor and recorded on his time sheet. To
admit that he worked would have made his presence on the scene
of the kidnapping unlikely, almost impossible, so the time sheets
were altered (quite obviously so, as a reproduction shows), and the
supervisor changed his evidence. The famous rail on the home-
made ladder was almost certainly faked by a detective who
occupied the Hauptmann apartment after his arrest, by cutting out
a piece of wood the right size, and then hammering holes to fit
those in the rail. An FBI report after Hauptmann's death concluded
that the ladder/attic connection had been 'fabricated by the joint
efforts of the New Jersey State Police and the New Jersey
Prosecutor's Office in co-operation with Arthur Koehler'. In the
handwriting tests Hauptmann had been asked to misspell words as
in the ransom notes, then these spelling errors were used against
him. A dozen witnesses were browbeaten and cajoled to say the
right things, or change their evidence after saying the wrong ones.

Kennedy is particularly good in showing why the prosecution
and police (all honourable men) were ready and even eager to
fabricate evidence. Lindbergh, young, shy, an airman hero, person-
ified one aspect of the American dream. Colonel Schwarzkopf,
chief of the New Jersey State Police, worshipped Lindbergh and
said he would break any oath for him. Hauptmann, a man of
foreign origin, was found guilty long before the trial by press,
public and police. From the moment of his arrest he had little
chance of escaping the electric chair. Kennedy shows conclusively
that if the evidence had not been faked, and if witnesses had
abstained from evident lies, Hauptmann would almost certainly
have been acquitted.

Yet to admit this is not to say, as Kennedy does, that Hauptmann
had no part in the kidnapping. The most damning evidence against
him was the money found in the garage. Hauptmann said it had
been given him for safe keeping by a fellow German named Isidor

Fisch, a business associate. Fisch was primarily a con man, but also one ready to turn a crooked dollar in any way he could. He died of consumption on a trip to Germany in March 1934, owing Hauptmann money. The carpenter's story was that when he suddenly found the money left by Fisch he began to spend it. *Natural enough, says Kennedy.* But on being questioned Hauptmann lied about the money, saying he had only 300 dollars at home. *Not surprising when he was frightened, says Kennedy.* And after the 14,000 dollars had been found, he still failed to mention another little cache which he had hidden 'in holes drilled for bits beside his pistol'. *He was concerned about the pistol, not the money, says Kennedy.*

The fact is that Kennedy makes from the beginning an assumption of Hauptmann's complete innocence, even imagining his thoughts at times. He accepts that this 'business partner' of Fisch was also his naïve victim, something hard to believe. Much of Kennedy's case was made originally by an American journalist, Anthony Scaduto, in a book called *Scapegoat* which caused little stir in this country when published here. Kennedy acknowledges the debt. He has built on Scaduto's discoveries, and presents the result with great skill. But Scaduto didn't make that assumption of Hauptmann's total innocence, and he offers one piece of evidence Kennedy ignores. A maid at the Lindbergh home, Violet Sharpe, committed suicide within a few days of the body being found. Scaduto was told that Violet, with an English couple named Whately who also worked for the Lindberghs, had been seen several times with a man identified as Fisch. This was secondhand evidence, but the same applies to some of Kennedy's case for Hauptmann. At the end of this book doubts remain, not about police corruption and perversion of the evidence, which is amply proved, but about Hauptmann's innocence.

(1985)

Two Spies

(i) Prince of Spies: Henri le Caron*

The spy working for Them must always be a villain (Philby, Blunt), but any man working for Us in an enemy stronghold does the state some service: this crude rule of thumb is used by all governments, echoed by their newspapers, with the effect of making the spy's career seem glamorous rather than dingy. In fact spying, public or private, is a fairly disgusting occupation, involving continual deception of oneself and others. The perfect spy is the perfect liar.

On this basis Henri le Caron, who penetrated the Irish revolutionary movement for more than twenty years in the nineteenth century, has some claim to be called the perfect spy. Or at least he is one who was never found out. He was born Thomas Billis Beach in 1841, son of a strict Methodist in Colchester. Thomas followed his father in being a lifelong teetotaller, but had no taste for the humdrum. At eighteen he was working in a Paris banking house, two years later enlisted on the Northern side in the American Civil War under the name of Henri le Caron. He finished the war as a major, and soon afterwards struck up a friendship with a Fenian named General O'Neill. Major le Caron expressed strong Fenian sentiments, then reported their plans back to England. His spying career had begun.

The Fenian movement in America, then as now, supplied the cash for rebels back home in Ireland. It was full of factional plotting and financial fiddling, ripe for penetration by spies. Mr Cole is an expert and amusing guide through the world of refugee politics in which le Caron speedily became O'Neill's right-hand man, and was promoted first to Colonel and then Brigadier-General. He helped plan O'Neill's invasion of Canada, while meticulously reporting all details of arms and troop movements to

* *Prince of Spies: Henri le Caron*, by J. A. Cole, Faber & Faber.

the Canadian Chief Commissioner of Police. O'Neill was a drunken blusterer, and no doubt his invasion would have failed like his first one five years earlier, but le Caron's activities made it a ludicrous affair. He removed the breechpiece of the Fenians' only gun, and was able to delay the arrival of some reserve troops. In the end O'Neill was captured, and not a single Canadian was even wounded.

Le Caron often said he suffered financially through his spying activities, and Mr Cole seems to endorse this. He and his family (he eventually had six children) were hardly on the bread-line, however. He had qualified as a doctor, and at this time earned ten to twelve dollars a day from his practice. In addition he got one hundred dollars a month from the Fenians, and another hundred from his paymasters Canadian and British, plus a $2000 bonus for his work in preventing the invasion. He remained O'Neill's trusted friend, while 'laughing to myself at his coming discomfiture' during the invasion, and noting that after defeat and disgrace the General 'made my life a burthen'. With O'Neill out of the way he became the colleague of other important Fenians, many of whom liked the brisk cocky little fellow who smoked sixteen cigars a day. He very readily took all sorts of bloodthirsty oaths, occupied important positions, made speeches at conventions, expressed approval of plans for violent activities, avoided criticism by always voting with the majority. He reported everything back to his paymaster Robert Anderson, later head of the CID. In between Fenian activities and writing reports he continued to practise medicine, and managed three drug stores. His reports had little or no effect in checking the dynamiting of buildings in London during the early 1880s.

The climax of le Caron's career came in 1889, with his evidence to the Special Commission investigating the *Times* articles linking Parnell to the encouragement of violence. The treatment of this episode is distinctly odd. The collapse of the *Times* case with the proof in court that the so-called Parnell letters were forgeries, and the flight and suicide of the forger Pigott, are moved to the wings, and instead le Caron's evidence takes centre stage. By giving evidence, of course, he blew his cover and 'came out in my true colours, as an Englishman' as he put it. He told many tales of Irish villainy, and gave an account of an interview with Parnell endorsing terrorism, which the politician totally denied. It was le Caron's moment in history, and he enjoyed it fully. He was a splendid witness, brisk and precise about names and dates, unshaken in cross-examination. Mr Cole, who must be one of the few people to think some of the Pigott letters may be genuine, believes also that le Caron was moved to give evidence by pure patriotism. It is far more likely that the Government attempted through him the destruction of Parnell. But for the exposure of the forged letters they would have succeeded.

His occupation gone, le Caron wrote his memoirs, which went through sixteen editions in a year. He settled down with wife and family, first in Sydenham, then in Kensington. He was constantly guarded by detectives, but the Fenians never made the expected attempt on his life, and he died prosaically of peritonitis in 1894. Was he a true patriot as Mr Cole thinks, or a disgusting moral monster as the Fenians asserted? An adventurer without many scruples, I should say, who liked excitement and positively enjoyed deception. Another Fenian verdict is not much in dispute, for what it is worth. They called him the champion spy of the century.

(1984)

(ii) Colonel Z*

What link was there in the thirties between millionaire Calouste Gulbenkian and his son Nubar, *Manchester Guardian* foreign correspondent Frederick Voight, Alexander Korda the film maker, art dealer Geoffrey Duveen, and Sichel the famous wine shipper? All were part of the Z Organization set up in 1936 by Claude Edward Marjoribanks Dansey, then a Colonel, and seven years later Sir Claude Dansey, KCMG.

Opinions varied, and vary still, about Dansey. He was, Hugh Trevor-Roper told the authors of this book, 'corrupt, incompetent, but with a certain low cunning'. Malcolm Muggeridge, whose view

---

* *Colonel Z*, by Anthony Read and David Fisher, Hodder & Stoughton.

is also quoted on the dust wrapper, thought him the only real professional in MI6. Dansey emerges from this book as devious, ruthless and wholly unscrupulous. He was also, and most notably, a ham actor. He made a cult of secrecy but still had his particular luncheon table at the Savoy. A new recruit might be told that he was to meet an unnamed man wearing a dark suit with a red carnation buttonhole and carrying a copy of *The Times*, but the waiters knew it was Colonel Dansey. Unmoved by such considerations, Dansey gave one raw recruit a card which told him that he had been lunching with Captain James Pomfret-Seymour. A con man tells lies to other people, but a professional spy is a con man who never tells the truth even to himself. By such a definition Dansey was indeed a real professional.

He was born in 1876, the eldest son of a Captain in the Life Guards. Taken away from Wellington because of trouble with the drains (two boys died of suspected diphtheria) he was sent to a school in Belgium where he was seduced by Oscar Wilde's first male lover Robert Ross. The experience seems to have had no lasting effect. He married twice, although the authors seemed to regard these events as minor disturbances of his professional career. Sent to South Africa as a youthful remittance man, Dansey joined the sketchy Army Intelligence Department in 1900, and emerged as a fully fledged spy before World War I. He controlled the entry of aliens into the UK, and played a part in setting up an American Intelligence service. Messrs Read and Fisher suggest that he may have been a model for Maugham's 'R' in *Ashenden*, but provide no evidence. Hard evidence, indeed, is lacking for many assertions and suggestions in a slapdash book which, when it strays from Dansey, repeats hoary myths about such figures as Lenin and Trotsky.

Dansey seems not to have flourished in the twenties, although at one time he acted as agent for an American robber baron named Ryan, who wanted to win an English classic race. Dansey, 'a fine judge of horseflesh', bought several horses for him, but had no luck. He was re-engaged by the SIS (Secret Intelligence Service) in 1929, but sacked a few years later, it was said for fiddling finances. The authors believe the sacking to have been a cover, under which it was arranged that Dansey should set up the Z Organization. In true showman style he was known as ZI, the spymaster.

The Z Organization was planned as an alternative intelligence service, working in parallel with the SIS but unknown to it and, Read and Fisher say, ready to replace it if a country was overrun so that the SIS ceased to exist there. It seems an extraordinary idea, ripe with the possibility of confusions like agents using the same source independently of each other. However, in the pre-War period Dansey built up a considerable network of German anti-Nazis. Some said that when information was thin Z agents often invented intelligence for London, and in spite of Z1's readiness to order the deaths of traitors and informers, there was a strong flavour of musical comedy about some of Dansey's agents, not only those linked with show business.

About, for example, Captain Sigismund Payne Best, Z man at The Hague, who was chiefly responsible for the sudden catastrophic end of the Z Organization. Best, who wore spats and a monocle, had been an agent of Dansey's during and after World War I. He had a prosperous import-export business in Holland, plus his expenses claims for a team of thirteen agents, most of whom did not exist. When World War II began, Best was conned into believing that he was negotiating with a group of German dissidents plotting to overthrow Hitler. In fact they were Nazi agents and Best, along with Major Stevens, the SIS man on the spot, was trapped on the Dutch side of the border. They were whisked into Germany, and under interrogation told all or most of what they knew. This was the Venlo incident.

Venlo was the end of the network, but not of Colonel Z. Dansey was by now Assistant Chief of the whole SIS, and according to his biographers was worshipped by his boss Stewart Menzies. Detested by some, distrusted by many, but loved by those who admired his barking bravura and called him Uncle Claude, he survived the War triumphantly, unscarred by errors like the occasion when he briskly pronounced as fakes two hundred telegram flimsies presented by a German defector, with the result that the man found a home with American and not British Intelligence. He retired with honour in 1945, and died two years later. One can agree with his biographers when they say that Dansey had one inviolable rule: 'Whatever happens, however disastrous it may appear, you must always look for a way of turning it to your own advantage.' Success in doing so was the prime achievement of Colonel Z.

There is a third view about Dansey on the dust wrapper. Edward Crankshaw, the eminent Kremlinologist, says that he was 'the sort of man who gives spying a bad name'. But whoever supposed it had a good one?

(1984)

Peter Sutcliffe*

Much press behaviour in the Peter Sutcliffe case was so disgusting (according to this book, the 'signing up' of his wife a couple of days after his arrest, for a rumoured £200,000 plus sixty per cent of syndication, was celebrated by the *Daily Express* by bucket after bucket of champagne) that it is tempting to dismiss any new book out of hand as one more wade through a lake of blood. That would be a pity, for Gordon Burn's book is a serious study. The casually horrific murders are detailed, the abysmal police work receives attention, but this is primarily a study of Sutcliffe and his background. Much of the material comes from what must have been dozens of interviews, and a close relationship with Sutcliffe's father, brothers and sisters. One can believe that Mr Burn has spent two years on the book. No money was paid for information. Many people, he says, wanted to put the record straight, and the story will never be told straighter or less sensationally than here. Even the off-putting title has its relevance, for Sutcliffe's character was largely shaped by his upbringing.

The Sutcliffe family is a group in which one is certainly glad not to have been born. Peter's father John had a humble enough job as a mill weaver, but away from work was a sporty fellow, good cricketer, ready drinker, amateur actor, wearer of hounds-tooth checks and paisley cravats. A tremendous eater too, saying, 'This should keep the Biafran army on the march for a month' as he attacked meat, vegetables and gravy 'with a fortress of Yorkshire pudding on the top'. This genial figure, however, bullied and sometimes beat up his wife and children, groped any girls who came to the house, and occasionally had trouble with the police for petty theft and burglary. His second son Mick was arrested at thirteen, and thereafter had convictions for robbery, assault and

---

* . . . *Somebody's Husband, Somebody's Son: The Story of Peter Sutcliffe*, by Gordon Burn, Heinemann.

grievous bodily harm. Like his father he was a great womanizer and would, it was said, have fucked a pig in knickers. Carl, the youngest, was in an approved school by the time he was fifteen, one of the girls was pregnant at sixteen, and another at the same age had the reputation of being 'lively as a lop'. Even their placid mother was discovered by her outraged husband to have been nipping off for afternoon bedding by a police sergeant who lived nearby.

By a nice irony the runt of this noisy litter, Peter, was the eldest son. A small sickly baby, a weedy child with ankles so thin that they needed support from special reinforced boots, shy and quiet, he spent hours in the lavatory or the bathroom. When he left school and began to earn he dressed conspicuously in all-white or dead-black suits, drainpipe trousers, and cuban heels to compensate for his lack of height. He worked as a gravedigger and made graveyard jokes, throwing a rock on a coffin and saying: 'That'll waken you, you bugger.' When he helped to lay out corpses, he took rings from the bodies. He bought a motor-bike, then a car, which he drove well but too fast.

Peter Sutcliffe went around little with girls, and when he appeared with one named Sonia his pub friends, most of them petty criminals and mill girls, didn't like her. Her parents were Czechs, she was short, plain and serious, studying to be a teacher. She had a mental breakdown during which she saw the stigmata on her hands, and after recovery still for a while tore off her clothes at home, or in the middle of a meal. Peter did not give her up and they were married in 1974, groom and best man wearing the same two-toned platform shoes. Sonia became a teacher, and filled their house with abstract pottery. Her husband was the star driver at a small engineering firm. His picture, at the wheel of his wagon, hung in the vestibule. The first murder occurred in the year after the marriage.

It seems clear that Peter Sutcliffe was a closet homosexual, unable to admit his inclinations to a family for whom sexual aggressiveness was a badge of manhood. His personal prudishness and fastidiousness (he was much upset by his sweaty feet, and even after marriage washed all his own clothes by hand), his frequent jeering at prostitutes and boasts of going with them without payment, suggest fear and dislike of sexual activity between men and women. The other men in the family copulated as easily and thoughtlessly as animals. Carl's story about bringing a girl home, 'giving her one' on the floor, and being interrupted by his father who when Carl went out tried to give her one too, is typical.

Mr Burn concentrates on Sutcliffe's character. He has little new to say about the murders, but his account of the police investigation emphasizes the administrative incompetence that left them utterly unable to organize the mass of information they had collected. Peter and Sonia Sutcliffe were visited time and again by different officers, but none of them knew about the earlier visits. When Sutcliffe's close friend Trevor Birdsall went to the police and gave information identifying him as a prime suspect, he was ignored. The police continued to believe in the famous Sunderland tapes, long after the voice experts who first identified them had decided that they were a hoax.

Should such studies, obviously painful to the families of victims, be published? The answer must be yes, when they are as detached, temperate and informative as this one. The book takes its prime justification from Piers Paul Read's remarks, quoted here, that at the trial prosecution and defence explanations 'both seemed inadequate explanations for what had happened', and that the inadequacy arose because in such accounts the jurors were inevitably denied 'quite crucial information . . . notably about Sutcliffe's childhood and married life'. Mr Burn's great merit is that he gives us facts which make intelligible what would otherwise seem meaningless crimes.

(1984)

The MacDonald Case*

Jeffrey MacDonald was voted at High School the Most Popular Student, and the one Most Likely to Succeed. He married his schoolgirl sweetheart Colette, became a doctor, an Army officer, a volunteer for the Green Berets, 'L'il Abner with straight-A marks' somebody said. The all-American boy had married the all-American girl. They had two girls aged five and two, another child on the way. This young and apparently happy family – husband and wife were both twenty-six – was destroyed in February 1970, when Colette and the two children were found savagely beaten and stabbed to death. The alarm was given by MacDonald, who had a bruise on his forehead, some superficial stab wounds, and another which had punctured his lung. There had been four attackers, he said, two white men, one black, and a woman with long blonde hair who wore a floppy hat.

The MacDonald story is a farcical tragedy in two acts, with a long interval. Joe McGinnis was invited to write the book by MacDonald himself, who imposed no restrictions, and made freely available lengthy tape recordings giving his version of his life and character. These are intercut with the progress of investigations, official and private, and finally by McGinniss's own conclusions. The result is not a minor work of art like *In Cold Blood*, but a sprawling, repetitious yet compellingly readable story. It shows American crime investigation at its worst, American legal procedure often at its most ludicrous, American sentimentality at its most blatant.

Act One is MacDonald victorious. The crime took place at Fort Bragg, Northern California, the biggest military base in the United States, and was investigated by the Army CID. They soon decided that MacDonald's story was implausible. There were bloodstains of the wrong type in the wrong places. MacDonald said he had

* *Fatal Vision*, by Joe McGinniss, André Deutsch.

attempted resuscitation, but there was no blood on the two
telephones he had used to call for help. And why had the intruders
not killed him too? The detectives decided that his one severe
wound was self-inflicted.

At the preliminary Army hearing, however, the appalling errors
and omissions of the CID were gleefully revealed by MacDonald's
flamboyant attorney Bernie Segal. Garbage cans had been left
unexamined, MacDonald's pyjamas thrown away, a bloody foot-
print destroyed. Skin found under Colette's nails had been lost in
the lab, and the pathologists had forgotten to take hair or fingerprint samples from the bodies. Fingerprints photographed on the
scene of the crime came out hopelessly blurred. No road block had
been set up to catch the Manson-type hippies described by
MacDonald, no attempt was made to follow up information about
a possible blonde drug-taker with floppy hat. With the prosecution
case in ruins, all charges were dismissed.

The interval followed, years of almost uninterrupted success.
MacDonald appeared on the Dick Cavett Show, became assistant
to a showbiz physician known as Doctor Broadway. Colette was
often mourned in lachrymose passages of the tapes, but she was
replaced as bed partner by Joy, 'a gorgeous receptionist, one of the
most sensual women I've ever seen'. Joy was succeeded by Bobbi,
'this very, very gorgeous redhead, taller than Joy, though not as
busty, not nearly as sensual'. When Bobbi started making demands
'both verbally and in body language', the surprisingly named
Sherree Sizelove, an airline stewardess, came on the scene. Suggestions to various writers that they should co-operate in work on the
MacDonald story had all been turned down, but this gap was filled
by McGinniss. By now it was 1979, and MacDonald was controller
of a group of fourteen doctors in Long Beach, California, lectured
nationally on child abuse, and had an honorary lifetime member-
ship of the local Police Officers' Association. But the long interval
was over. When McGinniss first met him, MacDonald had a
Citroën-Maserati in the front drive, a thirty-four-foot yacht at the
back. He was due to stand trial for the nine-year-old crime.

The last act might be called The Mills of God. They had ground
very slowly, moved chiefly by Colette's mother and her husband,
who pursued MacDonald implacably. He was indicted in 1975,
the charges thrown out on the ground that he should have been

tried earlier, and then that ruling rescinded. Absurdities abounded at both indictment and trial. The richest passage was the TAT (Thematic Apperception Test), in which MacDonald was presented with nineteen pictures and a blank card, and asked to make up stories about them. Almost equalling it was the moment when, to demonstrate a point, one prosecuting attorney lunged at another with an ice pick so realistically that he effected a cut on the forearm. The floppy-hatted blonde, a hopeless drug addict, had been discovered, but told a different story every time she was questioned.

MacDonald's witnesses – doctors, nurses, nuns and policemen – did what they could, one comparing him to Albert Schweitzer. 'You don't have to be Laurence Olivier,' Bernie Segal (still pitching after nine years) said the night before MacDonald took the stand. 'Just be yourself and you'll be fine.' And MacDonald did not let his admirers down. He wept frequently on the stand, and when Segal showed him a photograph of his daughter Kimberly wearing a nightgown with 'Little Angel' on it, the attorney and others including jurors wept too. But he had been found out in too many lies. The weeping jurors found him guilty, and he is now serving a life sentence.

It must be a bitter blow that MacDonald's chosen biographer finds him guilty too, remorselessly recording his verbal and emotional twists and turns, the departure of Sherree and arrival of Dolores ('an incredibly tumultuous relationship'), and then the twenty-year-old Randi Dee. What was the motive for murder? It seems likely that the all-American boy was an emotionally inadequate figure unable to bear the strain of family life, disliking pregnancy, finding refuge from latent homosexual feelings in a parade of toughness. But the only certainty is that Jeffrey MacDonald was a great ham actor. After hearing one of his maudlin tapes about discovering the bodies, one psychiatrist said: 'If he's guilty he deserves an Academy Award.' Perhaps he should get one.

(1990)